ECONOMICS OF CROP DIVERSIFICATION

ECONOMICS OF CROP DIVERSIFICATION

UTPAL KUMAR DE

AKANSHA PUBLISHING HOUSE
NEW DELHI

AKANSHA PUBLISHING HOUSE
R 37-B, Vani Vihar, Uttam Nagar,
New Delhi-110 059, India
E-mail: ektabooks@yahoo.com
Ph.: 91-11-25640621

Economics of Crop Diversification

First Edition, 2003

ISBN 81-87606-22-3

PRINTED IN INDIA

Published by M.P. Misra for Akansha Publishing House, New Delhi and Printed at Tarun Offest Press, Delhi.

TO
MY PARENTS

Foreword

The dominant role of agriculture in economic progress of developing committees is highly acknowledged and several doctrines have been formulated in this sphere, Copious literature providing knowledge about farmers' response to changes in different economic and meta-economic variables is also available. In recent years, the study of cropping choice has become a particularly prominent issue for its environmental implications, namely the long-term productivity of soil and sustainable development. In India too, this issue has emerged from the secular pattern and impact of agricultural transformation in the post-Green Revolution period. Although yield expansion of individual crops initially contributed to the growth of agricultural income it eventually subsided to a large extent. This has been truer in the case of extension of area under cultivation.

The present study by Dr. Utpal De a very talented, young economist University, teacher offers an in-depth analysis of the nature of crop diversification and its contribution to the growth of cultivators' income in West Bengal over the post-Green Revolution period. The study reveals how with the limited available resources farmers can maximize the returns from agriculture by utilizing & care land in the best possible manner.

The book also aptly analysis the basic reason underlying crop diversification along non-traditional lines. There is no denying that the available discourses in the area are far from adequate. Traditional theories and analysis have considered prices of crops, availability of irrigation and technological factors, as well as government policies as the crucial determinates of changes in cropping pattern. These have not taken into account the inter and intra-seasonal factor's, and the consequences of crop selection in one season on the return and cropping choice in the following seasons. Thus Dr. De has admirably extended the concept of competing crops grown in the same season to competition among crops raised in different seasons. This approach of the author, which is buttressed by first hand and meaningful empirical observations will materially help future researchers coupled with policy makers concerned with sustainability of agricultural development.

In my view, this volume will be a valuable acquisition for any institution or individuals interested in applied economics in general and agriculture in particular.

Prof. Gautam K. Sarkar
Former Member, Scientific Panel (ESM)
and the Society of the ICAR, New Delhi.

PREFACE

This study analyses the fundamental socio-economic problems of crop diversification that has paramount importance for the agricultural development of developing economies. The developing countries in Asia experienced a remarkable change in agrarian structure after the arrival of new varieties of seeds and technology. The idea of cultivation further changes with the extension of commercial farming. This book is written on the basis of my thesis work that earned me Ph.D. from the University of Burdwan, West Bengal and on some of my other research papers and Project Reports. I hope the book will be useful to the students, researchers and teachers of economics, especially agricultural economics.

A number of agricultural economists have analysed the land allocation problem among the competing crops. But no previous study has considered the impact of crop chosen in a particular season on the allocation in the following period apart from the other factors influencing the allocation of land for the cultivation of crops. This book gives a special emphasis on the analysis of allocation of land towards different combination of crops grown in successive seasons of the year. The first and second chapters give a brief outline of the problem and the methodology of the study. Chapter three and four deal with the analysis of crop diversification in West Bengal during 1970-71 to 1994-95 in terms of acreage and production and its regional pattern. Chapter five explains briefly the spatio-temporal variation in productivity. At macro level impact of crop diversification on the agricultural income of West Bengal is analysed in chapter-6. Chapter seven to nine is devoted to the statistical analysis of basic causes for diversification especially, chapter nine tries to link between flow of acreage in successive seasons with the net-return from a plot of land excepting its long run environmental consequences for a developed multiple cropping system of West Bengal. The last one incorporates the whole observations in brief and the policy implications.

Though the idea to take up the issue of crop diversification primarily emanated from my subjective experience as a student of economics having a first hand knowledge in this field of work, I would like to put on record my sincere gratitude to them who encouraged me to nurture it and also helped me in various ways to complete the writing. My debts of gratitude are many. At first I owe my extreme gratitude to my Ph.D. supervisor Dr Soumyendra Kishore Datta, of Department of Economics, University of Burdwan who was of continuous source of suggestions and assistance. I would also like to express my deep sense of gratitude to my teacher Prof. Goutam Sarkar, former professor of economics of University of Burdwan who paid a great attention to my work from the very beginning and gave invaluable suggestions. I am also indebted to Prof. M. Chattopadhyay, Prof. D. Coondoo of Economic Research Unit, ISI, Calcutta and Prof. M. Dasgupta of Tripura University who spared their valuable time and gave important clues for the analysis. I also received full cooperation from the Additional Director of Evaluation Wing, Directorate of Agriculture, Government of West Bengal, District Statistical Officer, Burdwan; Bureau of Applied Economics and Statistics, Government of West Bengal, Calcutta; Commercial Library, Calcutta; Central Library of University of Burdwan and Library of ISI, Calcutta for the collection of Data and other information. For all of them I express my deep gratitude. I am also grateful to Mr. Dulal Chatterjee, Santanu Banerjee of Department of Minor Irrigation, Government of West Bengal for providing me accesses to their official documents. I wish to acknowledge my sincere thanks to the members of computer centre of Tripura University, Mr. S. Debbarma, Mr. M. K. Debbarma and Mr. Shyamal Saha who helped me in different ways at the time of processing of data and composition of work and also to the Department of Economics, North-Eastern Hill University to get computer facilities for some typing. I am also thankful to Dr G. Das of Department of Economics, North Eastern University who encouraged me in various ways for publishing this book.

My sincere gratitude is also due to Tripura University and U. G. C. for providing me a Minor Research Project that was too helpful for conducting my study. I am also thankful to Akansha Publishing House for taking interest in publishing this work. However I would like to take the whole responsibility for any error remaining in my study.

The last but not the least I wish to mention my parents who were the major source of inspiration in all times.

Shillong **UTPAL KUMAR DE**

March 15, 2002

CONTENTS

List of Maps and Figures

List of Tables

Abbreviations

BAES	Bureau of Applied Economics and Statistics
DTW	Deep Tubewell
DW	Dug Well
FAI	Fertiliser Association of India
FP	Filter Point
GATT	General Agreement on Tariffs and Trade
GCA	Gross Cropped Area
GDP	Gross Domestic Product
HDTW	High Capacity Deep Tubewell
HYV	High Yielding Variety
LDTW	Low Capacity Deep Tubewell
MDTW	Middle Capacity Deep Tubewell
NA	Not Available
NCAER	National Council of Applied Economic Research
NSA	Net Sown Area
NSS	National Sample Survey
NT	No Trend
Neg	Negligible
ODW	Open Dug Well
RHS	Right Hand Side
RLI	River Lift Irrigation
SDP	State Domestic Product
STW	Shallow Tubewell
USA	United States of America
WD	World Development

CHAPTER 1
PROLOGUE

1.1 Introduction

It needs no large explanation that growth of agriculture is closely related to the general economic development of a developing economy like that of India. Most of the Indians live in rural areas and earn their livelihood primarily from agriculture and its allied activities. In the early years of the post-Independence period, India faced an acute food crisis and was largely dependent upon the import of food articles to feed its growing population (Government of India, 1959)[1]. Agricultural production and productivity were very low and insufficient to meet the domestic demand. In order to tackle the problem, the new seed-fertiliser-irrigation technology was adopted. Improved varieties of seeds were imported and cultivated to grow more food. The major breakthrough in agricultural production came in the wake of the Green Revolution. After the mid-1960s, initially the revolution came in Punjab and Haryana and was mainly confined to wheat and then rice. Gradually, the process spread all over the country and the country became self-sufficient in food production and later turned into a food-exporting country. Gradually, agricultural farming became commercial, leaving its traditional self-sufficient production structure, with emphasis shifted to more remunerative varieties of crops.

West Bengal, one of the important agricultural states of India, also observed the Green Revolution and its agricultural sector started growing fast in the early 1970s reaching a peak level during the early 1980s. During the last three decades there has been a great change in the agricultural scenario of the state. Before the Green Revolution the growth of agriculture was contingent upon the expansion of agricultural land, and gradually found momentum with the growth of the yield level or the general productivity-growth that depends partly on individual yield-growth and cropping-pattern growth (Boyce, 1987; pp. 276-77)[2]. The growth of agriculture has been closely associated with the changes in the cropping pattern. The traditional crops have been gradually replaced by the new varieties of crops – a phenomenon that has an important bearing on the growth of the returns from the limited land holdings of the farmers in the short as well as in the long run.

The present study concentrates on the investigation of the nature of crop diversification in West Bengal during 1970-71 to 1994-95 and the analysis of its impact on the rural economy of the state, and to bring out the major causes of crop diversification which would help in policy formulation to guide the agricultural economy along a desired path.

The idea of the proposed investigation into crop diversification in West Bengal emanates from the personal experience of a student of economics having some first-hand knowledge regarding this field of work. The agricultural sector, especially the crop-growing sector, has an important bearing on the development of an economy, particularly an economy, which has a large rural sector. With the development of the economy, the crop-generating sector is found to be associated with the changes in cropping pattern. The dynamics of 'cropping system' or intra-year variation in crop combinations is thus an important issue of research.

Crop diversification is of paramount importance in a developing economy like that of India in general and the state of West Bengal in particular. Not only area and yield but inter-crop changes in area are also of immense importance in the growth of resources generated from this sector. Before going into a detailed discussion, it is pertinent to understand at the very outset the concept of diversification.

1.2 Concept of Diversification

The term diversification is associated with the structural transformation of an economy. It may mean various kinds of changes at different level. (i) Diversification at the macro level, which is a broad concept. It means a change in the contribution of different sectors (viz. primary, secondary and tertiary) to national income, as well as the disposition of the working population. This type of diversification is in the nature a shift of activities, from the farm (agricultural) to the non-farm (non-agricultural) sector or *vice versa*. The former is the basic characteristic of the sectoral diversification in rural economies as distinct from the diversification of agriculture. (ii) Again, there is the concept of diversification within agriculture, which may be of two different types:

(a) enterprise diversification and (b) crop diversification. The first involves inter-enterprise shifts of resources such as, crop raising to livestock, while the latter involves inter-crop shifts of resources (e.g. food crop production to non-food crop production etc.) (Sawant, 1993).[3]

In addition to these, another kind of diversification may take place over time, which is in the nature a shift in resource use to diverse but complementary activities. This type of diversification emerges from the farmers' response to a slack in the system, leading to an addition of complementary crop activities or enterprises to the main enterprise for exploiting the unemployed and underemployed resources, whenever the opportunity to do so arises (Sawant, 1997).[4]

1.3 Diversification at the All India Level

The aforesaid three types of changes are generally noticed with the development of any economy and thus India is also no exception in this regard. The Indian experience of past few decades reveals a change (like the other developing countries) at the macro level with non-agricultural sectors (industry and services) becoming progressively more important in terms of contribution to national income as well as disposition of total workforce than the agricultural sector (Vyas, 1996).[5] The share of agriculture in Gross Domestic Product (GDP) of the country has declined from 34.7 per cent in 1980-81 to 27.7 per cent in 1993-94 (both at constant prices). In terms of resource use the diversification means that more and more resources in the economy are being diverted to non-agricultural activities. As in other developing economies, in India also the share of workers engaged in agricultural activities is declining, while that of non-agricultural (industry and services) sectors is increasing. The pace of increase is however much slower than in several other countries. During the period 1972-73 to 1987-88 the number of workers in agriculture in rural India declined by 7.3 per cent (Visaria, 1995).[6] Within agriculture, share of output and employment of the non-crop sectors i.e. animal husbandry, forestry, fishery etc. though very small (around 10 per cent of the total agricultural output) is gradually increasing.[7] More significant changes have taken place within the crop-producing sector, which has been denoted earlier as crop diversification.

1.4 Crop Diversification

Diversification of crop means the production of increased variety of crops. It can be defined broadly as a structural change in crop-mix in any geographical area. In terms of input use, it means a change in the use of basic agricultural inputs (land and labour) from one combination of crops to another. In a particular region changes in the crop-mix over time can be described either by a change in acreage distribution per crop or value-wise contribution of each crop to total agricultural production.

Changes in the crop-mix over time within the crop growing sector is one of the basic characteristics of a progressive agricultural economy. In India, particularly after the mid-sixties, diversification within the 'cropping sector' has been taking place in terms of a shift in area broadly, from food crops to non-food crops (Pandey and Sharma, 1996).[8] Area under so called commercial crops (non-food crops) has doubled since the 1960s and now equals half the area under food crops (Vyas, op. cit. 1996).[9] Within food crops, area under superior cereals (i.e., rice and wheat) is increasing while that under inferior cereals (like jowar, bazra, pearl millet etc.) is declining. Moreover, during pre-nineteen eighties period foodgrains experienced a marginal increase in area due to the growth of superior cereals and the non-food crops like potato, oilseed, sugarcane have exhibited a moderate growth. But during the decade of nineteen eighties those non-food crops experienced a quite high rate of growth in their area, while some other non-food crops like cotton, total fibre, tobacco and foodgrains as a whole witnessed negative growth rates (Pandey and Sharma, op. cit.).[10]

1.5 The Case of West Bengal

Among all other states, West Bengal occupies an important position in the agricultural front of India. Since 1970, it has been contributing around 15 or 16 per cent of total rice production and around 7 per cent of foodgrains production in India. Besides this, the proportion is still increasing.[11] The economy of the state is predominantly agricultural. Though contribution of agriculture to total state domestic product (SDP) had decreased from 41.46 per cent in 1970-71 to 27.52 per cent in 1980-81, it registered slight increase (29.24 per cent) in 1994-95. The contribution is still notably high as is evident from Table 1.1.

Table 1.1 reveals that proportion of forestry and fishery to state domestic product has been increasing over time and agriculture, forestry and fishery together constitutes more than one-third of state domestic product in 1994-95 and earlier periods also. Till now, around two-third of population earn their livelihood from agricultural activities.[12] Of the total workforce more than half is engaged in agriculture.[13]

The agricultural situation of the state has undergone significant changes during the past few decades. From the eastern region, West Bengal represented the most outstanding performance with the highest acceleration in the growth rate of agricultural production during the post-Green Revolution period. During 1968-69 to 1981-82 state domestic product originating in agriculture had increased by 2.46 per cent per annum. But the rate of growth achieved, especially after mid-eighties soared to a high level. Average annual compound rate of growth attained during this period was 6.1 per cent. Though the state gathered momentum in agricultural production during eighties, the rate of growth started declining after 1992 and thus raised the question of sustainability. Weather aberrations were identified to be the prime cause for this temporary setback in recent past.[14] Another explanation may be that the resources have already been optimally exploited with the help of existing state of technology and hence another breakthrough of agrarian technology is called for in order to maintain the tempo of increasing growth rate of production. Deceleration of this high growth rate was observed in West Bengal along with two other highly growing states, Tamil Nadu and Punjab, where irrigation and fertiliser consumption were at a very high level.[15] Despite this the agricultural sector still remains the backbone of the economy of West Bengal.

Table 1.1: Contribution of Agriculture and its Allied Sectors to State Domestic Product (SDP)

(in crore)

Year/ Item	Agri-culture	Forestry	Fishery	(Col. 1+2+3)	State Domestic *Product*	Percent-age of *1 to 5*	Percent-age of *4 to 5*
(0)	(1)	(2)	(3)	(4)	(5)	(6)	(7)
1970-71	1313.4	7.42	57.69	1378.51	3168.1	41.46	43.51
1980-81	2640.6	109.7	283.85	3034.15	9594.0	27.52	31.63
1994-95	14554.34	551.6	1687.71	16793.65	49780.31	29.24	33.74

Source: *Statistical Abstracts of India* (*various issues*).

1.6 Importance of the Study

(i) The importance of agriculture on the economy of West Bengal has been well recognised. Though the relative contribution of agriculture to the state domestic product (SDP) has declined slightly, it still remains significant. Rapid population growth, along with the sluggish progress of industrialisation has necessitated the growth and increase in efficiency of agriculture. Major breakthrough came in the wake of 'Green Revolution'. The advent of new seed-fertiliser technology (widely known as the technology of the Green Revolution) after mid-sixties has brought a revolutionary change in the agricultural production of the state. Attendant on this mechanisation (application of labour saving technology leading to a rise in efficiency of labourer), rising irrigation potential, increasing application of electricity in agriculture and changing institutional factors (including land reforms) have added a new dimension to the agriculture of the state particularly after 1970.

Emphasis was primarily given to rice and wheat production to meet the excess demand for foodgrains. But after having attained self-sufficiency in foodgrains and with the development of market, agriculture of the state became increasingly commercialised. The agrarian growth has been marked by significant change in cropping pattern. Cropping pattern has changed in conformity with the changes/progress in technology and in keeping with the objective of maximising net gain from agriculture. Traditional varieties of crops have been replaced by new high yielding varieties and relatively more remunerative crops. The change associated with the redistribution of land resources to different crops ultimately has a bearing on accelerating growth and efficiency of agriculture in West Bengal.

(ii) The change in cropping pattern is not uniform not only, across the states but also within the state. The regional character of agriculture in West Bengal has reflected a significant inter-crop and intra-crop variation in production and productivity. It may be hypothesised that the complex inter-play of changes in economic, technological, institutional, organisational and social factors has caused these inter-district variations of production and productivity. A reasonably elaborate analysis at a disaggregated (district) level would thus help in bringing out the nature and underlying causes of crop diversification in West Bengal during 1970-71 to 1994-95 as well as its contribution towards changes in agricultural output of the state.

(iii) The breakthrough in agrarian technology through changing opportunities have changed the cropping pattern but with some time lag.[16] Though Green Revolution is known to have started in mid-sixties in Punjab and Haryana, in West Bengal it has started yielding results much later (in early seventies). Thus the period 1970-71 to 1994-95 is chosen for the purpose of study.

(iv) Moreover, no rigorous study at the disaggregated level has been made so far, to examine the nature and implication of crop diversification in West Bengal. A few scattered studies whichever are available do not offer full justice to the problem outlined so far.

(v) A special consideration of the district of Burdwan because of its pristine position in the agricultural economy of West Bengal is also well warranted. As is well known, because of its very large contribution to the state's food crop production the district has been described as the granary of West Bengal.

1.7 Scope of the Study

The contents of the study are divided in ten chapters. Excluding this introductory chapter, the next chapter contains the methodology of the study undertaken. Changes in cropping pattern in terms of acreage distribution during 1970-71 to 1994-95 have been discussed in chapter-3. Chapter-4 deals with the analysis of changes in geographical distribution of output growth of major crops in West Bengal. In chapter-5, changes in inter-district disparity of agricultural productivity have been considered. Chapter-6 is devoted to the analysis of contribution of cropping pattern component to total variation in agricultural output in West Bengal in terms of a component analysis. Thereafter, the statistical analysis of basic determinants of crop diversification is undertaken in chapter-7. Chapter-8 pertains to the brief discussion of regional variation/ disparity of changes in basic agricultural inputs in relation to cropping pattern. An empirical study with respect to the district of Burdwan is contained in chapter-9. The last chapter will give a brief reorientation of the whole study and illuminate the policy implications emanated from the throughout discussion.

NOTES AND REFERENCES

1 Government of India (1959), Report of the Food grains Enquiry Committee.

2 Boyce J. K. (1987), *Agrarian Impasse in Bengal: Agricultural Growth in Bangladesh and West Bengal 1949 - 1980*, Oxford University Press, Pp. 276-77.

3 Sawant S. D. (1993), "Rural and Agricultural Diversification", paper submitted to the orientation workshop in Rural Development, organised by the Adhoc Committee for courses in Rural development, University of Mumbai, Mumbai, April 6-13 *(mimeo)*.

4 Sawant S. D. (1997), "Performance of Indian Agriculture with Special Reference to Regional Variations", *Indian Journal of Agricultural Economics*, Vol-52, No. 3, July-Sept., pp. 353-373.

5 Vyas V. S. (1996), "Diversification in Agriculture: Concept, Rationale and Approaches", *Indian Journal of Agricultural Economics*, Vol-51, No. 4, Oct.-Dec., pp. 636-651.

6 Visaria P. (1995), "Rural Non-Farm Employment in India: Trends and Issues for Research", *Indian Journal of Agricultural Economics*, Vol. 50, No. 3, July-September.

7 It is also obvious from the table-1.1.

8 Pandey and Sharma (1996), "Diversification of Agriculture and Food Security in the Context of New Economic Policy", *Indian Journal of Agricultural Economics*, Vol. 51, No. 4, Oct.-Dec., pp. 644-650.

9 Vyas V. S., (1996), op. cit.

10 Pandey and Sharma, op. cit.

11 Government of India, Directorate of Agriculture, Ministry of Agriculture, Statistical Abstracts of India, (various issues) and Agricultural Situation in India.

12 Government of India, Census Report (1991), Series-1, Primary Population Total.

13 De U. K. (1993), "Changes in Population, Employment and the Pattern of Occupational Distribution in West Bengal, 1981-91", M. Phil Dissertation, Submitted at the University of Burdwan, (unpublished).

14 Sawant S. D., (1997), op. cit.

15 Sawant S. D. (1997), op. cit. and Fertiliser Association of India, *Fertiliser Statistics, (various issues)*.

16 Johl and Kahlon, (1963), pp. 132-142.

CHAPTER 2

METHODOLOGY, DATA AND THEIR LIMITATIONS

Inquiry into the economics of crop diversification in West Bengal during 1970-71 to 1994-95 has been done in several parts. Here, three major aspects of crop diversification viz. Nature, causes and consequences have been examined rigorously. In the next part of the analysis, nature of crop diversification that has taken place in West Bengal during 1970-71 to 1994-95 has been discussed from different angles. Thereafter, impact of crop diversification, mainly on agricultural production has been evaluated and finally an attempt has been made towards the analysis of important reasons behind this diversification.

2.1 Nature of Diversification

Nature of crop diversification is first examined through changes in allocation of land towards the cultivation of different crops grown in different seasons over the years. Inter-crop variations in output are also considered in contrast to the changing acreage allocation and also to know the regional pattern of diversification. In addition to that, inter-district disparity in agricultural productivity and its movement over time has been analysed in relation to cropping pattern change in chapter-5.

Changes in acreage distribution is explained by comparing the proportion of area under different crops to gross cropped area (GCA) during 1970-73, 1977-80, 1984-87 and 1991-94. Triennia average values of area under crops and that of GCA have been calculated for those years. Then the average proportion of area under each crop has been computed. The years 1970-73 and 1991-94 are considered, because they are the initial and final year of the period of discussion. The years 1977-80 represent the years of change of political scenario, when the Left-front government took over the power of the state. The establishment of the left-front led government has enforced the redistribution of land resources among the people through rigorous implementation of land reform measures. Moreover, a close look at the data on area, production of major crops reveals that there was a remarkable shift in area and production of various crops during mid-1980s.

Average annual exponential rate of growth of area under crops is estimated by fitting regressions of the type $LnY_{it} = \alpha+\beta t$, where Y_{it} represents the value of dependent variable (here it is area under i^{th} crop at time t), α and β are the two parameters and t is the time in years. The coefficient α represents the exponential rate of growth of Y. The trend equations have been fitted by ordinary least square method (OLS) for the whole period. Truncated regressions have also been fitted, by dividing the entire period into different sub-periods. Those are 1970-71 to 1978-79, 1979-80 to 1994-95, 1970-71 to 1981-82, 1982-83 to 1994-95 and 1986-87 to 1994-95.[1] Thereafter the change in rate of growth is estimated by forming the trend equations of the type $Ln\ Y = \hat{a}_0 + \hat{a}_1 t + \hat{a}_2 t^2$ where Y_i is the area under i^{th} crop, t is the time in years and $\hat{a}_0$, $\hat{a}_1$, $\hat{a}_2$ are the coefficients. Here $2\hat{a}_2$ represents the rate of change in the rate of growth. If the estimated value of it is positive and significant then growth is accelerating. On the other hand, a negative value of $\hat{a}_2$ represents a deceleration in the rate of growth.

Having considered the rate of growth and changes in the rate of growth of acreage of different crops, analysis has been done to consider the substitution and expansion of area under different crops. First of all, to ensure whether the area under any crop has been changed due to the inter-crop shift of area or because of changes in total area under cultivation, a simple elasticity method is followed. The elasticity of area under each crop with respect to GCA is calculated to identify the crops that have a gain in area from other crops and those, who lose area to formers. If the elasticity is greater than unity for any crop then it can be said that the area under that crop has increased due to both expansion of area under cultivation as well as substitution for area under decreasing crops. On the other hand if the elasticity is negative for any crop then it can easily be asserted that the crop has lost area to crops having elasticity greater than one. However if the elasticity is positive but less than one then it is very difficult to assert whether the rise in area is due to the expansion of total area under cultivation or due to substitution of area from other crops. Here one can only say that the area of the crop has increased at a rate less than that of the GCA.

The absolute quantity of gain or loss of area under each crop can be approximated in the following way:

Suppose a_0 and a_t are the area under an individual crop in the base and final period and A_0 and A_t are the gross cropped area in the base and final period. Then actual change in area under that individual crop during the period is $(a_t - a_0)$. If the proportion of area under that crop to GCA remains same throughout the whole period as was in the initial year (a_0/A_0) then $(a_0/A_0)A_t$ would be the final year area under that crop. Therefore, $(a_0/A_0)A_t - a_0$ may represent the change in area under an individual crop due to expansion of gross cropped area. It is then subtracted from the actual change in area under the reference crop (a_t-a_0) to get the change in area due to substitution effect. In other words, absolute amount of change in area due to substitution effect is estimated by subtracting from the final year area under each crop, the initial year area under it multiplied by the ratio of final and base year GCA, i.e., $\{a_t - a_0 .(A_t /A_0)\}$.

Variability and instability of acreage growth of different crops are also considered at district level. Variability of acreage growth around trend is tested by using Goldfeld-Quandt test[2] while instability of the same is tested by Chow test.[3]

Inter-crop and intra-crop variation in production of different crops is considered in chapter-4. Crop-wise changes in contribution of each district to total production of the state (in terms of proportion to total state's production) during 1970-71 to 1994-95 is considered first. Inter-district disparity has been measured by the coefficient of variation of proportion to state's total production. Then rate of change in production of each crop, during last two and half decades is measured by simple growth rates. Average annual exponential rate of growth of production of each crop has been estimated by least square regression, for the whole as well as all sub-periods, as was done in case of area under crops.

Inter-district disparity in agricultural productivity has been considered in chapter-5. Here log-linear trend equations are fitted for the estimation of annual exponential rate of yield-growth for major crops as was done in case of area and production. Then triennia average yield of different crops has been calculated for four discrete years 1970-73, 1977-80, 1984-87 and 1992-95. Inter-district disparity of crop-yield and its change during 1970-71 to 1994-95 has been considered in terms of cocfficient of variation and its change over time. Change in absolute yield of major crops in terms of simple growth rates during 1970-71 to 1994-95 has also been considered and compared. Finally, in order to show the inter-district disparity in agricultural productivity in aggregate and its variation over time a composite productivity index is formed at the district level for various years. The index is formed in the following way:

First of all, a *yield index* or *yield relative* has been calculated for different crops for each district and that in the state is calculated. Suppose Y_{ij} and Y_{io} are the average yield of ith crop in the jth district and in the state respectivrly. Then yield relative (K_{ij}) when expressed in percentage can be written as $K_{ij} = (Y_{ij}/Y_{io})* 100$. K_{ij} is the yield relative for i[th] crop in the jth district. Thereafter, these values are multiplied by the proportion of area under corresponding crop to total cropped area in the district and then added up to get the composite productivity index (CPI). Then *composite productivity index* (CPI) for the jth district can be written as $CPI_j = \Sigma(Y_{ij}/Y_{io}).(A_{ij}/A_{io}).100$, where $A_{io} = \Sigma A_{ij}$ and A_{ij}/A_{io} = proportion of area under i[th] crop in the jth district, j =1, 2, ..., 15. The index is calculated for the year 1970-71, 1978-79, 1985-86 and 1993-94. Inter-district disparity has been considered by coefficient of variation of these district level indices. The same index is also constituted for the food and non-food crops separately.

2.2 Impact of Changes in Cropping Pattern

Major impacts of cropping pattern change are explained with a special stress to its impact on agricultural production in chapter-6. In order to analyse the impact of changes in cropping pattern on agricultural production (crop output only) in west Bengal during 1970-71 to 1993-94, the seven factor additive scheme as suggested by Minhas, is used.[3] For this purpose, output of major crops in any year is computed first from the log linear trend equations.

Value of each crop-output at each point of time is then calculated by multiplying with base year price (triennia average of 1969, 70 and 71). Thereafter they are added to arrive at the total value of agricultural output. Thus the change in agricultural output during 1970-71 to 1993-94 has been computed and split up according to the source of variation by using additive scheme of decomposition. The same analysis has also been done for the two sub-periods namely, 1970-71 to 1981-82 and 1982-83 to 1993-94. The decomposition is done in the following way:

$$Q_t - Q_0 = A_t \Sigma C_{it} Y_{it} P_i - A_0 \Sigma C_{i0} Y_{i0} P_i ,$$

$$\text{Or, } Q_t - Q_0 = (A_t - A_0) \Sigma C_{i0} Y_{i0} P_i + A_0 \Sigma(C_{it} - C_{i0}) Y_{i0} P_i + A_0 \Sigma C_{i0} (Y_{it} - Y_{i0}) P_i + (A_t - A_0) \Sigma(C_{it} - C_{i0}) Y_{i0} P_i + (A_t - A_0) \Sigma C_{i0} (Y_{it} - Y_{i0}) P_i + A_0 \Sigma(C_{it} - C_{i0}) (Y_{it} - Y_{i0}) P_i + (A_t - A_0) \Sigma(C_{it} - C_{i0}) (Y_{it} - Y_{i0}) P_i .$$

Where Q_0 and Q_t represent base and final year value of gross agricultural output at constant prices (P_i), A_0 and A_t are the *gross cropped area* during period 0 and t respectively. C_{i0} , C_{it} and Y_{i0}, Y_{it} represent respectively the proportion of area under i[th] crop to the *gross cropped area* in the base and final period and yield of ith crop in the base and final year. P_i is the price of ith crop in the base (triennia average of harvest price in 1969, 70 and 71) year. The first three components on the right hand side of the equation represent direct effect of area, cropping pattern and yield on output. The next three are the interaction effects of area and cropping pattern, area and yield, cropping pattern and yield. The last one shows the interaction effect of changes in all these three area, yield and cropping pattern in the growth of output.

Alternatively, change in total agricultural output due to inter-crop substitution of acreage is estimated in the following way:

Total change in output over a period can be written as $Q_t - Q_0 = \Delta Q_{(A.C.Y.P)} = \Sigma A_{it} Y_{it} P_{it} - \Sigma A_{i0} Y_{i0} P_{i0} = f(A, C, Y, P)$ where P_{i0} and P_{it} are the prices of ith crop in the base and final period. A_{i0} and A_{it} are area under i[th] crop in the base and final period respectively. $\Delta Q_{(A.C.Y.P)}$ represents the change in output due to changes in above mentioned four responsible factors, area, cropping pattern, yield, and price. The other symbols are used in the same sense as used in former analysis. This methodology is followed because it is necessary and easily possible to eliminate the effects of other factors from the total change for isolating the cropping pattern effect.

From the total change in output, effect of changes in yield rates and prices can be eliminated by multiplying the areas in the final period with the respective yield rates and prices as in the base period and then subtracting from it the total production (value) in the base period. Therefore, $\Delta Q_{(A.C)} = \Sigma A_{it} Y_{i0} P_{i0} - \Sigma A_{i0} Y_{i0} P_{i0}$ represents the change in output due to changes in GCA and cropping pattern. From this again the effect of change in *gross cropped area* can further be eliminated, assuming that the increase or decrease in area under the crops has changed in the same proportion as that of *total cropped area*. Therefore, the effect of cropping pattern changes on agricultural output alone, is given by $\Delta Q_{(A.C)} - \Delta Q_{(A)} = \Delta Q_{(C)} = \Sigma A_{it} Y_{i0} P_{i0} - \Sigma A_{i0} Y_{i0} P_{i0} (A_t / A_0)$. $\Delta Q_{(C)}$ represents the effects of area changes of different crops occurred due to substitution effect, on total value of output. The same sort of analysis was earlier followed by National Council of Applied Economic Research (NCAER, 1966) in order to explain the impact of Cropping pattern change in Punjab.[4]

2.3 Reasons behind Diversification

Having considered the nature and consequences of crop diversification, an analysis of basic causes of crop diversification has been made in chapters 7-9. In the present study mainly, the reasons behind the growth of area under crops those have experienced a remarkable growth during the period under consideration is considered first. To find out the impact of basic determinants for rapid increase in area under some crops than others, price and non-price factors are identified. The methodology applied has been explained elaborately with justification in the relevant section. Here a precise description of the steps follows.

First of all, impact of some basic factors on area under fast growing crops is analysed by regression method. Since both price and non-price factors like, rainfall, irrigation, availability and use of chemical fertiliser, yield of crops etc. have some kind of influence on the acreage allocation by the farmers for the production of different crops, all of them are incorporated in the regression analysis. The regression analysis has been done in two parts. First of all, only the non-price factors like rainfall, irrigation, chemical fertiliser (which are essential for the cultivation of crops) and yield, are included in the analysis. Thereafter, the price factor is introduced in the extended version.

Firstly, area under a crop or crop-group is expressed as a function of rainfall (R), irrigation (I), chemical fertiliser (C) and yield (Y). The stochastic form of relationship can be written as

$$Ln\ A_{it} = b_0 + b_1\ LnR_t + b_2\ LnI_t + b_3\ LnC_t + b_4\ LnY_{it} + U_{0t} \qquad (1)$$

where A_{it} is the acreage of ith crop in the year t, R is the level of rainfall measured in millimetre, I is the area under irrigation, C represents consumption of chemical fartiliser, y, the yield of the particular crop. All of them are the explanatory variables. b_js are the coefficients representing elasticities of acreage growth with respect to the corresponding explanatory variables and U_{ot} is the conventional random disturbance term with usual classical linear regression properties.

A dummy variable (D_t) is also included as another explanatory variable, which is assumed to incorporate the effect of land reform measures undertaken by the Government of West Bengal on the acreage variation of crops. Then, the new stochastic form of equation will be

$$Ln\ A_{it} = b_0 + b_1\ LnR_t + b_2\ LnI_t + b_3\ LnC_t + b_4\ LnY_{it} + b_5\ D_t + U_{1t} \qquad (2).$$

Where, D takes value 0 in a pre-land reform year and it assumes value 1 in the post-land reform years starting with 1979. The equation is called the modified Cobb-Douglas form. Here it may be observed that explanatory variables are more or less correlated as yield of a crop is influenced by the quantity of rainfall, irrigation and chemical fertiliser or there is a complementarity between the level of irrigation and use of chemical fertiliser. So the multicollinearity problem and related issues would arise. In such a situation it is very difficult to form a consistent and perfect model, free from any kind of limitation. Any of the explanatory variables that have a strong correlation with some others may be excluded from the expression. But later (from the data) it is found that the correlation coefficient is not exactly equal to one. Moreover the identified variable has a particular type of influence on farmers' decision on acreage allocation. So all the variables are retained despite the presence of nearexact multicollinearity to avoid the specification bias. The regression is run on shifting basis. At first, only one independent variable is included and then number of explanatory variables are increased. By doing so it is possible to examine the increase in percentage of total variation explained after the introduction of additional variable. Simultaneously significance of the coefficients can be judged.

Prices of crops are also incorporated into the regression analysis in the same way, as the other explanatory variables were included in the model. Initially area under crops has been regressed only on price lagged one year or total proceeds per acre (price lagged one year multiplied by yield) to know the direct impact of price or per acre revenue on the planning of acreage. In the multiple regression equations price of the crop itself and that of its competing crops, yield of the competing crops along with the others are included in the extended version. In this context three different forms of extended versions are considered. These are:

$$\text{Ln } A_{it} = a_0 + a_1 \text{LnR}_t + a_2 \text{LnI}_t + a_3 \text{LnC}_t + a_4 \text{LnY}_{it} + a_5 \text{LnP}_{i-1} + a_6 \text{LnY}_{jt} + a_7 \text{Ln P}_{j-1} + a_8 D_t + U_{2t} \quad (3)$$

$$\text{Ln } A_{it} = a_0 + a_1 \text{LnR}_t + a_2 \text{LnI}_t + a_3 \text{LnC}_t + a_4 \text{LnT}_{it} + a_5 \text{LnT}_{jt} + a_6 D_t + U_{3t} \quad (4)$$

$$\text{Ln } A_{it} = a_0 + a_1 \text{LnR}_t + a_2 \text{LnI}_t + a_3 \text{LnC}_t + a_4 \text{Ln } (P_{i-1} Y_{it} / P_{j-1} Y_{jt}) + a_6 D_t + U_{4t} \quad (5)$$

Here P_{i-1} and P_{j-1} represent respectively price of ith crop and j^{th} crop lagged one year. Suffix j is used to denote the crop or crops that can be grown during the same season on the same field on which i^{th} crop is cultivated, U s are the random disturbance terms. a_6 and a_7 in Eq. 3

are the cross yield and price elasticities of area under i^{th} crop with respect to yield and price of jth crop. $T_i = (P_{i-1}.Y_i)$ and $T_j = (P_{j-1}.Y_j)$ are the proceeds per hectare of ith and j^{th} crop evaluated at the previous year's prices. a_4 and a_5 in equation-4 represent direct and cross elasticities of area under i^{th} crop with respect to proceeds per hectare of ith and j^{th} crop respectively. In equation-5 total turnover in ratio form are introduced, as explanatory variables on the presumption that, farmers would still continue to produce i^{th} crop if its relative revenue remains higher than the others (competitors), irrespective of the direction of price movement. This is done to examine whether the cultivators are much concerned with the relative revenue of crop or price, whatever be the cost. It is however true that; variation in yield and thus revenue is also associated with a change in cost per unit of area. The implicit assumption is therefore that, the cost of production per unit of area either has not changed or even if it has happened, had affected all the crops in a similar fashion and/ or the farmers had taken it at a discount.

Two other forms of equations

$$\text{Ln } (A_{it}/A_{jt}) = a_1 + b_1 \text{ Ln } (P_{i-1}/P_{j-1}) \quad (6)$$

and

$$\text{Ln } (A_{it}/A_{jt}) = a_2 + b_2 \text{ Ln } (P_{i-1}.Y_i/P_{j-1}.Y_j) = a_2 + b_2 \text{ Ln } (T_i/T_j) \quad (7)$$

are also considered and these estimated forms are compared with the earlier results to have a firm idea about the relative importance of price and non-price factors on the acreage allocation decision of the farmer.

An alternative approach is also considered along with the earlier versions. The alternative explanation is based on the actual interdependence that is observed among the yield and cost (simply profitability) of different crops, grown in successive seasons on the same plot of land. In the earlier approach, actually price and yield of crops those can be grown during the same season are considered for the explanation of acreage variation of any crop i.e., the crops, which are directly competitive in production, are considered. However profitability of crops grown successively on the same plot are partially dependent because of their overlapping harvesting and sowing season. With identical applicaion of all inputs yield of any crop would be different due to differences in crops cultivated in the earlier season on the same plot. So focus of attention should be turned towards the profitability of different combinations of crops that can be grown on the same plot of land where the objective of the farmer is to allocate land in successive seasons over the year in such a way as to maximise net benefit over the years. Having identified the basic inputs, the growth of which has enabled the farmers to expand area under some lucrative crops, profitability of different combinations of crops that can be tried throughout the whole crop-year on a particular plot has been calculated and compared.

Farmers are interested not only in the profit earned from the cultivation of crops in each season but also in the profit earned throughout the whole crop-year. Since choice of crops to be grown in any season may affect the revenue and cost of the next possible crops, the farmer may not choose one for cultivation even if it gives highest profit in that season but it hampers the cultivation of the next season's crops and hence the profitability in such a way that the total profit earned in a year is less than that if any other crop is chosen in the current season. The other one may yield somewhat less profit but may not disturb the yield or profit of the next season's crop. Their other objective is to secure that farm income at least possible risk. They can reduce the risk by proper choice of crops to be grown in successive seasons.

Profitability of different combinations of crops that can be grown on a particular plot of land in a crop year is calculated on the basis of the data on cost and revenue of different crops available from *the Study on Farm Management and Cost of Production of Crops in West Bengal, during 1993-94*. This was the latest study available, conducted by the Evaluation Wing, Directorate of Agriculture, Government of West Bengal. Here cross section study is followed because the combinations, which are seen now a day, were not practised in the early years of nineteen seventies. So it is not possible to compare the relative profitability of same combination during 1990s with that of 1970s after the adjustment of price indices. Here, just by comparing the profitability of different combinations it is possible to show that the crops involved in the highest remunerative combination occupies the most important position in the land allocation over different seasons of the year.

The aforesaid study however has one weakness that needs attention. Here profits of alternative combinations are calculated only by adding the profit of different crops incorporated in different combinations. This is because the data available do not present the cost or benefit of each crop for different cases i.e., corresponding to different preceding crops. Here data offered by Farm Management Study show the average cost and benefit of each crop, that is cultivated in combination with any of the possible combinations. Thus, for the purpose of analysis in the way desired, a primary survey has been conducted in the district of Burdwan.

Burdwan is one of the important agricultural districts of West Bengal[5]. The southern part of the district is highly dominated by agricultural activities than the northern part. Over past few decades agricultural development in the district has taken place at rapid rate. A sample of 60 farms is chosen 20 from each of the three villages in Madhabdihi block of southern Burdwan. The block is well developed in the agricultural sphere and the three contiguous villages are selected purposively as those villages were known for several years, where cultivation takes place intensively. Most of the plots are under multiple cropping. So it is possible to have data on cost and benefit of each crop with different preceding and succeeding crops on separate plots of land. Cropping is done for direct consumption as well as for marketing. There is good marketing facilities as well as co-operative and banking facilities. There exists well-organised irrigation infrastructure, mostly under private ownership and a part under government canals, river lift irrigation and deep-tubewells. Most of the plots can receive water for most of the time of the year. Farming is done with the help of both hired as well as own family labour.

From each village, 20 farms have been selected by simple random sampling without replacement. From each of the scientifically selected farm various data relating to the availability of irrigation facilities, topology of plots, price about the inventory and live stock with its value and the repair, if any etc. are collected. Information like utilisation of family labour and hired labour, quantity and value of seeds, fertilisers used, manures, quantity and share of landowner (if leased in), cost of machineries (pump-set, power tiller etc.) incurred for each crop (hired or own) are gathered. Data on quantity of land allocated for different crops in a particular season and the portion of area under each crop that had been used for which particular crop in the preceding season and in the succeeding season during the last crop-year has been collected. All the information relating to expenditure and revenue have been collected for each crop separately with different preceding crops. From the collected information, profitability of each crop with different preceding crops has been calculated. Using those, profitability of different combinations has been estimated. Thereafter a flow chart showing the flow of acreage in aggregate of all the sixty farms together in successive seasons has been drawn. Then a comparison has been made between the profitability of alternative combinations of crops in contrast with the acreage allocation towards different combinations to show the nature of relationship if there exist, between the flow of land allocation and profits of alternative competitive crop-combinations. Therefore the rationale behind the increasing allocation of land towards the most remunerative combination has been explained.

2.4 Data and Their Limitations

Data on area, production and yield of different crops have been collected from various issues of *Statistical Abstracts* and *Economic Review* of west Bengal, published by Bureau of Applied Economics and Statistics, Government of West Bengal. Data relating to those matters were furnished for North and South 24-Paraganas and Uttar and Dakshin Dinajpur separately for last few years. The values of area and that of production for the corresponding two districts are added to get the corresponding values for the 24-Paraganas and West Dinajpur as a whole and to have a consistency and comparability of data. Accordingly yield of crops have been recalculated. Data on gross cropped area at district level were not available for all the years. So an approximation is made by aggregating the area of major crops grown in West Bengal, which roughly covers more than 95 per cent of actual gross cropped area. Information regarding the area under high yielding varieties of crops is not available for major crops at district level and for all the years. So district-wise pattern of use of improved seeds over time cannot be explained. Area of tea is also not included in the gross cropped area calculation, though it is an important cash crop of the state and grown on a large scale in Darjeeling, Jalpaiguri and on a few places of Cooch Behar. It is not taken into consideration because it is not grown in all the districts and so it will have little relevance in explaining inter-district variation in cropping pattern change. But there may be some inconsistencies in the explanation of cropping pattern movement for those districts where it is the main cash crop. Explanation of inter-crop acreage substitution would be somewhat different from the actual case in those districts. But for the state as a whole it is not a matter of great concern.

Data on area under minor irrigation set-up like deep-tubewell, submersible pump, shallow-tubewell, river lift irrigation etc. are not available for all the years and hence they cannot be utilised along with area under canal irrigation to explain fully the role of irrigation development on the changes in cropping pattern. But minor irrigation set-up comprises an important part of total irrigation potential of the state. In the regression analysis of growth of area under crops on different factors, data on area under government canals only have been used instead of total area under irrigation potential from all sources in the respective season. It is true that canals cannot supply water with identical capacity in all the seasons of the year.

Minor irrigation in West Bengal has experienced a substantial growth during the last two and half decades. Whatever data are available have been used in chapter-8 to explain inter-district differences in cropping pattern change. Capacity of each irrigation set-up are always subject to some kind of change with the progress of technology and some are not able to provide water with equal capacity throughout the whole year. In this case using conversion-table, obtained from the office of the Directorate of Irrigation and Waterways, Government of West Bengal, area under minor irrigation sources has been calculated. In the calculation of potential irrigation, shallow-tubewell, submersible pumps and deep-tubewells are supposed to irrigate in all the three seasons of the year with almost equal capacity. River pumps are assumed to function with full potential twice of the three seasons of the year, whereas open dug well, filter points are assumed to function only in one season of the year. Government canals are also able to irrigate with full potential only in one season of the year. However there is always a possibility of error remaining in the estimation of potential capacity of irrigation in the state while converting the number of irrigation set-up into area-wise contribution. This is because all the deep-tubewells, shallow-tubewells are not of equal capacity and there is a large variations of capacity and power due to differences in quality of machinery, power set-up (if electrified) and level of water table, which differs across the places. Still there is no other alternative way but to follow the above methods and data available in the manner noted above.

NOTES AND REFERENCES

1. For some crops, data are not available for 1994-95 and hence the periods for them are considered up to 1993-94 for regression analysis.
2. Gold-feld Quandt Test:

$$F_{n_1-k,\, n_2-k} = \frac{\Sigma\, e_1^2/(n_1-k)}{\Sigma\, e_2^2/(n_2-k)}$$

Actually it is done after eliminating some central observations and comparing residual sum of squares (RSS) of two sub-periods. In this study, at first it is calculated without omitting any observation and then RSS of 1970-71 to 1978-79 sub-period is compared with the RSS of 1985-86 to 1993-94 sub-period. The two statistics are represented by F_1 and F_2 respectively.

3. Chow test,

$$F_{k,n_1+n_2-2k} = \frac{\{\Sigma e_p^2 - (\Sigma e_1^2 + \Sigma e_2^2)\}/k}{(\Sigma e_1^2 + \Sigma e_2^2)/(n_1 + n_2 - 2k)},$$

where $n_1+n_2 = n$. Here Σe_p^2 is the residual sum of squares considering the whole period or set of data and Σe_1^2 and Σe_2^2 are the residual sum of squares of first and second sub-periods, k is the number of parameters.

4. NCAER, (1966), *Cropping Pattern in Punjab*, New Delhi.

5. Not only that, Burdwan is one of the two agriculturally richest districts in India (the other in Punjab).

CHAPTER 3

NATURE OF CHANGES IN CROPPING PATTERN IN WEST BENGAL DURING 1970-71 TO 1994-95

3.1 Introduction

Cropping pattern is defined as a mix of agricultural crops that are grown in a particular geographical area. It can be viewed either in terms of area allocation per crop or production composition in value terms in an area. Therefore, changes in cropping pattern can be seen as changes in the proportion of area or value of production under different crops to total agricultural area or production. The cropping pattern may and usually change over time with the development of agriculture. Thus, no wonder that the development of agriculture in India is associated with the changes in cropping patterns over time[1]. The change is largely characterised by an increasing trend towards commercial crops over the years[2]. There are spatial variations in cropping pattern and its change not only across the states but also within a state. Taking the case of West Bengal the change in cropping pattern during 1970-71 to 1994-95 has not been uniform throughout all the districts. It has been characterised by great regional disparities.

Cropping pattern change is of great interest to the agricultural economists for its notable impact on agricultural output[3]. It is well known that the growth of agricultural production depends on both area and productivity growth[4]. The latter can be further decomposed into two parts. One is yield growth and other is the cropping pattern change. The former measures the impact of changes in output per unit of area while the latter captures shift of acreage from crops with relatively low values of output per unit of area to higher value crops[5].

Now area under all crops or gross cropped area (GCA) can be increased either through an increase in net cropped area or intensity of cultivation. Rise in intensity of cultivation is brought about by the extension of area under multiple cropping system. In the post-Green Revolution period increase in gross cropped area was made possible by the development of high-yielding, short-period crops or introducing multiple crops' production in a year, while the net cropped area ceased to grow significantly since most of the cultivable area have already been brought under cultivation[6]. The marginal expansion of net cropped area as well as introduction and expansion of multiple crop production have been possible due to the extension of area under irrigation in all seasons of the year. The introduction of high yielding crops and crops with short period maturity accompanied by the Green Revolution through rising intensity of cultivation has been a significant source of output expansion.

Bhalla and Singh (1997) has observed that the average annual compound growth rate of *gross cropped area* in West Bengal during 1970-73 to 1992-95 was only 0.57 per cent. During 1970-73 to 1980-83 period the growth rate was merely 0.11 per cent per annum while the rate increased to 0.95 per cent during 1980-83 to 1992-95 period. The net sown area growth that they have been calculated was negative, -0.09 per cent per annum for the whole period. It was 0.23 per cent during the period of 1970-73 to 1980-83 and -0.42 per cent during 1980-83 to 1992-95[7]. This was mainly due to the exhaustion of most of the available agricultural land and expansion of urban areas over agricultural lands[8].

It is important to note that adoption of a scientific cropping pattern best suited to the technological changes and that maximises net agricultural production in value terms is extremely essential. The decision of the cultivators to allocate available resources to different crop production in a particular region depends on the economic, geographical, technological, social and institutional factors. Thus impact of changes in these factors can be felt only when the existing cropping pattern changes. Generally the farmers have a tendency to stick to a stable cropping pattern under any given agro-climatic region unless they are dictated by the price factors in adjusting acreage allocation[9]. A breakthrough in agrarian technology through changing production opportunities do change the cropping pattern but with some time lag[10]. A shift from traditional varieties of crops to new high yielding and relatively more remunerative crops has added a new dimension to the agriculture of West Bengal. The change is associated with the redistribution of land resources to different crops, which ultimately has a bearing on accelerating growth and efficiency of agriculture in West Bengal.

Changes in absolute and proportion of area under different crops may reasonably be considered for the analysis of change in cropping pattern; since farmers' interest in producing different crops is primarily reflected in the acreage of each crop in most cases[11]. Generally farmers are guided by the relative profitability of crops in the system of commercialised agriculture and thus area under crops change depending on past prices and the changes in technology, expansion of irrigation and possibility of productivity change in the respective region or districts.

One could have considered the changes in relative contribution of each crop output to total agricultural production after evaluating their value of production. But the farmers in each region respond to the local prices of crops and the regional variation of agricultural prices is so large that, it is very difficult (if not an impossible one) to bring all of them into consideration. Moreover, output in value terms of any crop and its contribution to total agricultural output may not move in the same direction as the area does. This is because; the value depends on the relative change in price as well as quantity of output, which is attributable to change in area and yield. With same or even lower area under any crop, production of that crop may increase due to increase in yield. Similarly despite increase in area, output of any crop may fall because of sudden setback in yield. Again, with increased quantity of output of any crop, absolute and relative contribution of that crop to total agricultural production in value terms may decrease if price decreases sufficiently. Therefore, the change in relative contribution of each crop to total agricultural production in value terms in different districts or region depends on complex interplay of relative change in area, yield and prices of the respective region[12]. Thus it is relatively much easier to consider the movement of acreage distribution.

3.2 Some Earlier Considerations

Various studies have been devoted to analyse the nature of cropping pattern changes in several places at different times. Bhalla and Singh (1997) have explained the cropping pattern change at the state level in terms of area allocation among different crops[13]. Taking a sum of 43 major crops produced in India they have shown that the changes have taken place in favour of high value crops. They observed that the change was rapid after 1980 than the early post-Green Revolution years. During 1962-65 to 1980-83 substantial increase in area under wheat in West Bengal had taken place at the cost of pulses but after that area under wheat continued to decline. However rice remains the main cereal crop and its share to total cropped area has increased slightly. They have also considered the relative share of crops to total value of output in different regions for explaining the changes in cropping pattern.

Acreage allocation has changed in favour of high value crops at all India level and also in Eastern states including West Bengal as well[14]. The growth of area under different crops and their proportions have exhibited different trends over time as well as in different regions. The primary causes of this regional disparity of cropping pattern or changes in inter-crop variations in proportion of area are the differences in relative yield of different crops, relative price advantage, climatic condition, development of irrigation and technological innovation. Along with these, the expansion of market and rapid transformation of subsistence to profit oriented agricultural production have led to the disproportionate change in production and contribution of individual crop to total agricultural crop production and area under crops in different places.

Dhindsa and Sharma (1995) have studied the aggregate changes in cropping pattern in Punjab during 1965-66 to 1990-91 in terms of "*expansion and substitution effects*"[15]. The two effects have been measured by *area - gross cropped area elasticities* of various crops[16]. They have divided the whole period into two sub-periods and calculated the same for each sub-period also. They have also shown the impact of change in cropping pattern on total returns of agriculture in Punjab with the help of a seven factor additive model, as suggested by Minhas[17].

C. G. Ranade (1980) has used a cropping pattern index to observe its variation and impact on agricultural production over time in India[18]. Taking inter-district data on crop output for the state of West Bengal, J.K.Boyce (1987) has shown that cropping pattern component displays a very strong effect on output growth during the post- Green Revolution period. Using the method of Minhas and Parikh (1966) he has shown that the cropping pattern effect is different in different districts of West Bengal and Bangladesh[19]. The effect was found to be much stronger in the fastest growing districts Hooghly, Malda, Nadia and Murshidabad.

Bhalla and Alagh (1979, pp.48, 51, 54); who has decomposed the output growth in 289 Indian districts for the period 1962-65 to 1970-73 using point to point estimates based on the triennia average, have shown a negative cropping pattern effect in thirteen of West Bengal's fifteen districts and positive yield-cropping pattern interaction component in all but one[20]. Studies have also been conducted to distinguish factors responsible for crop diversification. Narayanamoorthy (1997) has identified the irrigation as very important factor for increasing area under non-food crops[21]. He also argued that the changes in the system of farming (from subsistence to commercial) were closely associated with the crop diversification in India. The details have been considered in the latter chapters of this book.

3.3 Changes in Cropping Pattern in West Bengal during 1970-71 to 1994-95

This section is devoted to the examination of cropping pattern change in West Bengal during 1970-71 to 1994-95. For the purpose of analysis, first of all, changes in proportion of area under different crops to total agricultural area is considered. Since data on gross cropped area are not available throughout the whole period, an approximation is made by aggregating the area of major crops grown in West Bengal and for all districts separately from 1970-71 to 1993-94[22]. Then relative changes in the proportion of area under each crop to total cropped area[23] for all districts have been considered and compared. For the rigorous presentation, the whole period is divided into two broad sub-periods: 1970-71 to 1981-82 and 1982-83 to 1994-95. Moreover, for comparing the relative change before and after the implementation of land reform measures the sub-periods 1970-71 to 1978-79 and 1979-80 to 1994-95 have also been considered. A close look at the acreage data of different crops reveals a spectacular shift that has taken place for major crops since mid-nineteen eighties. So growth during post- mid-eighties is considered and again compared with that during the first (1970-71 to 1978-79) sub-period.

Log linear trend equations by least square regression of the type $LnY_i = \alpha+\beta t$, have been tried on area under each crop in different districts and in different sub-periods to examine their relative growth and the ups and downs of importance of different crops over time in the state's agricultural scenario.

3.3.1 Relative Changes in Proportion of Area under Different Crops

Inter-crop variation in growth of area and proportion of area is discernibly large over time in West Bengal. It is reflected from Table 3.1 that rice still continues to remain the most important crop of the state. This is because of the well-known great plain land, fertile and suitable for the cultivation of paddy, which is the staple food crop of the majority of the inhabitants of the state. The table represents the three-year moving average value of absolute and proportion of acreage.

Proportion of area under foodgrains as a whole declined but at a diminishing rate. It was 89.0 per cent in 1970-73 and decreased to 86.56 per cent in 1977-80. It further decreased to 83.9 and around 83 per cent in 1984-87 and 1991-94 respectively. Though during the first and second eight years it had declined by 2.44 per cent and 2.66 per cent, during the last eight years period, the proportion declined by only 0.92 per cent. Within the foodgrains, cereal registered a declining trend through 1970-73 to 1984-87 while it has increased afterwards. The proportion declined by 1.5 and 0.16 percent during 1970-73 to 1977-80 and 1977-80 to 1984-87, while it increased by 0.88 per cent during 1984-87 to 1991-94. Above all, the proportion of area under cereals continued to remain around 80 per cent of the gross cropped area. Though during 1977-80 to 1991-94 proportion of area under foodgrains had declined, that of cereal registered an opposite trend. It can therefore reasonably be surmised that the proportion of non-cereal food crops i.e., pulses must have suffered a serious setback. The fall in the proportion of area under pulses was large because cereals occupied the major portion of area under foodgrains as well as gross cropped area and so even a smaller percentage increase in area under it implies a large increase in absolute area under cereals and hence the proportion of *gross cropped area* allocated to pulses registered a concomitant decline. Share of pulses in total area have been decreasing continuously from 8.77 per cent in 1970-73 to 7.83 per cent in 1977-80 and again to 5.78 and 3.53 per cent respectively in 1984-87 and 1991-94. The proportion of other cereals including jawar, bazra, ragi, small millet etc. also, has experienced a steady decline. The percentages were 1.96, 1.48 and 1.02 in 1970-73, 1977-80 and 1991-94 respectively[24].

Among cereal crops, share of paddy had decreased by 1.48 per cent, from 72.7 per cent in 1970-73 to 70.22 per cent in 1977-80 before it increased steadily but slowly to 74.85 per cent during 1991-94. Proportion of wheat experienced just opposite trend to that of rice throughout the whole period. It had increased first from an average of 5.57 per cent during 1970-73 to 7.03 per cent during 1977-80 (i.e., by 1.46 per cent) before it declined continuously to 3.58 per cent (i.e., by 3.45 per cent) in 1991-94.

Within paddy different pattern of trend have been observed by its different sub-categories. Among aus (bhadoi rice), aman (winter rice) and boro (summer rice) proportion of aman has been the largest and thus changes in its share was largely reflected in the movement of share of paddy as a whole. Considering the entire state, share of area under aman has declined, first by 1.68 per cent; from 57.31 per cent in 1970-73 to 55.63 per cent in 1977-80 and then remains more or less stable or some times increased marginally. Proportion of aus (bhadoi rice) has declined persistently from 11.73 per cent in 1970-73 to 6.98 per cent in 1991-94. The rate of decrease throughout the whole period has been 4.75 per cent. On the other hand, there has been a tremendous increase in the percentage share of area under boro (summer rice). It is evident from the table that the share has increased by 7.17 per cent throughout the entire period. The proportions were 4.13, 4.67, 7.68 and 12.3 per cent respectively in 1970-73, 1977-80, 1984-87 and 1991-94.

Among the non-food crops, proportion of area under oilseed registered a sharp increase during the whole period. The share was 2.55, 3.2, 5.48 and 7.05 per cent in 1970-73, 1977-80, 1984-87 and 1991-94 respectively. Among oilseed the maximum beneficiary has in general been mustard and then til. Proportion of area under mustard has increased from 1.50 per cent in 1970-73 to 5.14 per cent in 1991-94. Potato has also experienced a significant rise in proportion of area during the period under consideration. Proportion of gross cropped area allocated for the cultivation of potato has increased from merely 1.03 per cent in 1970-73 to 1.84 per cent in 1977-80 and then to around 3 per cent (three times of 1970-73) in 1991-94. Jute, once the most important cash crop of Bengal began to lose its importance after the arrival of relatively more profitable crops and reduction of its prospect owing to great setback in the market resulting from the emergence of non-agricultural synthetic substitutes. In 1970-73 the proportion of area under jute was 5.98 per cent. It increased to 7.07 and 8.23 per cent respectively in 1977-80 and 1984-87 but then it started declining for the last ten years. The proportion was around 6.68 per cent during 1991-94. Sugarcane also experienced a continuous decline throughout the whole period.

Within each crop it was found that the acreage moved from low yielding to high yielding varieties. Table 3.2 reveals that high-yielding varieties of aus, aman and boro rice were 11.23, 8.67 and 60.93 per cent in 1972-73 in terms of acreage. The proportion to total area under those crops were respectively 34.38, 23.97 and 97.19 per cent in 1978-79 but then growth rate of high-yielding varieties decreased. In 1985-86 the proportions were 37.88, 31.98 and 99.94 per cent respectively. After 1985-

86 again the proportions have increased rapidly. The proportions were found to be 90.81, 50.73 and 100 per cent for aus, aman and boro rice in 1993-94. Proportion of HYV rice, as a whole was 13 per cent in 1972-73. The figure was 32.28, 39.4 and 63.17 in 1978-79, 1985-86 and 1993-94 respectively. Proportion of area under high yielding varieties of wheat was 92.61 per cent in 1972-73 but reached to almost 100 per cent after 1978-79. The above results indicate that though proportion of non-food crops has increased, the benefit has not been accrued equiproportionately to all non-food crops. Inter-period and inter-crop variation in proportion of acreage growth has been observed to be significant.

3.3.2 Growth of Absolute Area under Different Crops

In this section the growth of absolute area under each crop has been examined. From the semi-logarithmic trend equations,

$$\text{Ln } Y_{it} = \alpha + \beta t$$

(where, Y_{it} represents area under i^{th} crop at time t, t represents time in year and α, β are the two parameters, β gives the annual exponential rate of growth of area and its fluctuation around trend can be estimated by using standard error) an idea about the changes in relative importance of different crops in terms of absolute area can be formed. The result displayed in table- 3.3 reveals a quite different pattern of change to that of inter-crop proportion of area.

The table reveals that annual exponential rate of growth of area under foodgrains was only 0.04 per cent during 1970-71 to 1994-95. The sub-period growth rates indicate an increasing trend[25]. Though rate of growth of absolute area under foodgrains was positive, proportion of the same to total cropped area declined during the period of discussion (from table 3.1). This is a clear indication of relatively lower rate of growth of area under foodgrains than that of total cropped area.

Within foodgrains, area under cereals registered a positive rate of growth during 1970-71 to 1994-95. This was accounted for by a moderate rate of growth of rice which more than counter balanced an even moderate negative trend rate of growth of wheat and other cereals[26]. The overall rate of growth of total cereals was only 0.36 per cent per annum. A comparison of sub-period growth rates indicates the accelerated pattern of growth of cereals in terms of absolute area devoted to the cultivation of the same. During 1970-71 to 1978-79 the rate of growth was 0.71 per cent per annum while the rate was 0.96 per cent during 1979-80 to 1994-

95. Like foodgrains as a whole, cereals also experienced a negative rate of growth during 1970-71 to 1981-82 and then upturned during 1982-83 to 1994-95 period. During 1986-87 to 1994-95 average annual exponential rate of growth was 0.60 per cent.

The rise in the area under cereals was also at the cost of area under pulses. Acreage allocated to pulses decreased by 4.4 per cent per annum during 1970-71 to 1994-95 period. In spite of having a tremendous growth of more than 5 per cent per year during 1970-71 to 1978-79, area under wheat registered an overall decline at the rate of 1.86 per cent per annum throughout the entire period. Area under rice increased at the annual exponential rate of 0.58 per cent per annum throughout the entire period. The rate was 0.31 and 0.90 per cent respectively during the first and last nine-year period. The rate of growth was found to be increasing from the comparison of sub-period growth rates[27].

Among different kinds of paddy, boro (summer rice) has recorded a maximum gain in the sense of rate of rise in acreage under crop. A great part of land that formerly used to remain uncropped (those were not suitable for boro cultivation because of absence of irrigation facilities without which production of it is unimaginable) during summer season have been brought under cultivation after the gradual development of irrigation infrastructure. Traditionally some amount of land was used for sowing til during summer but harvested at the mercy of rain-god. With the spread of irrigation the area coverage under boro cultivation galloped on a vigorous scale after having replaced some other relatively less remunerative crops. Rate of growth of area under boro rice had been 6.21 per cent per annum throughout the entire period (1970-71 to 1993-94) and the rate continued to increase subsequently. During 1979-80 to 1993-94 the growth rate was around ten per cent per annum, almost twice that of the earlier period. Aman (winter rice) has registered a marginal increase in terms of absolute area throughout the whole period, whereas aus (bhadoi rice) was a moderate loser. During the whole period 2.33 per cent per annum rate of decline was found for aus and in case of aman the rate of growth was noticed as merely 0.24 per cent per annum.

Among others, notable increase was noticed in case of potato, and oilseed (whose principal component is mustard). The rate of overall increase for area under potato was around 5.3 per cent and that of oilseed was nearly 5.8 per cent per annum during 1970-71 to 1993-94 period. Acreage of mustard has increased by an average exponential rate of 7.74 per cent per annum. During 1970-71 to 1978-79, 1970-71 to 1981-82 and 1982-83 to 1993-94 average annual rate of growth was -1.75, 2.34 and 9.4 per cent respectively. Area under jute cultivation has increased by 2.28 per cent per annum during 1970-71 to 1978-79. Quantity of land allotted for jute cultivation however declined since 1979-80. Annual average exponential rate of reduction was 0.66, 0.20 and 1.8 per cent respectively during 1979-80 to 1993-94, 1982-83 to 1993-94 and 1985-86 to 1993-94 sub-periods. The overall trend indicates an increase in area under jute at an annual average rate of 1.11 per cent[28]. Sugarcane continued to wither out of the agricultural field throughout the whole period despite a mild increase during immediate post mid-eighties.

From the above analysis of the results obtained, it is clear that the cropping pattern in West Bengal in terms of allocation of acreage has been skewed towards boro paddy, potato and oilseeds (especially mustard), the three important emerging cash crops during the last two decades. Cropping pattern turned against pulses, coarse cereals and sugarcane throughout the period of discussion. After 1980, the second important food-crop, wheat and erstwhile most preferable cash crop, jute continued to lose their importance along with pulses, inferior cereals and sugarcane in the agricultural scenario of West Bengal. From the values of standard errors it is found that variations in the acreage growth rate were greater for the rapid growing crops. For each individual crop in most cases the variations in growth rates were on the average greater in the early years (first nine-year sub-period) compared to that of latter years (last nine-year sub-period). This is mainly because, during the early years, irrigation development was at the primary stage and consequently agriculture was highly weather dependent.

3.4 Acceleration and Deceleration in the Rate of Growth of Acreage

The change in rate of growth of area allocated to the cultivation of different crops can directly be measured from the estimation of the quadratic equation of the type

$$\text{Ln } Y = \hat{a}_0 + \hat{a}_1 t + \hat{a}_2 t^2$$

where, Y_i is the area under i[th] crop, t is the time in years and $\hat{a}_0$, $\hat{a}_1$, $\hat{a}_2$ are the coefficients. Here $2\hat{a}_2$ represents the rate of change in the rate of growth. If the estimated value of it is positive and significant then growth is accelerating. On the other hand a negative value of $\hat{a}_2$ represents a deceleration in the rate of growth. The results are depicted in Table 3.4.

Table 3.4 reveals that the state observes an increasing rate of growth of area under foodgrains. This was due to increasing rate of growth of cereals which more than offset the significantly decreasing rate of reduction in area under pulses. Among cereals paddy especially boro rice has experienced significantly increasing rate of growth. The district of Bankura, Midnapore, Howrah, West Dinajpur, Malda, Cooch Behar and Purulia have seen faster rate of growth of acreage under boro rice over time. West Dinajpur, Jalpaiguri, Cooch Behar, Darjeeling in the northern Bengal registered significantly decreasing rate of growth (i.e., deceleration) of area under wheat while Malda witnessed the opposite trend. Foodgrains and cereals as a whole have shown significantly accelerated rate of growth in acreage distribution in most of the southern districts. Deceleration in area under jute was found at a decelerating rate in all the districts except in Malda and Cooch Behar. Oilseed and potato have also registered significantly declining rate of growth in most of the districts. Only in Midnapore, an accelerated growth of acreage of potato was noticed.

3.5 Comparative Ranking of Crops in West Bengal in terms of Acreage Distribution

A glimpse of comparative ranking of different crops at different time can be had from the comparison of inter-crop proportion of area under cultivation. The results are shown in Table 3.5.

From Table 3.5, it is observed that rice is at number one position throughout the entire period. Oilseed as a group became the second most important crop of the state from its number five position in 1970-73. Proportion of area under mustard, which is the principal component of oilseeds, has increased from 1.5 per cent of total cropped area in 1970-73 to around 5.14 per cent in 1991-94. Wheat, jute and sugarcane have been more or less stable at their relative position of 4, 3 and 8 respectively but they are the great losers in terms of absolute and proportion of area under each of them. Potato was elevated just one step to number 6 position in 1991-94 from its number 7 position in 1970-73. However, it is a huge gainer of area in absolute sense. Pulses as a whole registered a demotion to the fifth position from its second position in 1970-73. Therefore, it is obvious that potato and oilseeds improved their positions at the cost of pulses, coarse cereals and wheat[29].

3.6 Districtwise Changes in Cropping Pattern

Districtwise pattern of changes in area-wise composition of crops over time in West Bengal has been varied and divergent. In the districtwise acreage distribution, foodgrains specially the aman rice remains the most important item of all the districts occupying the major portion of total as well as of net cropped area. The proportion of area under foodgrains has however declined in almost all the districts during 1970-73 to 1977-80 and also during the entire period. In the district of Howrah however it decreased during 1970-73 to 1977-80 and then increased slightly. In Jalpaiguri and Cooch Behar it had experienced an increasing trend during 1970-73 to 1977-80 before the inception of declining trend in the beginning of the rest of the period. Among food crops proportion of area under rice decreased in the districts of Bankura, Midnapore, Hooghly in the southern West Bengal and Jalpaiguri, Darjeeling and Cooch Behar in the north. In the districts of Birbhum, Howrah, 24-Paraganas, Nadia, Murshidabad and Malda rice has experienced a rise in terms of proportion of area over time; whereas Burdwan experienced a decrease first during 1970-73 to 1977-80 and again an increase later. In absolute terms, area under rice has increased during 1970-71 to 1994-95 in all but one though the pattern is different for different districts and sub-periods. Over different sub-periods area under different sorts of rice reflect divergent pattern of trends. Proportion of area allocated for the cultivation of boro rice registered a notable increase persistently but the rate was different for different districts. Significantly larger rate of increase was found in Nadia, Bankura, Howrah, Hooghly, Burdwan, Birbhum, Midnapore, 24-Paraganas and Murshidabad i.e., almost in all the south-Bengal districts except Purulia and Malda, West Dinajpur, and Cooch Behar in the north. The rate of growth was higher during 1970-71 to 1981-82 sub-period than in 1982-83 to 1993-94 sub-period in Burdwan, Hooghly and Nadia; while the case is reversed for other districts. In other words deceleration in the rate of growth is observed in those three districts and acceleration for other cases.

One possible reason would be that these three districts had easy accessibility to irrigation sources. So most of the potential sources had already been tapped in the immediate post-Green Revolution years with the help of simple irrigation technology available at that time and at cheaper cost. Thus, expansion of irrigation had taken place at a rapid rate in the early years. But with the passage of time, speed of extension of further irrigation despite improved technology became slower. This has slackened the rate of growth of cropped area in these districts, as irrigation is the most important precondition of boro cultivation[30]. On the other hand, in the districts with vast drought-prone areas like Purulia, Bankura etc., Government and private irrigation development programmes started later owing to the difficulty and long gestation period of those irrigation projects (those districts are mainly dependent on canal irrigation because ground water irrigation is very difficult and costly affairs for those areas). Moreover, in the districts like Burdwan, Hooghly etc. irrigation (especially ground water) is comparatively much cheaper and so even the ordinary (middle or small farmers) farmers could easily set up shallow, tubewell, submersible pumps or any other system for the exploitation of ground water on their own account which was not possible for the same category of people in the arid or semi-arid region. For this reason private irrigation development was rapid in Burdwan, Hooghly and Nadia than that of other districts during the early years. Districtwise pattern of development of irrigation infrastructure has been elaborately discussed in chapter-8.

Aman has been the major cereal and paddy crop of all districts of West Bengal. Proportion of its area though decreased in most of the southern part, it had increased in Birbhum, Nadia and Murshidabad. The northern districts experienced an increase in proportion of area under aman during the later years after having suffered squeezes during the early period. In absolute terms the trend was negative during the whole period in Burdwan and during the second period in Birbhum, Midnapore, 24-Paraganas respectively. During sub-period 1970-71 to 1978-79 the trend was negative in Murshidabad, West Dinajpur, Jalpaiguri, Darjeeling and Purulia. In other cases trend rate of growth was positive. During the sub-period 1985-86 to 1993-94 the growth of area under aman was positive but insignificant in all but Jalpaiguri and Darjeeling of West Bengal's fifteen districts. Area under aus in absolute term also saw a decelerating trend throughout the entire period in all the districts except Darjeeling. The net effect of trend rate of growth of aus, aman and boro was however positive but not significant.

Among rabi crops, sharp reduction in area under wheat were noticed in central region (Burdwan, Birbhum, Bankura, Howrah and Hooghly) while the northern districts experienced a positive trend of the same in terms of proportion and absolute area. Sizeable growth in absolute and proportion of area under potato have been noticed in a descending order in central and southern districts like Hooghly, Burdwan, Midnapore,

Howrah and only Jalpaiguri in the northern region. Here potato has replaced wheat and rabi pulses as a major rabi crops because of its higher yield, higher possible remuneration and possibility of yielding greater profit in combination with the other crops during a whole crop-year on the same field i.e., higher expected total profit on the same plot of land. Innovation of new technology has expedited and made the cultivation of potato much easier. So with the passage of time more and more land have been brought under the cultivation of potato within the desired time interval [31].

Sowing and harvesting seasons also stand as some important factor through which the interdependence of production and productivity of crops is felt. Therefore, these are the other important factors playing a vital role in determining the combination of crops to be chosen for growing on a particular plot of land on the merit of its *total profitability in a crop year*[32]. Generally, it is optimal to grow three crops on most plots of land where sufficient irrigation, an important (essential during winter and summer season) precondition of agriculture is available. That means three successive seasons in which crops can be grown successively on a particular plot (e.g., aus, potato and boro rice) in a cyclical order can constitute a complete crop year. They are grown in a cyclical order year after year. However, the crops grown within a cycle may change over time on the basis of their merit of changing remuneration in accordance with the changing circumstances. The *optimal combination* chosen each year is determined by the *total and net remuneration expected* by the cultivators. Though the blueprint of cycle in many cases is prepared in the beginning of each crop year or much earlier than that, cultivators may switch over (totally or partially) to other combination owing to the changing circumstances (such as availability of fertilisers, prices of seeds, changing weather conditions etc.). *It is empirically found that cultivation of boro rice preceded by the harvest of wheat in February-March on the same plot of land is a late-running performance and its productivity would be much lower even with usual applications of other factors, than that if it had been sown earlier. Moreover, harvesting of boro rice may be confronted with problems if monsoon arrives earlier and the profitability of wheat is not so high that it can compensate the expected loss of boro rice emanating from its late sowing. On the other hand, if jute is cultivated after wheat, then its usual productivity is not affected due to this problem of matching of time. Again, if boro rice is preceded by potato on the same plot then its cultivation is also delayed slightly and its normal yield is likely to be affected adversely. But the farmers may still choose the combination if the expected profitability of potato is substantial (in spite of costly affairs) and can compensate (or even more than offset the loss of profit incurred due to late running performance of boro) the reduction of profitability of boro rice.* In other words, it may be the best choice combination if the expected profit of the combination is not less than that of any other alternative combination. The choice of combination of crops to be grown on a particular plot of land is guided by the *expected total or net remuneration* from that holding in a *crop year*. The farmers will prefer that one where there is a greater possibility of recovering the loss incurred for any crop failure (either due to natural calamities or market failure) by the production of next alternative crop and the peasants are left with the possibility of earning more from their limited field. However, some farmers by virtue of their managerial ability, availability of resources may pursue different combination or cycle on different plots within their own area (the reasons for diversification will be elaborately discussed in chapter-7). From the above discussion it is clear that, over the years, farmers in the developed agricultural regions increasingly switched over to the best profitable and convenient/ combination like high yielding aus/aman in the kharif season, potato/ mustard in the rabi season and then boro rice in the summer from their traditional combination of either local aus, wheat/pulses/other rabi crops and til/jute or aman and til/jute in the respective season by one circulation.

Among the districts a negative trend of absolute area under foodgrains is observed in Birbhum, Murshidabad in the southern region and West Dinajpur, Malda, Jalpaiguri in the northern region throughout the entire period. The lowest positive trend rate of growth has been found in case of Hooghly. In spite of high rate of growth of boro rice and moderate rate of growth of area under aman, Birbhum registered a net decrease in absolute area under foodgrains due to the huge loss of area under wheat and pulses. The district now has become a major oilseed producer instead of pulses and is thus coping with the tempo of other oilseed producing districts in southern West Bengal.

3.7 Substitution and Expansion Effect in Acreage Changes

One may have doubt, whether the big swing of area in favour of boro rice, potato and oilseed was only due to the increase in total agricultural area i.e., bringing more land under cultivation or at the cost of the area under other crops which have been losing area under them.

It has already been noted in chapter-1 that net-cropped area has not increased significantly during the period under consideration. Land that used to remain fallow during off-monsoon seasons might have come under cultivation. Still one can investigate whether the importance of those three crops has increased. This may be viewed in a simple way. Even if the rise in area is supposed to have occurred due to increase in area under cultivation i.e., gross cropped area, it can still be argued that these increased areas were not devoted for the production of crops other than the aforesaid crops. So, there is no doubt that their importance relative to the other crops has increased. However, it is possible to show both at the state level as well as district level that, a part of increased area under the newly emerging important cash crops happened to be at the cost of losers. Whether the growth of area under different crops was due to *expansion* of area under cultivation (net or gross cropped area) or due to *substitution* for area under other crops can be shown in the following way[33].

3.7.1 Crop-area—Gross Cropped Area Elasticity

In order to have an idea about the acreage change of each crop due to inter-crop substitution of areas and expansion of gross cropped area, the method of *crop-area--gross cropped area elasticities* are resorted here. The elasticity for ith crop is measured by the ratio of proportional change in area under ith crop and gross cropped area[34]. Suppose E_i represents area-gross cropped area elasticity of ith crop. Then if (i) $E_i > 1$ it indicates the rate of growth of area under ith crop is greater than the rate of growth of total cropped area. So the increase in area under ith crop occurred not only due to the expansion of total cropped area i.e., expansion effect but also owing to the substitution effect, (ii) if $E_i < 0$ that is, elasticity is negative, there is loss of area under ith crop due to substitution effect. All these crops registered negative rates of growth of area under them during the period. Again (iii) if $0 < E_i < 1$ i.e., the rate of growth of area under ith crop is positive but less than that of gross cropped area, there arises ambiguity as to the identification of the gain attributable to substitution and expansion effect. May it be the fact that a part of increased gross cropped area have been devoted to the production of ith crop but substitution effect went in reverse direction and still the net effect is positive or the substitution effect may even be zero[35]. The two effects may act in opposite direction or same direction but yield a net positive change in acreage. The values of crop-area -- gross cropped area elasticities are displayed in Table 3.6.

The Table shows that elasticity is greater than one during the entire period in case of boro rice, total rice, mustard, total oilseed, potato and jute. The value is negative for aus, wheat, pulses and sugarcane. Elasticity is positive but less than one in case of aman, total cereal, total foodgrains for which it is very difficult to say from the elasticity whether the increase in area is due to substitution or expansion effect. The same sort of result is obtained in all subperiods and for each crop or crop group, except jute for which elasticity is less than one during 1979-80 to 1993-94 and wheat whose elasticity is greater than one during 1970-71 to 1978-79 period.

Since E > 1 for boro rice, mustard, potato and jute, their acreage was enhanced by both the *substitution* and *expansion effect*. Pulses, wheat and sugarcane have lost areas due to substitution by other crops. But it is ambiguous to say whether area under aman has increased due to the substitution of other crops or expansion of gross area under cultivation. Here, significant positive elasticities are obtained in decreasing order in case of mustard, boro rice and potato respectively.

3.7.2 Changes in Area under Individual Crop due to Substitution and Expansion Effect

Though an idea of substitution and expansion effect may be gathered from the elasticity of acreage changes of each crop with respect to gross cropped area, it is not possible to desegregate the total changes in absolute area under different crops caused by substitution and expansion effect through the aforesaid elasticity approach. Moreover, if elasticity is positive but less than unity then it is not possible to definitely comment on, whether the increased area of the crop was caused by expansion of gross cropped area or substitution for other crops. Absolute changes in area under different crops due to substitution and expansion effect has been calculated in the following way. First, area under any crop in the base period (triennia average of 1970-73) is subtracted from the final year (1991-94) gross cropped area multiplied by base year proportion of area under that crop to gross cropped area, that is (a_0/A_0). A_t - a_0 . Where a and A represent area under an individual crop and gross cropped area respectively. The suffix 0 and t represent base and final year. The result gives the expansion of area under the crop due to variation in gross cropped area, holding the proportion constant at its base year value and thus the change measures the expansion effect. Thereafter this value (expansion effect) is deducted from the total change in area (a_t - a_0) under the crop, during the whole period. That gives the change in area due to substitution effect. In mathematical jargon the change in area due to substitution effect is $\{a_t - (a_0/A_0).A_t\}$ or $a_t - a_0 (A_t/A_0)$. The results obtained for different districts are presented in Table 3.7.

From the table it is observed that area under aus has decreased during 1970-71 to 1991-94 due to substitution in all the districts except Purulia. The substitution effect also leads to reduction of acreage under Pulses in all but Darjeeling. Substitution effect went in favour of boro rice, oilseed as a whole and potato. It was in favour mustard in most of the southern districts. Substitution effect led to a squeeze in area under jute, though by a small amount in all the major districts except Nadia, Murshidabad, West Dinajpur and Malda. Sugarcane was also adversely affected though by a little amount due to substitution by growing crops. Expansion effect worked in reverse direction in Birbhum and Malda. Above all major changes in area due to substitution effect have been observed in case of boro rice, oilseed as a whole, mustard and potato in most of the districts of West Bengal.

3.8 Variability and Instability of Acreage Growth

Analysis of inter-crop and intra-crop variation in acreage growth, in West Bengal, has already been presented in the earlier sections. The differential growth in area under crops is also associated with an inter-crop and intra-crop variation in *instability and variability*. Now the change in *Variability and Instability* in acreage growth of different crops is examined very closely.

Several earlier studies have already been conducted in regard to the growth of instability of agricultural output in India. Prominent among them are the studies of Mehra (1981), Hazel (1982), Nadkarni and Deshpande (1984), Dhawan (1988), Majumdar et al (1988), Narayana and Ganesh (1993) and Vani and Vyasulu (1996) in Karnataka. Most of them have used the concept of variability and instability in more or less same sense, to measure the year to year fluctuation of output and yield etc. In econometric sense however, variability is referred to as the heteroscedasticity of error. In other words variability means the degree of deviation of actual values from the trend or expected values. However, instability means the structural change in parameters. In the present section the interest is to consider the stability of the growth parameter. The stability of the trend rate of growth is judged by using the *Chow test*[36] and variability is tested by the use of *Gold-feld Quandt test*[37]. The results are presented in Table 3.8.

The result reveals that instability of acreage growth of foodgrains is significant in most of the south Bengal districts. But the variability is insignificant except in Murshidabad, West Dinajpur, Jalpaiguri and for the state as a whole. Area under rice also reflects the same pattern. Instability is much greater in the fastest growing districts; where substitution of boro rice, oilseeds and potato in place of other crops was rapid. Variability of area under boro rice was much significant in the earlier period than the latter period in the districts where the growth was also rapid but irrigation was uncertain in the early years of development. In the districts of drought-prone areas like Bankura and Purulia variability and instability both are not significant because there was very little possibility of boro cultivation in the earlier periods due to the lack of assured irrigation. The development of irrigation though started later, the growth was rather slow but smooth. The districts with high growth of acreage under non-food crops also saw greater instability in all those crops. Growth of acreage of wheat was positive and significant in the northern districts except Cooch Behar where instability was also significant. Instability of cereal crops' acreage growth was significant in the southern districts where the growth was significant. Variability of leading agricultural crop aman has been reduced over time in major agricultural districts like, Burdwan, Midnapore, Nadia, Murshidabad in the south and West Dinajpur, Malda and Jalpaiguri in the north.

3.9 Observations

From the overall analysis it is clear that crop diversification in West Bengal has taken place largely in favour of boro rice, potato and oilseeds, the principal component of which is mustard. The diversification has always taken place in favour of high valued crops or the crops those seem to give higher relative remuneration than the others grown during the same season to the cultivators. This will later be considered in detail in chapter-7. Table 3.2 also shows the shift of area increasingly towards the high yielding varieties of rice and wheat categories.

The growth of these crops originates from the expansion of area under assured irrigation. Crops like boro rice, potato are highly dependent on irrigation, as they are grown in off-monsoon seasons. Not only that the high yielding crops (varieties of rice) are generally found to be more irrigation intensive and modern technology dependent. Even in the rainy season irrigation may facilitate good cultivation if it is kept ready to insure for any breaks in the monsoon and to ensure a smooth flow of water. As the pace of diversification is partly determined by the expansion of irrigation capacity, diffusion of and application of modern technology (which has been changing) over time and the development of irrigation potential as well as upgradation of technology has not taken place uniformly throughout the state (as will be seen in chapter-8) inter-district variation in the growth rates of newly emerging leading crops are much significant. The change in area-wise allocation was much rapid in the early years when much of land were under single cropping (thus were available for the cultivation of crops in off-monsoon seasons if irrigation permits). In those districts where irrigation potential was fast developing with diffusion of technology taking place at rapid strides. It will be seen later in chapter-8 that the districts of Hooghly, Burdwan, Nadia and Howrah have been running faster than the others in using scientific methods of cultivation, with the intensive use of mechanical devices to exploit more ground water as well as surface water, to protect the crops and finish the task of insemination and harvesting in a much shorter time alongside saving much labour and hardship. It is also worthnoting that in those regions invasion of bacteria and pests are highly aggressive in nature due to likely heavy moisture content and other reasons and hence farmers have been searching and moving towards most pest-resilient crops. Crops with short period maturity are increasingly preferred[38] and injected with more priority or importance (particularly in the summer season) in every places as those varieties require less irrigation, power etc. This helps better utilisation and conservation of resources in addition to the maintenance of a balancing profit. These are the clear indication of growing commercialisation of agriculture in different regions of West Bengal.

In the districts of drought-prone areas (Purulia and parts of Bankura) the same pattern of change was observed but the change took momentum much later. Earlier, in those areas, vast areas of land used to remain idle during winter and summer seasons and even during rainy season in the years of very low rainfall [39]. Sometimes, planted areas would have been abandoned in the middle of the season owing to the scanty water supply. Later, gradually those areas were also brought under multiple cropping system when cultivation started in an integrated way. In the developed districts most of the easy access of irrigation were exhausted in earlier periods after which it was very difficult to maintain the tempo of irrigation development, because of difficulty and cost involved in the use of lesser accessible sources of irrigation despite much technological innovation. Similarly, the variability of acreage growth of water-intensive crops (cultivation of which requires continuous flow of water) in areas formerly having limited access to artificial irrigation was high in the earlier periods. Moreover, the crops cultivated exclusively for making profit had greater variation than the others.

In the early stage of Green Revolution wheat and paddy had received priority to fulfil the target of foodgrain production and to remove the scarcity of foodgrains. The use of high yielding varieties of seeds, irrigation and synthetic fertiliser made India and the state self-sufficient in foodgrains production. Agriculture became increasingly commercialised over the years and thus market oriented specification of crop production started. Thus variability of acreage under commercial crops was far greater than their counterpart because the former absorbs the shock of market fluctuation in addition to other uncertainties which affect all the crops in a more or less uniform way.

After mid-eighties when several high productive varieties of different crops were brought under rigorous cultivation and irrigation opportunity became pervasive in nature, there occurred a massive shift of production of different crops with a skewed acreage distribution. Now even the food crops are produced on a commercial basis. Thus the traditional definition of commercial crops (as the non-food crops) no longer remain a valid proposition. Any crop, which is produced mainly for market and a small fraction of which is used for direct consumption by the producer (as the boro rice, potato in the present day) would be treated as the commercial crop.

The newly emerging commercial crop is found to occupy the position of traditionally important commercial crop like jute, owing to the reduction of its relative profitability. This was due to the stiff competition faced by jute after the arrival of its synthetic substitutes. Sugarcane has lost its importance due to the non-possibility of multiple cropping in the sugarcane field. The development of many short period crops has led to widespread reallocation of land for multiple crop production as the new system raised the probability of earning more with a substantial reduction in risk involved in the production of crops.

Traditionally, the areas of land (full of clay and hard soil) thought to be non-useable for potato cultivation, were brought under the same with the help of sophisticated machinery like, power tiller, tractor, machine-operated harrow etc. But there was a limit beyond which it was not possible to expand the cultivation of potato at a uniformly rapid rate. It is true that the capacity of management has increased manifold in the wake of expansion of use of modern technology, the benefits of which has reached even the small farmers as they can hire it now in accordance with their requirement (e.g., a few hours or even a few minutes of tractor can be hired in cooperation with others for ploughing field). So the small peasants are now not required to maintain a large stock of fixed capital in the form of machinery or cattle and thus can minimise the diseconomies of scale. But still there are some other constraints for which the area growth rates have decreased under certain crops (like potato, oilseeds etc.) slightly during nineties. Those are the suitability of market, uncertainty of price movement, availability of credit to the real (particularly small) tillers and the timing of Government helps.

In many cases Government subsidised seeds, fertilisers, provided for the small farmers (who generally suffer from resource crunch) come through proper channel so belatedly that they can not be utilised notwithstanding the fact that vast areas remain uncultivated which could be sown if the aids had been disbursed timely. This is because; by this time the sowing season has already passed over. Though the large farmers usually do not suffer from the lack of resources and operate in response to their expectation regarding the market price, storage capacity for crops with low durability, Government's price policy and their managing capability, they also take into consideration the probable adverse effect of uneven natural disturbance alongside their profit motive.

Above all, it is found that over the years share of non-food crops as a whole increased as the growth of their acreage was relatively much greater than their counterpart. Within foodgrains however, boro rice emerged as an important commercial crop. Fluctuations of growth around trend have decreased over time. This kind of temporal variation is due to the decline of nature- dependence and better water management coupled with other advanced facilities, which help keep some crops' yield steady and attractive. Among the crops, larger variation was found amongst the high valued crops though inter-district variation of growth rates have decreased significantly with the passage of time.

NOTES

1 Vyas V.S. (1996), "Diversification of Agriculture and Food Security in the context of New Economic Policy", *Indian Journal of Agricultural Economics*, Vol. 51, No. 4, Oct-Dec., pp. 636-673.

2 Nadkarni and Vedini (1996), "Accelerating Commercialisation of Agriculture", *Economic and Political Weekly*, June 26, pp. A63- A73.

3 Ranade C. G. (1980), "Impact of Cropping Pattern on Agricultural Production" *Indian Journal of Agricultural Economics*, Vol. 35, No. 2, April-June.

4 Here, agricultural production means the total value of agricultural output of any region. This is the sum of individual crop output in value terms. Therefore, total output of a particular area depends on the area and yield of individual crops, assuming prices are constant. Thus the growth of agricultural output of any region is contingent upon the growth of total cultivated area (GCA), yield of each crop and a shift of area from low yielding to high yielding crops, with prices remaining constant. The term productivity is used to denote the composite productivity of a region. In symbol, at = Qt/At, Qt and At are total value of output and gross cropped area at time t. at includes the effect of any cropping pattern shift along with individual yield changes.

5 Boyce J. K. (1987), *Agrarian Impasse in Bengal: Agricultural Growth in Bangladesh and West Bengal 1949 - 1980*, Oxford University Press, ch. 3, pp. 74-81.

6 Gross cropped area (GCA) = net cropped area (NSA). cropping intensity. So even if NSA has not increased significantly, GCA has expanded due to the introduction of multiple cropping (i.e., due to increase in cropping intensity).

7 Bhalla G.S. and Singh G., (1997), " Recent Development of Indian Agriculture, A State Level Analysis", *Economic and Political Weekly*, March 29, pp. A.2 to A-18.

They have calculated three-year moving average of area under 43 major crops for different states from 1962 to 1995. They have also divided the whole period into three sub-periods, 1962-65 to 1970-73, 1970-73 to 1980-83 and 1980-83 to 1992-95 and shown the cropping pattern changes during the whole as well as different sub-periods across the states.

8 Expansion of population has necessitated the conversion of cultivated land to homestead and thus partly responsible for deceleration in the growth of net cropped area.

9 Murthyunjaya and Kumar, (1989), pp. (A159 - A166).

10 Johl and Kahlon (1963), pp. 132 - 142.

11 In some cases farmers are forced to cultivate some crops on account of agro-climatic condition, institutional reasons and also for their own consideration. Such as, in spite of high price, farmers in the southern districts of West Bengal can not cultivate tea due to unfavourable climatic condition and opium due to legal prohibition.

12 Sagar Vidya (1980), " Decomposition of Growth trends and Certain Related Issues", *Indian Journal of Agricultural Economics*, Vol. 35, No. 2, April-June, pp. 42-48.

13 Bhalla G.S. and Singh G.,(1997), op cit.

14 Bhalla G.S. and Singh G., (1997), op cit.

15 Dhindsa K. S. and Sharma A., (1995), "Analysis of Cropping Pattern Changes in Punjab During 1965-66 to 1990-91" *Indian Economic Review*, Vol XXX, No.1, Jan-June, pp. 69-87.

16 Dhindsa K. S. and Sharma A., (1995), op cit.

17 Dhindsa K. S. and Sharma A., (1995) , op cit.

18 Ranade C. G. (1980), "Impact of Cropping Pattern on Agricultural Production" *Indian Journal of Agricultural Economics*, Vol. 35, No. 2 , April-June.

19 Minhas and Parikh, (1966) proposed an index number for isolating yield and cropping pattern component by:

$$\frac{Q_t}{Q_o} = \frac{\Sigma a_{it}\, y_{it}\, p_i}{\Sigma a_{io}\, y_{io}\, p_i} = \frac{\Sigma a_{it}}{\Sigma a_{io}} \frac{\Sigma c_{it}\, y_{it}\, p_i}{\Sigma c_{io}\, y_{io}\, p_i}$$

$$= \frac{A_t}{A_o} \frac{(\Sigma c_{io}\, y_{it}\, p_i)}{(\Sigma c_{io} y_{io}\, p_i)} \frac{(\Sigma c_{it}\, y_{it}\, p_i)}{(\Sigma c_{io}\, y_{it}\, p_i)}$$

where, $c_{it} = \frac{a_{it}}{A_t}$, the share of ith crop in gross cropped area at time t and the subscript o refers to the base period. The last two terms on the right hand side represent respectively, the index of yield per unit of area evaluated at initial cropping pattern and the index of change in cropping pattern evaluated at final yield. Here, qit = output of ith crop at time t. Similarly, a_{it} and y_{it} represent area and yield of ith crop at time t . p_i is the constant price weight of ith crop. Aggregate output $Q_t = A_t . \gamma_t$, where $\gamma_t = \frac{Q_t}{A_t}$ or $Q_t = \Sigma q_{it} \cdot P$ and

$A_t = \Sigma ait$ = gross cropped area .

20 Bhalla G. S. and Alagh Y. K., (1979), *Performance of Indian Agriculture: A Districtwise Study,* Sterlng Publisher, New Delhi.

21 Narayanamoorthy, (1997), " Crop Diversification and Yield Response to Fertiliser ", *Productivity,* Vol. 38 No-1 , April-June , pp. 121-126 .

22 Tea is excluded from the aggregation because it is not a general crop of all the districts and largely produced only in Darjeeling and in some parts of Jalpaiguri and Cooch Behar. Moreover, area under tea in the state has been only around 1.2 per cent to 1.3 per cent of gross cropped area throughout the entire period despite the fact that it brings a good amount to state's revenue.

23 In this analysis, the term total cropped area and gross cropped area are used interchangeably. Similarly, net sown area and net cropped area are used in the same sense.

24 This is clear from the changing proportion of area under other cereals, (which is exposed in the table). Superior cereals have been gradually replacing the inferior cereals from the food basket of the residents of the state.

25 Though growth rate during 1970-71 to 1978-79 was positive, average rate of growth during 1970-71 to 1981-82 was negative. This was due to sudden fall in area during 1979-80 to 1981-82. The growth rate was highest during 1982-83 to 1994-95.

26 Other cereals include inferior cereals like, jawar, bazra, ragi, small millet etc.

27 In the later part of this section the change in growth rate (acceleration *and*

deceleration) has also been estimated by forming the trend equations of the type $\text{Ln } Y = \hat{a}_0 + \hat{a}_1.t + \hat{a}_2.t^2$, where Y, t and â's have their usual meaning. Here, $2\hat{a}_2$ is used as an estimate of change in rate of growth. A positive value of it implies the acceleration in the rate of growth and vice versa.

28 The results obtained for different periods differ because of the points of division of periods. In this type of regression divergence of coefficients are significant not only due to observations of different years but also due to the magnitude of observations around the two ends of the sub-periods. So the values around the cut-off points (years) have a bearing more on the results than the others.

29 In the later part of this chapter an attempt has been made to show the acreage expansion of boro rice, oilseed and potato in terms of Substitution and expansion effect.

30 A breakthrough in technology from time to time has led to sudden shift in area under boro cultivation as long as many of available plots remain uncultivated during summer and its profitability has increased more relative to that of other summer crops.

31 Here desired time interval means, the normal space of time in the rabi season within which sowing of potato is desired by a rational cultivator. If potato were cultivated within this period then yield would be optimum, if application of inputs in optimum proportion is maintained and favourable weather condition prevails.

32 It is implied that the farmers are rational and hence their objective is to maximise net profit expected from their limited land holding.

33 The same thing has also been explained in the study conducted by NCAER (1966) in terms of elasticity of individual crop area with respect to gross cropped area.

34 Gross cropped area increases due to the change from monocropping to multiple cropping system and conversion of fallow and cultivable wasteland into cultivated land.

35 This methodology was also followed by Dhindsa and Sharma (Dhindsa and Sharma p. 72). The basic drawback from which their argument suffers is that they have argued the crops falling in category $0<E<1$ have a fall in area due to both expansion of gross cropped area and at the expense of area under $E<0$ category crops. But one can not assure that substitution effect will be positive. One can say that the net effect is positive. Any of the two effects may be positive, negative or even zero.

36 Chow test,

$$F_{k,n_1+n_2-2k} = \frac{\{\Sigma e_p^2 - (\Sigma e_1^2 + \Sigma e_2^2)\}/k}{(\Sigma e_1^2 + \Sigma e_2^2)/(n_1 + n_2 - 2k)},$$

where $n_1 + n_2 = n$. Here Σe_p^2 is the residual sum of squares considering the whole period or set of data and Σe_1^2 & Σe_2^2 are the residual sum of squares of first and second sub-periods, k is the number of parameters.

37 Gold-feld Quandt Test:

$$F_{n_1 - k, n_2 - k} = \frac{\Sigma e_1^2 /(n_1-k)}{\Sigma e_2^2/(n_2-k)}$$

Actually it is done after eliminating some central observations and comparing residual sum of squares (RSS) of two sub-periods. In this study, at first it is calculated without omitting any observation and then RSS of 1970-71 to 1978-79 sub-period is compared with the RSS of 1985-86 to 1993-94 sub-period. The two statistics are represented by F_1 and F_2 respectively.

38 Adoption of short period but high yielding crop helps the farmers to produce more crops on the same plot in a year and effectively use the scarce resources, especially water in the dry season.

39 This is also clear from the low intensity of irrigation potential as is clear from the Table 8.2A and 8.2B.

REFERENCES

1. Bhalla and Singh, (1997), " Recent Development in Indian Agriculture: A State Level Analysis", *Economic and Political Weekly*, March, 29, pp. A.8-A.12.
2. Bhalla G. S., and Alagh Y. K., (1979): *Performances of Indian Agriculture: A Districtwise Study*, Sterling Publisher, New Delhi.
3. Bhalla G. S. and Tyagi D. S. (1989): Patterns in Indian Agricultural Development - A District Level Study, ISID, New Delhi.
4. Boyce J. K., (1987), *Agrarian Impasse In Bengal, Institutional Constraints to Technological Change*, Oxford University Press.
5. Chow G. C., (1960), " Test of Equality Between Subsets of subsets of coefficients in Two Linear Regression," *Econometrica*, 28, pp 591-605.
6. Dhawan B. D., (1988): *Irrigation in Indian Agricultural Development: Productivity, Stability, Equity*, Sage, New Delhi.
7. Government of West Bengal, Bureau of Applied Economics and Statistics (BAES), *Economic Review*, Various Issues.
8. Government of West Bengal, *Statistical Abstract*, Various Issues.
9. Government of India: *Area and Production of Principal crops in India* (Various Issues), Ministry of Agiculture, New Delhi.
10. Gulati A. and Sharma A. (1994), " Agriculture Under GATT: What It Holds for India", *Economic and Political Weekly*, July 16.
11. Johl S.S. and Sandhu H.S. (1970), Existing and Suggested Cropping Patterns by the Type of Farming Areas in Different Districts of Punjab and Haryana, 1969-70. Department of Economics and Sociology, Punjab Agricultural University, Ludhiana.
12. Koutsoyiannis A. (1977): *Theory of Econometrics* (2nd ed.), Macmillan Press, London.
13. Lahiri A. K. and Roy P., (1985): " Rainfall and Supply Response: A Study of Rice in India", *Journal of Development Economics*.

14. Mehra Shakuntala, (1981), Instability in Indian Agriculture in the Context of the New Technology, Research Report No. 25, International Food Policy Research Institute, Washington D. C., U. S. A.

15. Ministry of Agriculture, Government of India, *Agricultural Situation in India,* June, 1994.

16. NCAER (1966), *Cropping Pattern in Punjab*, New Delhi.

17. Srinivasan T. N., (1979), " Trends in Agriculture in India, 1949-50 to 1977-78", *Economic and Political Weekly*, 14(30-2), Special Number, 1283-94.

18. World Bank (1990), *Agricultural Diversification: Policies and Issues from East Asian Experience*, Agriculture and Rural Development Department, Washington, D.C., U.S.A.

Table 3.1: Proportion of Area under Each Crop to Total Cropped Area in West Bengal (Districtwise)

(in percentage)

District	Aus				Aman				Boro				Rice			
	1970-73	1977-80	1984-87	1991-94	1970-73	1977-80	1984-87	1991-94	1970-73	1977-80	1984-87	1991-94	1970-73	1977-80	1984-87	1991-94
Burdwan	5.60	4.39	3.81	4.57	71.67	65.48	63.92	60.87	7.80	11.00	15.13	18.63	85.14	80.87	82.85	84.06
Birbhum	11.88	1.92	1.93	2.70	60.01	67.68	70.21	69.96	1.54	4.35	5.92	8.19	73.50	73.95	78.06	80.81
Bankura	11.75	6.94	6.49	7.31	78.12	76.21	76.08	70.49	0.59	1.36	3.66	8.01	90.47	84.51	86.22	85.81
Midnapore	7.25	5.05	5.81	5.89	75.43	76.23	73.03	64.21	6.59	5.90	11.12	16.87	89.27	87.18	89.01	86.96
Howrah	3.48	1.16	2.33	0.87	66.54	64.6	58.19	54.18	11.34	10.57	17.82	36.25	81.36	76.32	78.34	91.30
Hooghly	5.31	3.64	3.56	3.22	52.81	52.03	51.65	47.37	14.87	13.43	14.14	16.13	73.02	69.10	69.36	66.72
24-Paraganas	4.07	3.19	2.99	2.97	75.65	72.43	70.51	67.01	3.28	5.44	9.55	15.47	83.0	81.06	83.05	85.44
Nadia	22.56	17.01	12.24	10.44	16.96	20.59	17.80	20.33	1.84	5.17	11.29	16.54	41.35	42.77	41.33	47.32
Murshidabad	13.68	14.55	12.09	10.12	28.05	25.87	21.85	34.25	1.91	3.04	5.80	9.27	43.64	43.46	44.85	53.64
West Dinajpur	18.46	16.75	11.07	4.96	50.81	45.70	52.61	57.13	0.74	0.97	2.62	9.28	70.02	63.43	66.30	71.37
Malda	17.33	18.03	13.32	8.24	27.54	31.56	36.07	40.41	4.52	6.71	9.88	15.66	49.39	56.31	59.18	64.31
Jalpaiguri	20.49	21.14	16.39	18.29	59.70	49.48	55.84	57.62	0.04	--	0.07	0.53	80.23	70.62	72.25	76.44
Darjeeling	6.83	9.64	8.84	10.23	43.27	36.53	37.42	36.59	0.20	--	--	0.26	50.30	46.17	46.25	46.99
Cooch-Behar	24.38	24.34	21.89	18.67	49.57	42.84	49.05	51.67	0.14	0.24	0.22	2.45	74.09	67.42	71.19	72.79
Purulia	1.50	1.15	0.65	1.68	83.41	84.38	74.16	83.96	0.34	0.22	0.28	0.58	85.25	85.75	85.85	86.30
West Bengal	11.73	9.91	8.09	6.98	57.31	55.63	56.52	55.57	4.13	4.67	7.68	12.90	72.70	70.22	72.29	74.85

Cont....

Table 3.1 contd.

District	*Wheat*				*Other Cereals*				*Total Cereals*				*Pulses*			
	1970-73	1977-80	1984-87	1991-94	1970-73	1977-80	1984-87	1991-94	1970-73	1977-80	1984-87	1991-94	1970-73	1977-80	1984-87	1991-94
Burdwan	4.85	4.46	1.39	0.39	0.11	0.24	0.07	0.01	90.10	85.52	84.32	84.46	3.91	3.75	1.74	0.23
Birbhum	14.42	12.54	5.33	2.55	0.44	0.34	0.20	0.40	88.36	86.84	83.59	83.75	7.89	7.06	3.92	2.16
Bankura	3.12	5.12	3.08	1.78	0.42	0.55	0.62	0.53	94.01	90.18	89.93	88.11	3.12	2.34	1.34	0.67
Midnapore	1.44	2.18	1.26	0.57	0.25	0.21	–	0.07	90.96	89.58	90.25	87.59	5.51	5.64	3.30	1.63
Howrah	4.55	3.71	0.72	0.13	0.01	–	0.03	–	85.91	80.04	79.07	91.44	6.73	9.98	9.30	1.10
Hooghly	7.01	5.21	2.17	0.37	0.03	–	–	0.002	80.05	74.31	71.53	67.10	4.19	2.68	1.50	0.12
24-Paraganas	2.31	2.24	1.34	0.97	0.05	0.04	0.004	0.005	85.36	83.35	84.39	86.42	6.59	6.55	4.53	2.68
Nadia	11.15	9.23	10.61	7.33	1.09	0.76	0.12	0.45	53.59	52.76	52.06	55.10	22.34	19.42	14.31	10.23
Murshidabad	15.71	16.87	15.41	13.50	3.12	2.05	1.32	0.54	62.47	62.39	61.57	67.68	60.16	18.24	12.84	6.61
West Dinajpur	4.09	7.50	6.00	4.42	1.97	1.16	0.60	0.43	76.08	72.10	72.91	75.92	6.41	6.61	3.61	3.29
Malda	7.04	8.88	8.47	11.06	9.86	5.81	4.58	3.41	66.29	71.00	72.23	78.78	22.43	15.52	12.08	14.21
Jalpaiguri	0.36	8.97	4.04	4.10	1.22	1.74	2.47	0.84	81.81	81.33	78.77	81.37	1.50	3.04	1.87	0.87
Darjeeling	0.52	4.37	1.17	3.33	39.94	38.33	41.89	35.88	90.76	88.87	89.31	86.20	1.57	1.94	1.21	2.09
Cooch-Behar	1.90	11.72	4.98	3.64	0.59	0.58	1.13	0.33	76.58	79.91	77.31	76.76	3.33	3.20	2.02	2.38
Purulia	0.96	2.85	1.39	0.51	3.22	2.34	5.12	4.27	89.43	90.95	92.36	91.09	7.84	6.27	5.51	5.73
West Bengal	5.57	7.03	4.80	3.58	1.96	1.48	1.48	1.02	80.23	78.73	78.57	79.45	8.77	7.83	5.78	3.53

Cont....

Table-3.1 contd.

District	*Total Foodgrains*				*Mustard*				*Total Oilseed*				*Potato*			
	1970-73	1977-80	1984-87	1991-94	1970-73	1977-80	1984-87	1991-94	1970-73	1977-80	1984-87	1991-94	1970-73	1977-80	1984-87	1991-94
Burdwan	94.01	89.27	86.06	84.69	0.56	1.50	5.01	7.08	0.80	3.05	6.54	8.54	2.49	4.45	4.64	4.93
Birbhum	96.26	93.90	87.51	85.91	0.43	0.91	8.18	7.93	1.54	2.41	9.84	8.45	1.13	1.63	1.99	1.75
Bankura	96.62	92.52	91.27	88.78	0.47	0.80	2.21	4.03	1.11	4.57	5.81	7.52	0.75	1.44	2.02	3.29
Midnapore	96.46	95.21	93.56	89.23	0.30	0.10	0.78	2.28	0.67	1.30	3.09	5.26	1.09	1.65	2.42	4.45
Howrah	92.64	90.02	88.39	92.53	0.19	0.11	0.54	1.14	2.53	3.07	3.96	3.88	1.99	3.04	2.77	1.90
Hooghly	84.24	76.99	73.03	67.22	0.79	0.81	2.95	2.70	1.46	2.94	5.65	9.18	5.97	9.59	12.32	16.44
24-Paraganas	91.95	89.90	88.92	89.10	1.16	0.98	2.71	4.52	1.25	1.58	3.43	5.56	0.40	0.74	0.77	0.71
Nadia	75.93	72.18	66.36	65.33	2.89	2.19	5.77	10.36	6.19	5.32	7.84	12.85	0.10	0.64	0.73	0.52
Murshidabad	82.52	80.62	74.41	74.29	1.99	2.03	5.75	8.60	4.39	4.79	7.82	9.25	0.56	1.04	1.05	1.02
West Dinajpur	82.48	78.70	76.53	79.12	3.37	3.70	6.27	8.66	4.27	6.51	8.73	9.40	0.55	1.13	0.83	0.92
Malda	88.72	86.53	84.31	84.16	3.6	2.99	4.00	6.63	4.56	4.56	5.68	7.16	0.18	0.50	0.36	0.48
Jalpaiguri	83.31	84.37	80.63	82.24	2.6	1.88	2.08	2.29	2.73	2.07	3.02	3.26	0.35	1.00	0.75	1.93
Darjeeling	92.33	90.80	90.51	88.29	0.80	0.52	0.41	0.76	0.60	0.97	1.44	1.44	2.89	4.26	4.05	7.24
Cooch-Behar	79.92	82.91	79.32	79.14	2.29	1.96	1.38	1.47	2.37	2.15	2.92	2.90	0.43	0.98	1.24	1.79
Purulia	97.27	97.21	97.86	96.81	0.56	0.22	0.19	0.46	1.31	1.18	1.57	2.58	0.13	0.54	0.20	0.38
West Bengal	89.00	86.56	83.90	82.98	1.504	1.50	3.56	5.14	2.55	3.20	5.48	7.05	1.03	1.84	2.13	2.95

Table-3.1 concld.

District	*Jute*				*Sugarcane*			
	1970-73	1977-80	1984-87	1991-94	1970-73	1977-80	1984-87	1991-94
Burdwan	1.67	2.58	2.48	1.67	0.58	0.39	0.13	0.13
Birbhum	0.08	0.09	0.14	0.07	0.84	0.84	0.35	0.36
Bankura	0.27	0.41	0.25	0.10	0.45	0.34	0.07	0.04
Midnapore	1.08	1.41	1.42	0.84	0.34	0.26	0.15	0.11
Howrah	3.32	3.90	2.82	1.66	0.57	0.32	0.08	0.03
Hooghly	7.94	10.34	8.98	7.14	0.31	0.08	0.03	0.02
24-Paraganas	5.23	7.27	6.69	4.49	0.19	0.14	0.07	0.08
Nadia	14.81	19.93	24.12	20.74	1.25	0.94	0.35	0.37
Murshidabad	10.89	12.10	15.93	14.82	1.14	1.16	0.62	0.59
West Dinajpur	9.38	11.11	12.29	9.86	0.29	0.25	0.09	0.02
Malda	4.99	7.15	9.00	7.23	0.60	0.67	0.34	0.72
Jalpaiguri	12.81	11.41	14.77	12.13	0.10	0.06	0.03	0.01
Darjeeling	3.98	3.78	3.95	3.02	0.12	--	--	--
Cooch-Behar	15.93	12.5	15.77	15.73	0.11	0.05	--	--
Purulia	0.03	--	0.03	--	0.26	0.57	0.06	0.17
West Bengal	5.98	7.07	8.23	6.68	0.51	0.43	0.18	0.18

Sources: (i) Government of West Bengal, Bureau of Applied Economics and Statistics, *Statistical Abstract (various issues).*
(ii) Government of West Bengal, Bureau of Applied Economics and Statistics, *Economic Review (various issues).*

Note: -- indicates the value is negligible.

Table 3.2: Area and Proportion of Area under High Yielding Varieties of Crops

Year crop	*Aus*	*Aman*	*Boro*	*Total Rice*	*Wheat*
1972-73	92.6 (11.23)	345.2 (8.67)	221.1 (60.93)	658.9 (13.00)	341.0 (92.61)
1978-79	239.2 (34.38)	869.5 (23.97)	429.5 (97.19)	1538.3 (32.28)	520.6 (99.92)
1985-86	183.0 (37.88)	1306.0 (31.98)	512.0 (99.94)	2001.0 (39.4)	305.1 (100)
1993-94	490.0 (90.81)	2176.6 (50.73)	1045.0 (100)	3711.6 (63.17)	306.9 (100)

Source: Government of West Bengal, Bureau of Applied Economics and Statistics, Statistical Abstracts, (various issues).

Note: Figures in the parentheses represent percentage to total.

Table 3.3 Exponential Rate of Growth of Area under Crops in West Bengal (Districtwise) During 1970-71 to 1994-95 and Different Sub-periods

	Aus						Aman					
Period	70/1-78/9	79/80-93/4	70/1-81/2	82/3-93/4	85/6-93/4	70/1-93/4	70/1-78/9	79/80-93/4	70/1-81/2	82/3-93/4	85/6-93/4	70/1-93/4
Burdwan	-.046	.023*	-.03	.036*	.032*	-.009	-.011	-.001	-.002	.002	.004	-.002
	(.035)	(.009)	(.02)	(.013)	(.012)	(.007)	(.013)	(.008)	(.003)	(.003)	(.002)	(.002)
Birbhum	-.302*	.08*	-.245*	.097*	.043	-.071	.023*	-.004	.019*	-.0002	.006	.004*
	(.096)	(.021)	(.056)	(.032)	(.05)	(.022)	(.008)	(.004)	(.005)	(.005)	(.009)	(.002)
Bankura	-.086*	.038*	-.071*	.064*	.043	-.02	.006	.006	.002	.009*	.01	.0015
	(.032)	(.013)	(.018)	(.016)	(.025)	(.009)	(.005)	(.003)	(.004)	(.003)	(.005)	(.001)
Midnapore	-.059*	.024*	-.049*	.025	.038	-.007	.004	-.002	.002	.0001	.001	-.0016
	(.018)	(.011)	(.011)	(.018)	(.03)	(.006)	(.004)	(.001)	(.002)	(.001)	(.001)	(.001)
Howrah	-.238*	-.028	-.111	-.083*	-.131	-.028	.027*	.004	.015	.012	.004	.001
	(.097)	(.03)	(.063)	(.04)	(.067)	(.022)	(.011)	(.006)	(.007)	(.008)	(.008)	(.003)
Hooghly	-.031	-.001	-.008	.012	.033	-.012	.017*	.008*	.012*	.014*	.014*	.005*
	(.086)	(.027)	(.047)	(.043)	(.073)	(.017)	(.006)	(.003)	(.004)	(.003)	(.003)	(.001)
24-Paraganas	-.01	.012	-.038	-.004	.009	-.014	.002	-.001	.001	.001	.005*	-.001
	(.033)	(.01)	(.021)	(.013)	(.018)	(.008)	(.005)	(.001)	(.003)	(.002)	(.002)	(.001)
Nadia	-.018	-.018	-.032	-.019	-.001	-.031*	.036	.018*	.028	.035*	.041*	.011
	(.023)	(.017)	(.014)	(.028)	(.048)	(.008)	(.027)	(.006)	(.015)	(.005)	(.008)	(.006)
Murshidabad	.022	-.021	.001	-.029	-.037	-.018*	-.03	.017	.002	.044*	.042*	.005
	(.021)	(.012)	(.013)	(.018)	(.032)	(.007)	(.03)	(.014)	(.019)	(.018)	(.009)	(.007)
West Dinajpur	.005	-.101*	-.011	-125*	-.107*	-.062*	-.015	.009*	.001	.012*	.005	.007*
	(.008)	(.012)	(.008)	(.014)	(.023)	(.007)	(.011)	(.002)	(.007)	(.003)	(.004)	(.002)

Contd. . . .

Table 3.3 contd.

Malda	.025	-.031*	-.034	-.05*	-.073*	-.036*	.009	.008*	.018	.012*	.018*	.014*
	(.019)	(.014)	(.021)	(.02)	(.034)	(.007)	(.014)	(.002)	(.008)	(.003)	(.003)	(.002)
Jalpaiguri	.042*	-.007	.008	.002	.02	-.013*	-.007	.002	-.001	.0004	-.01	.002
	(.014)	(.007)	(.012)	(.009)	(.009)	(.005)	(.013)	(.003)	(.008)	(.004)	(.004)	(.002)
Darjeeling	.075*	.044*	.029	.044	.022	.03*	-.017	.005	-.006	.004	-.004	.002
	(.017)	(.02)	(.016)	(.031)	(.057)	(.008)	(.01)	(.003)	(.006)	(.005)	(.009)	(.002)
Cooch-Behar	.034*	-.01	.008	-.015*	-.014	-.008*	.003	.016*	.004	.014*	.01	.01*
	(.012)	(.005)	(.01)	(.006)	(.012)	(.003)	(.009)	(.003)	(.005)	(.004)	(.008)	(.002)
Purulia	-.017	.103*	-.089*	.172*	.18*	-.015	-.005	.021*	-.008	.034*	.014*	.004
	(.015)	(.028)	(.022)	(.032)	(.05)	(.018)	(.005)	(.008)	(.004)	(.011)	(.005)	(.004)
West Bengal	-.009	-.012	-.026*	-.015	-.009	-.023*	.0013	.004*	.004	.008*	.008*	.0024*
	(.012)	(.006)	(.009)	(.009)	(.016)	(.004)	(.007)	(.001)	(.004)	(.001)	(.001)	(.001)

Note: (i) Figures in the parentheses represent standard error, (ii) * indicates the coefficient is significant at 5% level of significance by two tailed test.

Table-3.3 contd.

	Boro						Rice					
Period	70/1-78/9	79/80-93/4	70/1-81/2	82/3-93/4	85/6-93/4	70/1-93/4	70/1-78/9	79/80-94/5	70/1-81/2	82/3-94/5	86/7-94/5	70/1-94/5
Burdwan	.079	.086*	.008	.069*	.024	.047*	-.001	.013*	-.002	.015*	.014*	.007*
	(.045)	(.021)	(.039)	(.024)	(.022)	(.011)	(.01)	(.003)	(.006)	(.004)	(.004)	(.002)
Birbhum	.141	.098*	.08	.102*	.041	.069*	.004	.005	.003	.008*	.009	.0021*
	(.101)	(.025)	(.061)	(.033)	(.045)	(.014)	(.006)	(.003)	(.004)	(.0037)	(.007)	(.001)
Bankura	.137*	.202*	.064	.173*	.121*	.138*	-.0016	.016*	-.005	.02*	.02*	.005*
	(.062)	(.022)	(.045)	(.028)	(.035)	(.014)	(.004)	(.003)	(.004)	(.003)	(.005)	(.002)
Midnapore	-.004	.103*	-.018	.079*	.078*	.056*	-.001	.013*	-.003	.014*	.016*	.006*
	(.024)	(.01)	(.015)	(.011)	(.017)	(.008)	(.004)	(.001)	(.002)	(.002)	(.003)	(.001)
Howrah	.008	.145*	-.019	.119*	.109*	.082*	.021*	.031*	.008	.033*	.019*	.018*
	(.045)	(.013)	(.027)	(.011)	(.016)	(.011)	(.006)	(.005)	(.005)	(.007)	(.009)	(.003)
Hooghly	.142	.039*	.065	.037*	.04*	.034*	.013	.015*	.005	.02*	.021*	.007*
	(.092)	(.01)	(.056)	(.012)	(.018)	(.014)	(.008)	(.003)	(.006)	(.004)	(.005)	(.002)
24-Paraganas	.086*	.092*	.066*	.069*	.077*	.089*	.057*	.01*	.003	.01*	.012*	.007*
	(.015)	(.009)	(.011)	(.009)	(.012)	(.005)	(.004)	(.001)	(.003)	(.002)	(.002)	(.001)
Nadia	.175*	.102*	.157*	.091*	.063*	.125*	.018	.025*	.009	.03*	.01	.015*
	(.035)	(.009)	(.02)	(.013)	(.013)	(.007)	(.017)	(.005)	(.01)	(.007)	(.005)	(.003)
Murshidabad	.07	.091*	.07*	.083*	.05*	.08*	-.005	.012*	.007	.017*	.008	.01*
	(.044)	(.009)	(.024)	(.013)	(.015)	(.006)	(.022)	(.004)	(.012)	(.005)	(.007)	(.003)
West Dinajpur	.09	.193*	.041	.173*	.152*	.13*	-.008	.003	-.001	.004	-.002	.002
	(.045)	(.018)	(.03)	(.026)	(.032)	(.012)	(.009)	(.002)	(.006)	(.002)	(.002)	(.001)

Contd.. . . .

Table 3.3 contd.

Malda	.074*	.088*	.028	.091*	.056*	.05*	.02	.013*	.003	.012*	-.007	.006*
	(.024)	(.01)	(.018)	(.015)	(.021)	(.008)	(.012)	(.003)	(.008)	(.005)	(.004)	(.002)
Jalpaiguri	---	----	----	.290*	.271*	----	.007	-.003	.001	-.004	-.013*	-.002
	---	---	---	(.044)	(.079)	(.013)	(.002)	(.007)	(.003)	(.004)	(.002)	(.002)
Darjeeling	---	----	----	----	----	----	-.002	.011	-.001	.004	-.02	.007*
	---	---	---	---	---	---	(.01)	(.006)	(.005)	(.009)	(.013)	(.003)
Cooch-Behar	.103*	.359*	-.081	.416*	.319*	.136*	.014	.007	.005	.004	-.009	.006*
	(.017)	(.058)	(.068)	(.064)	(.09)	(.035)	(.01)	(.004)	(.006)	(.005)	(.009)	(.002)
Purulia	.002	.143*	-.083	.136*	.222*	.037	-.005	.019*	-.009	.023*	.012*	.005*
	(.094)	(.037)	(.058)	(.057)	(.08)	(.022)	(.005)	(.003)	(.004)	(.004)	(.005)	(.002)
West Bengal	.044	.098*	.0247	.086*	.069*	.062*	.003	.0115*	.0006	.013*	.009*	.006*
	(.03)	(.008)	(.0174)	(.01)	(.013)	(.006)	(.006)	(.002)	(.004)	(.002)	(.002)	(.001)

Note: (i) Figures in the parentheses represent standard error, (ii) * indicates the coefficient is significant at 5% level of significance by two tailed test.

Table-3.3 contd.

	Wheat						Cereal					
Period	70/1-78/9	79/80-94/5	70/1-81/2	82/3-94/5	85/6-94/5	70/1-94/5	70/1-78/9	79/80-94/5	70/1-81/2	82/3-94/5	86/7-94/5	70/1-94/5
Burdwan	.011	-.128*	-.082*	-.141*	-.161*	-.118*	-1.0(10-5)	.012*	-.004	.014*	.013	.038*
	(.019)	(.019)	(.032)	(.024)	(.048)	(.01)	(.01)	(.003)	(.006)	(.004)	(.004)	(.002)
Birbhum	-.027	-.057*	-.091*	-.052*	-.114*	-.078*	-.002	.0006	-.007	.006	.003	-.005*
	(.04)	(.019)	(.035)	(.021)	(.036)	(.01)	(.009)	(.003)	(.005)	(.0037)	(.007)	(.002)
Bankura	0.12	-.03*	-.009	-.037	-.049	-.043*	.004	.015*	-.005	.018*	.017*	.004
	(.039)	(.015)	(.041)	(.022)	(.043)	(.011)	(.005)	(.003)	(.005)	(.003)	(.005)	(.002)
Midnapore	.094*	-.027	-.021	-.014	-.021	-.047*	.001	.012*	-.003	.013	.016*	.005*
	(.026)	(.023)	(.038)	(.031)	(.066)	(.012)	(.004)	(.001)	(.002)	(.002)	(.0027)	(.001)
Howrah	.003	-.14*	-.125*	-.113*	-.072	-.158*	.02*	.029*	.005	.032*	.0184	.016*
	(.048)	(.041)	(.058)	(.052)	(.102)	(.019)	(.005)	(.005)	(.005)	(.007)	(.0087)	(.003)
Hooghly	-.009	-.189*	-.087*	-.211*	-.318*	-.152*	.011	.012*	-7.8(10-5)	.017*	.016*	.003
	(.03)	(.034)	(.032)	(.049)	(.09)	(.016)	(.006)	(.003)	(.005)	(.004)	(.0044)	(.002)
24-Paraganas	0.018	-.026	-.048	-.031	-.103*	-.039*	.006	.009*	.002	.009*	.011	.006*
	(.03)	(.016)	(.03)	(.018)	(.011)	(.008)	.006	(.005)	(.001)	(.003)	(.002)	(.001)
Nadia	4.0(10-5)	-.001	-.02	-.018	-.008	-.023*	.011	.021*	.001	.022*	.008	.011*
	(.043)	(.01)	(.025)	(.011)	(.017)	(.007)	(.014)	(.004)	(.008)	(.006)	(.006)	(.003)
Murshidabad	0.016	.003	-.009	.001	-.005	-.024*	-.002	-.0074*	.002	.011*	.003	.005*
	(.013)	(.006)	(.013)	(.006)	(.01)	(.003)	(.014)	(.003)	(.008)	(.004)	(.005)	(.002)
West Dinajpur	0.14*	-.025*	.052	-.037*	-.046*	-.043*	.001	-.0003	.001	-.0002	-.006*	-.0002
	(.034)	(.009)	(.032)	(.01)	(.019)	(.009)	(.009)	(.002)	(.005)	(.0022)	(.002)	(.001)
Malda	.05*	.05*	-.014	.06*	.039*	.016*	.012	.013*	-.006	.014*	-.003	.002
	(.022)	(.013)	(.027)	(.011)	(.016)	(.008)	(.01)	(.003)	(.007)	(.005)	(.003)	(.002)

Contd.. . . .

Table 3.3 contd.

Jalpaiguri	0.544*	.025	.273*	.039	-.058	.073*	.026*	-.003	.01	-.004	-.017*	-.001
	(.055)	(.026)	(.087)	(.026)	(.035)	(.025)	(.012)	(.002)	(.008)	(.004)	(.002)	(.002)
Darjeeling	0.34*	.023	.178*	.047	.177*	.048*	.01	.004	.0102*	.003	-.022	.007*
	(.043)	(.03)	(.056)	(.041)	(.05)	(.019)	(.008)	(.006)	(.004)	(.009)	(.015)	(.003)
Cooch-Behar	0.30*	.001	.128*	.008	-.082*	.026	.033*	.005	.013	.003	-.015	.006*
	(.047)	(.027)	(.065)	(.026)	(.039)	(.017)	(.008)	(.004)	(.003)	(.005)	(.007)	(.002)
Purulia	.235*	.002	-.023	-.004	-.119*	-.049*	-.002	.02*	-.01*	.022*	.007	.005*
	(.075)	(.034)	(.082)	(.048)	(.076)	(.022)	(.005)	(.004)	(.004)	(.005)	(.006)	(.002)
West Bengal	.052*	-.008	-.016	-.008	-.031	-.019*	.007	.001	-.0004	.011*	.006*	.0036*
	(.017)	(.011)	(.025)	(.0103)	(.018)	(.006)	(.006)	(.001)	(.004)	(.002)	(.0015)	(.001)

Notes: (i) Figures in the parentheses represent standard error, (ii) * indicates the coefficient is significant at 5% level of significance by two tailed test.

Table 3.3 contd.

	Pulses						Total Foodgrains					
Period	70/1-78/9	79/80-94/5	70/1-81/2	82/3-94/5	85/6-94/5	70/1-94/5	70/1-78/9	79/80-94/5	70/1-81/2	82/3-94/5	86/7-94/5	70/1-94/5
Burdwan	.0015	-.174*	-.044	-.191*	-.22*	-.124*	-.0001	.01*	-.0055	.0116*	.011*	.0013*
	(.028)	(.018)	(.021)	(.026)	(.045)	(.011)	(.01)	(.003)	(.006)	(.0042)	(.0046)	(.002)
Birbhum	.0266	-.084*	-.041*	-.082*	-.056	-.075*	-.0012	-.003	-.01	.0024	.001	-.008*
	(.024)	(.012)	(.02)	(.018)	(.035)	(.007)	(.009)	(.003)	(.0057)	(.0037)	(.007)	(.002)
Bankura	-.012	-.098*	-.037*	-.111*	-.164*	-.076*	.0035	.013*	-.0055	.017*	.016*	.0023
	(.025)	(.015)	(.015)	(.022)	(.039)	(.008)	(.005)	(.003)	(.0048)	(.003)	(.0046)	(.002)
Midnapore	.009	-.073*	-.009	-.057*	-.056*	-.057*	.0012	.01*	-.0037	.0116*	.014*	.003*
	(.017)	(.011)	(.011)	(.016)	(.022)	(.006)	(.004)	(.001)	(.0025)	(.002)	(.0026)	(.001)
Howrah	.094*	-.164*	.041	-.208*	-.256*	-.075*	.0262*	.023*	.0086	.026*	.011	.014*
	(.023)	(.024)	(.025)	(.029)	(.035)	(.016)	(.006)	(.007)	(.006)	(.01)	(.019)	(.003)
Hooghly	-.072*	-.223*	-.057*	-.246*	-.162*	-.147*	.008	.01*	-.0026	.014*	.016*	.0001
	(.034)	(.026)	(.02)	(.039)	(.069)	(.015)	(.007)	(.003)	(.0049)	(.003)	(.004)	(.002)
24-Paraganas	.006	-.06*	-.016	-.05*	-.041	-.049*	.0061	.0061*	.0011	.007*	.009*	.0031*
	(.02)	(.014)	(.016)	(.02)	(.035)	(.007)	(.005)	(.001)	(.003)	(.0018)	(.0025)	(.001)
Nadia	-.014	-.033*	-.025	-.028*	-.074*	-.033*	.0034	.0102*	-.0064	.013*	-.006	.001
	(.025)	.008)	(.014)	(.011)	(.008)	(.004)	(.015)	(.004)	(.008)	(.006)	(.0056)	(.003)
Murshidabad	-.01	-.077*	-.023*	-.083*	-.062*	-.057*	-.004	-.0044*	-.0038	-.0016	-.004	-.0051*
	(.012)	(.006)	(.007)	(.009)	(.013)	(.004)	(.012)	(.002)	(.0068)	(.003)	(.0048)	(.002)
West Dinajpur	.023	-.045*	.002	-.031	.029	-.037*	.0031	-.003*	.0013	-.002	-.004	-.0024*
	(.017)	(.012)	(.011)	(.017)	(.021)	(.006)	(.009)	(.001)	(.0048	(.002)	(.0023)	(.001)
Malda	-.053*	-.008	-.059*	-.001	-.027	-.031*	-.0022	.0031	-.012*	.0068	-.012	-.007*
	(.017)	(.008)	(.01)	(.012)	(.021)	(.005)	(.01)	(.006)	(.0069)	(.009)	(.016)	(.003)

Contd. . . .

Table 3.3 contd.

Jalpaiguri	.119*	-.093*	.079*	-.092*	-.052	-.036*	.028*	-.004	.0115	-.0038	-.013*	-.001
	(.034)	(.012)	(.023)	(.017)	(.033)	(.011)	(.012)	(.002)	(.008)	(.003)	(.003)	(.002)
Darjeeling	.016	.0104	.032	.051*	.052	.007	.01	.0043	.011*	.0036	-.021	.0071*
	(.024)	(.016)	(.017)	(.016)	(.033)	(.007)	(.007)	(.006)	(.0041)	(.009)	(.015)	(.003)
Cooch-Behar	.009	.013	-.026	.038*	-.007	-.014	.032*	.0055	.012	.004	-.015*	.005*
	(.039)	(.014)	(.028)	(.013)	(.016)	(.008)	(.008)	(.004)	(.0071)	(.005)	(.007)	(.002)
Purulia	-.073	.017	-.048	.0203	-.047*	-.005	-.0063	.02*	-.0126*	.0217*	.003	.0047*
	(.047)	(.011)	(.027)	(.016)	(.013)	(.008)	(.007)	(.004)	(.005)	(.005)	(.005)	(.002)
West Bengal	-.009	-.051*	-.025*	-.05*	-.052*	-.044*	.0046	.0061*	-.0028	.0082*	.003	.0004
	(.013)	(.006)	(.009)	(.008)	(.008)	(.003)	(.006)	(.001)	(.004)	(.002)	(.0016)	(.001)

Notes: (I) Figures in the parentheses represent standard error, (ii) * indicates the coefficient is significant at 5% level of significance by two tailed test.

Table-3.3 contd.

	Total Oilseed						Mustard					
Period	70/1-78/9	79/80-93/4	70/1-81/2	82/3-93/4	85/6-93/4	70/1-93/4	70/1-78/9	79/80-93/4	70/1-81/2	82/3-93/4	85/6-93/4	70/1-93/4
Burdwan	.1602*	.04*	.232*	.035	.035	.132*	.054	.006	.189*	-.061	-.181	.119*
	(.026)	(.012)	(.024)	(.013)	(.023)	(.013)	(.039)	(.055)	(.042)	(.084)	(.142)	(.027)
Birbhum	.047	.057*	.117*	.027	-.036	.092*	.0545**	.068	.1743*	-.0002	-.132	.155*
	(.025)	(.019)	(.026)	(.023)	(.027)	(.011)	(.025)	(.043)	(.0371)	(.059)	(.085)	(.0208)
Bankura	.208*	.041*	.171*	.044*	.049	.079*	.0647	.058	.077*	.006	-.123	.085*
	(.035)	(.01)	(.022)	(.016)	(.025)	(.011)	(.0355)	(.0518)	(.0206)	(.079)	(.1297)	(.0205)
Midnapore	.098*	.11*	.113*	.119*	.097*	.103*	-.012	.163*	-.011	.1418*	.075	.099*
	(.017)	(.014)	(.014)	(.013)	(.0176)	(.006)	(.0289)	(.027)	(.0175)	(.0418)	(.065)	(.014)
Howrah	.069	.013	.083*	.011	-.008	.052*	-.0347	.273*	-.059**	.2477*	.25*	.139*
	(.045)	(.021)	(.027)	(.021)	(.036)	(.011)	(.0455)	(.037)	(.0310)	(.0576)	(.104)	(.0232)
Hooghly	.117*	.063*	.138*	.049	.069	.098*	-.0248	.1361*	.033	.1243*	.104	.109*
	(.027)	(.019)	(.02)	(.025)	(.038)	(.009)	(.0373)	(.023)	(.0267)	(.0358)	(.065)	(.0122)
24-Paraganas	.007	.084*	.068*	.085*	.073	.085*	-.0586**	.1111*	.0259	.107*	.089*	.0932*
	(.038)	(.006)	(.026)	(.01)	(.015)	(.006)	(.033)	(.0077)	(.0298)	(.0108)	(.0165)	(.0093)
Nadia	-.033	.074*	-.003	.061*	.086*	.047*	-.0844	.1008*	.009	.0813*	.100*	.0864*
	(.048)	(.009)	(.03)	(.01)	(.013)	(.008)	(.0478)	(.0096)	(.0374)	(.0093)	(.0134)	(.011)
Murshidabad	-.002	.037*	.036*	.032*	.011	.048*	-.024	.095*	.0246	.0754*	.0228	.0807*
	(.023)	(.009)	(.018)	(.012)	(.017)	(.007)	(.031)	(.015)	(.0225)	(.0221)	(.0296)	(.0088)
West Dinajpur	-.041	.019*	.031	-.003	.006	.044*	.0232	.0342	-.0018	-.018	-.079	.035*
	(.098)	(.008)	(.057)	(.008)	(.012)	(.015)	(.0118)	(.0309)	(.0098)	(.0428)	(.0716)	(.0118)
Malda	.0021	.048*	-.015	.044*	.002	.019*	-.0198	.049	-.0586	.0211	-.110	.0111
	(.016)	(.013)	(.011)	(.02)	(.029)	(.006)	(.0137)	(.045)	(.0156)	(.0694)	(.11)	(.0178)

Contd.. . . .

Table 3.3 contd.

Jalpaiguri	-.035	.023*	-.013	-.003	-.0011	.024*	-.045	.0406*	-.0236	.0384	.093	.0202**
	(.029)	(.01)	(.017)	(.011)	(.019)	(.006)	(.0309)	(.0199)	(.018)	(.0315)	(.0506)	(.0094)
Darjeeling	.091	.034	.079*	.015	.014	.061*	-.0163	.152*	-.0535**	.1973*	.363*	.037
	(.059)	(.018)	(.035)	(.0236)	(.043)	(.013)	(.0238)	(.0574)	(.029)	(.0876)	(.139)	(.026)
Cooch-Behar	-.023	.01	.013	-.008	.0011	.029*	-.0302	.0237	-.0099	.0579	.1163**	.0036
	(.032)	(.008)	(.02)	(.01)	(.016)	(.008)	(.0339)	(.0257)	(.0199)	(.0376)	(.062)	(.011)
Purulia	-.027	.101*	-.036*	.117*	.063*	.036*	-.1415	.1792*	-.1417*	.2605*	.374*	.0188
	(.029)	(.017)	(.016)	(.026)	(.022)	(.011)	(.052)	(.0617)	(.0287)	(.0913)	(.153)	(.0316)
West Bengal	.038*	.054*	.058*	.049*	.034*	.058*	-.0175	.0993*	.0234	.094*	.05*	.0774*
	(.019)	(.007)	(.0128)	(.01)	(.015)	(.003)	(.0192)	(.0117)	(.0159)	(.0182)	(.016)	(.0072)

Notes: (i) Figures in the parentheses represent standard error, (ii) * indicates the coefficient is significant at 5% level of significance by two tailed test.

(iii) ** indicates the coefficient is significant at 10% level of significance by two tailed test.

Table-3.3 contd.

	Potato						Jute					
Period	70/1-78/9	79/80-93/4	70/1-81/2	82/3-93/4	85/6-93/4	70/1-93/4	70/1-78/9	79/80-93/4	70/1-81/2	82/3-93/4	85/6-93/4	70/1-93/4
Burdwan	.095*	.0285*	.068*	.022*	.0123	.004	.059	-.029	.0482*	-.026	-.059	-.0022
	(.013)	(.007)	(.0105)	(.01)	(.0168)	(.005)	(.0358)	(.015)	(.0201)	(.023)	(.039)	(.008)
Birbhum	.074*	.0253	.036*	.019	-.022	.0226*	.038	-.011	-.0127	-.0095	-.111	-.034*
	(.014)	(.014)	(.013)	(.022)	(.0337)	(.007)	(.044)	(.04)	(.031)	(.063)	(.097)	(.017)
Bankura	.115*	.096*	.078*	.102*	.0904*	.0804	.08	-.074*	.0361	-.038	-.137*	-.045*
	(.0246)	(.014)	(.018)	(.021)	(.026)	(.007)	(.049)	(.037)	(.0307)	(.056)	(.072)	(.017)
Midnapore	.076	.1034*	.048*	.108*	.1014*	.077*	.041	-.039*	.047*	-.023	-.066*	-.006
	(.017)	(.007)	(.012)	(.011)	(.017)	(.005)	(.022)	(.013)	(.0166)	(.017)	(.024)	(.007)
Howrah	.116*	.0321	.009	-.018	-.046	.024*	.038	-.055*	.055*	-.0348	-.064	-.02*
	(.019)	(.018)	(.0306)	(.0177)	(.0286)	(.009)	(.044)	(.015)	(.025)	(.02)	(.033)	(.009)
Hooghly	.085*	.0596*	.07*	.063*	.069*	.061*	.051	-.004	.0277	.0066	-.005	-.0003
	(.0117)	(.004)	(.008)	(.005)	(.009)	(.003)	(.037)	(.012)	(.022)	(.0177)	(.032)	(.006)
24-Paraganas	.133*	.0092	.072*	.0064	.0103	.024*	.061*	-.04*	.051*	-.031	-.053	-.0054
	(.016)	(.01)	(.019)	(.015)	(.0247)	(.007)	(.023)	(.014)	(.014)	(.02)	(.036)	(.008)
Nadia	.370*	.0093	.203*	-.0057	.0252	.061*	.046*	.0092	.049*	.01	-.003	.029*
	(.033)	(.025)	(.048)	(.04)	(.071)	(.019)	(.017)	(.01)	(.0103)	(.016)	(.0268)	(.006)
Murshidabad	.118*	-.0008	.071*	-.0012	.0014	.0216*	.0105	.0214*	.0164	.021	-.0008	.021*
	(.0113)	(.01)	(.014)	(.0157)	(.029)	(.006)	(.0289)	(.009)	(.016)	(.013)	(.02)	(.005)
West Dinajpur	.16*	.0165	.052	.0056	.0194	.019*	.0238	-.031	.0349*	-.023	-.025	-.0076
	(.0225)	(.012)	(.032)	(.018)	(.032)	(.008)	(.018)	(.017)	(.0107)	(.026)	(.046)	(.007)

Contd.. . . .

Table 3.3 contd.

Malda	.192*	.0352*	.072*	.037*	.0343	.0316*	.038	-.0193	.049*	-.0047	.0036	.008
	(.0247)	(.009)	(.035)	(.014)	(.026)	(.008)	(.0377)	(.022)	(.0207)	(.034)	(.06)	(.011)
Jalpaiguri	.227*	.1324*	.062	.1501*	.1326	.073*	-.015	-.0178*	.0241	-.0203	-.051	.01
	(.0425)	(.01)	(.051)	(.012)	(.015)	(.012)	(.0218)	(.009)	(.0167)	(.013)	(.019)	(.006)
Darjeeling	.0704*	.036*	.0614*	.048*	.062	.043*	-.024	-.0132	.0145	-.005	-.051	.005
	(.013)	(.012)	(.008)	(.018)	(.0308)	(.005)	(.022)	(.015)	(.0195)	(.021)	(.0315)	(.007)
Cooch-Behar	.196*	.1236*	.039	.107*	.0795	.0735*	-.0336	$6.0(10^{-5})$	.0136	.0041	.0004	.019*
	(.047)	(.018)	(.05)	(.0257)	(.045)	(.012)	(.0208)	(.007)	(.0185)	(.009)	(.016)	(.006)
Purulia	.228*	.1142*	.052	.1642*	.0904	.0508*	--	--	--	--	--	--
	(.059)	(.032)	(.062)	(.035)	(.049)	(.018)						
West Bengal	.108*	.058*	.063*	.0581*	.0548*	.053*	.0228	-.0066	.033*	-.002	-.0179	.0111*
	(.009)	(.004)	(.013)	(.006)	(.008)	(.003)	(.0186)	(.009)	(.0113)	(.014)	(.0236)	(.005)

Notes: (i) Figures in the parentheses represent standard error, (ii) * indicates the coefficient is significant at 5% level of significance by two tailed test.

(iii) ** indicates the coefficient is significant at 10% level of significance by two tailed test.

Table-3.3 contd.

	Sugarcane				
Period	70/1-78/9	70/1-81/2	82/3-93/4	85/6-93/4	70/1-93/4
Burdwan	-.048	-.076*	-.034	-.0448	-.061*
	(.027)	(.022)	(.0215)	(.0361)	(.0087)
Birbhum	.0067	-.023	-.0347	.0003	-.051*
	(.006)	(.0122)	(.023)	(.031)	(.0067)
Bankura	-.003	-.113*	-.1435*	-.083	-.143*
	(.017)	(.0347)	(.036)	(.059)	(.012)
Midnapore	-.039*	-.065*	.0022	-.039	-.038*
	(.013)	(.018)	(.04)	(.064)	(.011)
Howrah	-.053*	-.108*	--	--	--
	(.018)	(.03)			
Hooghly	-.191	-.22*	--	--	--
	(.026)	(.018)			
24-Paraganas	-.031*	-.049*	-.0525	.01	-.051*
	(.008)	(.013)	(.0447)	(.074)	(.011)
Nadia	-.036	-.04*	-.084	.076	-.0656*
	(.025)	(.0162)	(.069)	(.093)	(.017)
Murshidabad	.002	-.0246	-.0685	-.028	-.051
	(.0167)	(.0169)	(.0401)	(.069)	(.011)
West Dinajpur	-.019	-.067*	--	--	--
	(.0043)	(.019)			
Malda	.009	-.014	.009	.1104	-.012
	(.0197)	(.025)	(.043)	(.053)	(.012)
Jalpaiguri	-.053	--	--	--	--
	(.048)				

Contd.. . . .

Table 3.3 concld.

Darjeeling	--	--	--	--	--
Cooch-Behar	-.109*	--	--	--	--
	(.016)				
Purulia	.115	-.0123	-.074	.0795	-.066*
	(.066)	(.0576)	(.068)	(.124)	(.0244)
West Bengal	-.02	-.0477*	-.043	.005	-.053*
	(.01)	(.0159)	(.0226)	(.0245)	(.0068)

Notes: (i) Figures in the parentheses represent standard error,
(ii) * indicates the coefficient is significant at 5% level of significance by two tailed test.
(iii) ** indicates the coefficient is significant at 10% level of significance by two tailed test.

Table 3.4: Test For Changes in Growth Rate of Area under Different Crops in West Bengal (Districtwise)

District\Crop	*Aus*	*Aman*	*Boro*	*Rice*	*Wheat*	*Cereal*	*Pulses*	*Foodgrain*	*Oilseed*	*Jute*	*Potato*	*Sugarcane*
Burdwan	.004	.0002	.002	.001	-.006	.0012	-.012	.001	-.0144	-.006	-.004	.003
	(2.72)*	(.61)	(1.096)	(2.70)*	(-2.926)*	(2.948)*	(-6.98)*	(2.653)*	(-7.58)*	(-3.44)*	(-5.79)*	(1.723)**
Birbhum	.024	-.0016	-.0016	.0004	.002	.0008	-.004	.0008	-.0072	-10.6*10-5	-.0028	-.001
	(6.715)*	(-3.7)*	(-.461)	(1.202)	(.838)	(2.366)*	(−2.29)*	(1.971)**	(-3.39)*	(-.027)	(-2.056)**	(-.656)
Bankura	010	.0004	.007	.0018	-.004	.0016	-.006	.0016	-.0106	-.006	.0012	-.0026
	(5.731)*	(1.226)	(2.333)*	(5.60)*	(-1.585)	(4.455)*	(-4.91)*	(4.351)*	(-6.63)*	(-1.841)**	(.705)	(-.933)
Midnapore	.006	-.0002	.0074	.0012	-.0004	.0012	-.004	.0012	.00042	-.006	.004	.004
	(5.68)*	(-1.12)	(5.363)*	(7.404)*	(-1.405)	(6.74)*	(-3.155)*	(5.968)*	(.382)	(-4.05)*	(4.308)*	(1.55)
Howrah	.0002	-.0008	.01	.002	.0012	.0018	-.022	.0008	-.0054	-.006	-.004	NT
	(.054)	(-.914)	(5.278)*	(2.875)*	(.29)	(3.25)*	(-12.49)*	(1.062)	(-2.746)*	(-3.243)*	(-2.047)*	–
Hooghly	.002	7.0 $*10^{-5}$	-.004	.001	-.012	.0012	-.014	.0012	-.0064	.002	-.0006	NT
	(.466)	(.214)	(-1.28)	(2.672)*	(-3.75)*	(3.122)*	(-5.186)*	(3.044)*	(-3.428)*	(-.962)	(-1.167)	–
24 Paraganas	.0014	-5.8$*10^{-5}$	11.6$*10^{-5}$	.0004	-.0006	.0004	-.004	.0004	.0024	-.006	-.006	.0002
	(.755)	(-.313)	(.121)	(.274)	(-.316)	(2.524)*	(-2.23)*	(1.974)**	(1.465)	(-4.287)*	(-4.004)*	(.08)
Nadia	.0004	-1.5$*10^{-5}$	-.006	.0014	-.0002	.0012	-.001	.0012	.006	-.003	-.018	-19.2$*10^{-5}$
	(.178)	(-.012)	(-4.89)*	(1.927)**	(-.192)	(2.333)*	(-1.094)	(1.94)**	(3.501)*	(-2.754)*	(-5.17)*	(-.048)
Murshidabad	-.004	.0034	17.4$*10^{-5}$	.0006	.0004	.0006	-.004	6.84$*10^{-5}$	-2.6$*10^{-5}$	.0004	-.006	-.0028
	(-2.427)*	(2.024)**	(.111)	(.895)	(.438)	(1.137)	(-6.708)*	(.177)	(-.022)	(.431)	(-4.9)*	(-1.152)
West Dinajpur	-.01	.0008	.008	.0004	-.008	-19.8*10-5	-.0014	-.0002	-.002	-.0038	-.004	NT
	(-9.25)*	(1.671)	(3.26)*	(1.153)	(-5.043)*	(-.693)	(-1.128)	(-1.06)	(-.569)	(-2.248)*	(2.42)*	–
Malda	-.002	-.0002	.004	.0002	.004	.0012	.004	.0012	.0032	-.0034	-.004	NT
	(-1.215)	(.38)	(2.18)*	(.524)	(2.68)*	(2.306)*	(3.937)*	(1.767)**	(2.399)*	(-1.466)	(-1.933)**	–
Jalpaiguri	-.002	-19.8$*10^{-5}$	NA	-.0008	-.022	-.0014	-.006	-.0016	.001	-.003	.004	NT
	(-.99)	(-.367)	–	(1.845)	(-4.544)*	(-3.477)*	(-7.01)*	(-3.571)*	(7.53)*	(-2.36)*	(1.414)	
Darjeeling	-.0008	.0004	NA	10.54$*10^{-5}$	-.01	-.001	.002	-.0008	-.0046	-.0016	-.001	NT
	(-.367)	(.862)	–	(.178)	(-2.337)*	(-1.61)	(1.5)	(-1.571)	(1.93)**	(-.98)	(-.83)	–

Contd.. . . .

Table 3.4 contd.

Cooch Behar	-.002	.0006	.016	-.0004	-.012	-.0012	.004	-.001	-.0008	$3.4*10^{-5}$	.004	NT
	(-3.306)*	(1.039)	(3.426)*	(-1.11)	(-3.168)*	(-2.766)*	(2.22)*	(-2.386)*	(-.613)	(.058)	(1.01)	–
Purulia	.02	.0026	.034	.0022	-.003	.002	.004	.0022	.0106	NA	.004	.0036
	(6.7)*	(3.324)*	(5.307)*	(6.103)*	(-.595)	(5.024)*	(2.571)*	(5.058)*	(5.4)*	–	(1.079)	(.611)
West Bengal	$9.6*10^{-5}$	.0002	.0046	.0008	-.00046	.00068	-.002	.0006	-.0006	-.002	-.0012	.0008
	(.1004)	(.735)	(3.461)*	(3.467)*	(-.335)	(2.71)*	(–3.5)*	(2.55)*	(-.703)	(-2.354)*	(-1.336)	(.53)

Notes: (i) Figures in the parentheses represent t values.
(ii) * means significant at 5 % level by two tailed test and ** means significant at 5 % level by one tailed test.
(iii) + value indicates growth rate is increasing and (-) value indicates growth rate is decreasing.

Table 3.5: Ranking of Crops According to the Proportion of Area under Different Crops in West Bengal 1970-73 to 1991-94

Crop	1970-73	1977-80	1984-87	1991-94
Rice	72.7 (1)	70.22 (1)	72.29 (1)	74.85 (1)
Wheat	5.57 (4)	7.03 (4)	4.80 (5)	3.58 (4)
Other Cereals	1.96 (6)	1.48 (7)	1.48 (7)	1.02 (7)
Pulses	8.77 (2)	7.83 (2)	5.78 (3)	3.53 (5)
Oilseed	2.55 (5)	3.2 (5)	5.48 (4)	7.05 (2)
Potato	1.03 (7)	1.84 (6)	2.13 (6)	2.95 (6)
Jute	5.98 (3)	7.07 (3)	8.23 (2)	6.68 (3)
Sugarcane	.51 (8)	.43 (8)	.18 (8)	.18 (8)

Source: Government of West Bengal, Bureau of Applied Economics and Statistics, *Economic Review, (Various issues).*

Notes: (i) Here other cereals, pulses and oilseeds are represented as single crop (as a group). Other cereals include cereals other than rice and wheat, Pulses include gram & tur, oilseed includes mustard, til etc.

(ii) Figures in the parentheses represent ranks.

Table 3.6: Crop Area-Gross Cropped Area Elasticities

Crop	1970-71 to 1978-79	1979-80 to 1993-94	1970-71 to 1993-94
Aus	-2.97 (E < 0)	-3.26 (E < 0)	-2.8 (E < 0)
Aman	.25 (0 < E < 1)	.98 (0 < E < 1)	.713 (0 < E <)
Boro	4.34 (E > 1)	24.5 (E > 1)	19.68 (E > 1)
Rice	.13 (0< E < 1)	1.95 (E > 1)	1.28 (E > 1)
Wheat	7.7 (E > 1)	-6.07 (E < 0)	- 2.38 (E < 0)
Total Cereal	.52 (0 < E < 1)	1.133 (E > 1)	.91 (0 < E < 1)
Pulses	-1.73 (E < 0)	-6.93 (E < 0)	-4.65 (E < 0)
Total Foodgrains	.30 (0 < E < 1)	.40 (0 < E < 1)	.36 (0 < E < 1)
Mustard	.91 (0 < E < 1)	35.98 (E > 1)	28.83 (E > 1)
Oilseeds	7.45 (E > 1)	18.36 (E > 1)	17.65 (E > 1)
Potato	20.98 (E > 1)	9.65 (E > 1)	18.49 (E > 1)
Jute	5.68 (E > 1)	.19 (0 < E < 1)	2.1 (E > 1)
Sugarcane	-2.8 (E<0)	-7.24 (E< 0)	-5.01 (E< 0)

Table 3.7: Change in Area under Crop due to Substitution and Expansion Effect during 1970-71 to 1991-94 (in thousand Hectares)

Crop→	Aus		Aman		Boro		Rice		Wheat	
District	Subs.	Exp.	Subs.	Exp.	Subs.	Exp.	Subs.	Exp.	Subs.	Exp.
Burdwan	-7.0	5.54	-73.23	71.43	73.01	7.82	-7.30	84.85	-30.23	4.84
Birbhum	-39.46	-2.04	42.76	-10.53	28.58	-2.51	31.4	-12.5	-51.01	-2.45
Bankura	-21.53	8.0	-36.97	53.24	35.94	0.39	-22.6	61.67	-6.52	2.12
Midnapore	-16.50	13.14	-135.72	137.08	124.28	11.99	-27.95	162.22	-10.54	2.64
Howrah	-3.87	1.5	-18.37	28.74	37.04	4.89	14.79	35.15	-6.57	1.97
Hooghly	-8.53	5.17	-22.25	51.49	5.16	14.50	-25.74	71.21	-27.12	6.85
24-Paraganas	-9.34	4.11	-73.08	75.88	103.07	3.30	20.65	83.28	-11.33	2.3
Nadia	-77.56	30.99	19.74	18.30	86.0	2.0	34.90	44.56	-22.34	12.04
Murshidabad	-23.36	3.02	40.69	6.24	48.29	0.44	65.63	9.71	-14.52	3.52
West Dinajpur	-88.49	0.622	41.40	1.75	55.98	0.02	8.84	2.46	2.16	0.18
Malda	-34.29	-5.48	48.55	-8.68	42.04	-1.41	56.31	-15.57	15.17	-2.21
Jalpaiguri	-7.48	3.75	-7.07	10.94	1.66	0.006	-12.9	14.7	12.71	0.064
Darjeeling	3.30	0.96	-6.49	6.12	0.056	0.024	-3.21	7.11	2.73	0.075
Cooch-Behar	-24.44	17.8	8.99	36.24	9.9	0.10	-5.55	54.15	7.44	1.404
Purulia	0.60	0.44	1.84	23.63	0.82	0.08	3.56	24.15	-1.51	0.275
West Bengal	-365.7	95.27	-133.88	466.48	633.55	28.62	165.30	592.36	-153.09	45.28

Table 3.7 contd.

Crop→	Pulses		Mustard		Oilseeds		Potato		Jute		Sugarcane	
District	Subs.	Exp.	Subs.	Exp.	Subs.	Exp.	Subs.	Exp.	Subs.	Exp.	Subs.	Exp.
Burdwan	-24.92	3.89	44.24	0.56	52.48	0.79	16.55	2.48	-0.01	1.67	-3.0	0.57
Birbhum	-24.64	-1.36	32.25	-0.08	29.68	-0.251	2.67	-0.213	-0.044	-0.026	-2.08	-0.12
Bankura	-11.85	2.12	17.22	0.32	31.05	0.75	12.3	0.504	-0.84	0.178	-2.01	0.31
Midnapore	-46.86	10.03	23.97	0.53	55.53	1.23	40.65	2.011	-2.86	1.93	-2.68	0.612
Howrah	-8.38	2.91	1.42	0.08	2.01	1.09	-0.13	0.86	-2.47	1.437	-0.80	0.248
Hooghly	-16.62	4.09	7.80	0.76	31.56	1.44	42.80	5.83	-3.28	7.75	-1.19	0.30
24-Paraganas	-33.04	6.61	28.42	1.14	36.40	1.24	2.62	0.382	-6.21	5.28	-0.91	0.206
Nadia	-70.87	24.08	43.72	3.11	38.98	6.65	2.485	0.115	34.72	15.95	-5.14	1.34
Murshidabad	-351.47	13.37	43.41	0.43	31.92	0.945	2.99	0.146	25.82	2.45	3.62	0.283
West Dinajpur	-20.44	0.243	34.64	0.12	33.61	0.117	2.425	0.035	3.12	0.35	-1.8	0.001
Malda	-31.01	-7.065	11.45	-1.12	9.82	-1.42	1.151	-0.051	8.44	-1.57	0.44	-0.21
Jalpaiguri	-2.13	0.269	-1.04	0.47	1.79	0.51	5.38	0.06	-2.32	2.35	-0.29	0.01
Darjeeling	0.506	0.224	-.05	0.11	0.82	0.083	4.22	0.41	-0.93	0.56	--	--
Cooch-Behar	-4.09	2.43	-3.50	1.67	2.25	1.75	5.83	0.311	-0.87	11.63	--	--
Purulia	-7.13	2.23	-0.32	0.16	4.30	0.358	0.83	0.04	--	--	-0.31	0.08
West Bengal	-403.65	71.21	279.66	12.24	346.25	20.58	147.6	8.11	53.52	48.62	-25.04	0.37

Source: (i) Government of West Bengal, Bureau of Applied Economics and Statistics, Statistical Abstract (various issues).
(ii) Government of West Bengal, Bureau of Applied Economics and Statistics, Economic Review (various issues).

Note: -- means the value is negligible.

Table 3.8: Test For Variability and Instability of Growth of Area Under Different Crops in West Bengal During 1970-71 to 1994-95 (Districtwise)

Crop ®	Aus			Aman			Boro			Rice			Wheat		
District	F1	F2	F3	F1	F2	F3	F1	F2	F3	F1	F2	F3	F1	F2	F3
0	1	2	3	4	5	6	7	8	9	10	11	12	12	14	15
Burdwan	2.367	8.507*	5.236*	7.129*	18.75*	-.306	2.64	4.182*	.209	1.768	6.25*	4.537*	1.39	.157	1.494
Birbhum	3.063*	3.686	10.58*	1.00	.792	4.154*	3.423*	5.018*	-2.791	.916	.74	-4.25	2.191	1.232	1.416
Bankura	1.266	1.638	14.71*	1.769	1.00	-2.923	2.582	3.133	2.345	1.39	.64	20.2*	2.718	.823	.763
Midnapore	.372	.36	4.313*	4.00*	16.00*	25.39*	1.85	1.988	22.73*	.786	1.769	12.37*	1.181	.152	.834
Howrah	2.48	2.097	5.376*	.774	1.904	4.091*	6.003*	7.896*	15.19*	.401	.449	10.61	.977	.221	.585
Hooghly	1.195	1.392	2.60	1.769	4.00*	-2.923	21.81*	26.11*	.572	1.768	2.56	4.537*	.335	.109	2.316
24 Paraganas	2.608	3.349	8.562*	2.25	6.25*	3.61*	1.488	1.563	11.90*	1.768	4.00*	4.536*	2.191	7.453*	-.12
Nadia	.25	.230	1.554	9.00*	11.42*	1.548	2.372	7.236*	5.236*	1.604	11.56*	1.219	4.049*	6.401*	3.042
Murshidabad	.518	.436	7.585*	1.124	11.09*	2.656	3.423*	8.585*	-1.451	4.526*	9.86*	.538	3.70*	1.69	-1.494
West Dinajpur	.325	.121	23.34*	5.429*	7.563*	2.202	1.323	1.96	6.166	7.071*	20.25*	-5.223	8.046*	3.204	4.778*
Malda	1.103	.312	.0308	7.129*	21.81*	-.305	1.44	1.30	10.63*	2.001	9.00*	-1.629	4.716*	1.904	5.14*
Jalpaiguri	1.769	2.403	9.658*	4.00*	10.56*	-1.154	NA	NA	NA	4.266*	10.56*	3.754*	8.818*	2.465	5.614*
Darjeeling	.266	.09	-6.96*	1.44	1.232	1.602	NA	NA	NA	.238	.593	3.777*	1.475	.74	3.938*
Cooch Behar	2.789	1.00	1.708	1.563	1.266	7.261*	1.124	3.572	14.85*	1.131	1.232	1.869	4.911*	1.452	1.769
Purulia	.476	.09	28.01*	.132	1.00	10.66*	1.036	1.392	2.949	.786	1.00	12.37*	2.298	.980	.18
West Bengal	1.00	.563	7.474*	16.00*	49.00*	.407	3.61*	5.336*	3.816*	3.43*	9.00*	-.337	4.64*	.884	-.282

Note:

Where, $F_1 = \dfrac{\Sigma e_1^2/10}{\Sigma e_2^2/11} = F_{(10,11)}$ for rice, wheat, cereal, pulses and foodgrains, and $F1 = \dfrac{\Sigma e_1^2/10}{\Sigma e_2^2/10} = F_{(10\ 10)}$ for others.

Where, Σe_1^2 is the RSS for 1970-71 to 1981-82 and Σe_2^2 is the RSS for 1982-83 to 1994-95 sub-period.

$F_2 = \dfrac{\Sigma e_3^2/7}{\Sigma e_4^2/7}$ where, $\Sigma e_3^2/7$ and $\Sigma e_4^2/7$ represent RSS for the first and last nine year sub-period respectively.

Table-3.8 contd.

Crop	Cereal			Pulses			Total Foodgrains			Oilseed		
District	F1	F2	F3	F1	F2	F3	F1	F2	F3	F1	F2	F3
0	16	17	18	19	20	21	22	23	24	25	26	27
Burdwan	1.768	6.25*	4.537*	.512	.384	8.647*	1.603	4.725*	3.968*	3.408*	1.278	30.13*
Birbhum	1.432	1.664	9.383*	.968	.476	2.103	1.865	1.653	6.50*	1.278	.857	7.766*
Bankura	1.815	2.00	11.32*	.363	.41	5.067*	2.011	1.181	14.14*	1.89	1.96	18.93*
Midnapore	.786	.2.190	12.37*	.374	.593	5.987*	1.228	2.367	8.026*	1.159	.933	7.45*
Howrah	.401	.331	10.61*	.581	.436	20.68*	.283	.0997	.727	1.653	1.563	8.297*
Hooghly	1.228	1.85	4.136*	.204	.240	9.029*	2.096	3.063	13.49*	.64	.505	3.981*
24 Paraganas	1.768	6.25*	4.536*	.164	.325	2.683	2.183	4.00	5.72*	6.76*	6.418*	-1.792
Nadia	1.39	5.43*	6.772*	1.267	9.766*	-.887	1.397	7.175*	6.771*	8.999*	13.63*	1.323
Murshidabad	3.143*	7.84*	-.336	.478	.846	11.13*	4.037*	6.25*	4.425*	2.25	1.83	8.524*
West Dinajpur	4.049*	20.25*	-3.591	.332	.656	14.69*	4.526*	15.31*	-2.834	50.77*	66.69*	2.016
Malda	1.54	11.09*	-.045	.541	.656	7.698*	.462	.391	1.772	.303	.305	2.225
Jalpaiguri	3.143*	36.0*	-.336	1.432	1.061	17.95*	5.587*	16.0*	.964	2.389	2.33	5.535*
Darjeeling	.152	.281	4.77*	.883	.533	6.116*	.163	.218	4.675*	2.199	1.883	6.779*
Cooch Behar	1.54	1.30	-.045	3.682*	5.944*	3.267	1.54	1.306	-.218	4.00*	4.00*	12.65*
Purulia	.503	.689	6.719*	2.244	12.96*	2.421	.786	1.96	4.136	.379	1.738	12.97*
West Bengal	3.143*	.16	-.336	.994	2.641	1.082	3.143*	14.06*	-.336	1.638	1.604	-3.965

$$F_3 = \frac{\Sigma e_p^2 - (\Sigma e_1^2 + \Sigma e_2^2)/2}{(\Sigma e_1^2 + \Sigma e_2^2)/21}$$ is used for testing instability, where Se_p^2 is the RSS for the whole period.

· The symbol * indicates that the test statistic is significant at 5 per cent level of significance.

Table-3.8 concld.

District	Potato			Jute			Sugarcane		
	F1	F2	F3	F1	F2	F3	F1	F2	F3
0	28	29	30	31	32	33	34	35	36
Burdwan	1.102	.599	11.04*	.756	.843	2.189	1.047	.559	4.152*
Birbhum	.349	.173	3.276	.242	.206	.371	.281	.037	1.717
Bankura	.734	.895	1.332	.300	.463	2.537	.93	.083	.19
Midnapore	1.19	.786	6.691*	1.000	.84	4.999*	.203	.041	1.127
Howrah	2.988*	.441	1.468	1.563	1.778	3.981*	NA	NA	NA
Hooghly	2.56	1.69	7.891*	1.545	1.33	-2.011	NA	NA	NA
24 Paraganas	1.605	.42	4.794*	.54	.408	8.379*	.085	.012	-.1215
Nadia	1.44	.216	6.36*	.415	.402	7.590*	.055	.072	.178
Murshidabad	.795	.152	4.394*	1.515	2.09	.407	.178	.059	1.305
West Dinajpur	3.16*	.494	-1.60	.179	.153	.877	NA	NA	NA
Malda	6.25*	.903	-2.032	.370	.395	3.511*	.338	.138	.298
Jalpaiguri	18.06*	8.028*	-.719	1.65	1.316	4.22*	NA	NA	NA
Darjeeling	.197	.178	1.40	.862	.488	.556	NA	NA	NA
Cooch Behar	3.785*	1.091	-1.939	4.457*	1.69	4.41*	NA	NA	NA
Purulia	3.14*	1.45	1.309	NA	NA	NA	.718	.283	3.263
West Bengal	4.69*	1.27	-2.233	.617	.621	3.953*	.495	.167	.78

CHAPTER 4

GEOGRAPHICAL DISTRIBUTION OF AGRICULTURAL PRODUCTION OVER TIME IN WEST BENGAL

The objective of this chapter is to present a brief account of production of different crops and its growth during the period 1970-71 to 1994-95 in West Bengal as well as in its different districts. First of all the growth of production in the state will be analysed. Thereafter, districtwise pattern of agricultural production will be presented.

4.1. Introduction

Agricultural production in West Bengal is largely characterised by wide diversification among different crops within a particular district and also across the districts. Inter-crop and intra-crop variation in production over time has been substantial. This districtwise variation in the growth of output of different crops is due to disproportionate growth of area and yield. These two primarily determine the amount of output of any crop at any point of time. Major factors which may account for this regional variation in acreage and yield of different crops are the differential agro-climatic condition that depends on geographical location of the place, elevation, slope, chemical composition of soil, timing and quantum of rainfall, temperature, humidity on the one hand and availability as well as application of inputs in different proportions like, varieties of seeds, fertiliser, irrigation, plant protective chemicals etc on the other. Suitability of different varieties of crops to different agro-climatic conditions, adoption of technology of cultivation and the pattern of crops itself are thus the major important aspects of agricultural output growth of any region.

As agriculture constitutes an important part of the economy of West Bengal, from planning perspective it is essential to have an idea of geographical distribution of crop production and their regional pattern of growth over time in the past. Acreage allocation and its regional character have already been discussed in the previous chapter.

For the purpose of analysis trend rate of growth of production of different crops has been considered and compared for the whole and all sub-periods; as was done in case of area allocation to crops in the previous chapter. The same thing has been done here for all the districts to have an inter-district comparison of production growth of all major crops grown in West Bengal. This chapter also investigates the absolute growth of production during the whole period and the change in contribution of each district to the state's total production of each crop over time. Besides, here it is sought to examine whether the growth of output is associated with an increase or decrease in inter-district disparity in the production of each crop. Inter-district variability is considered here in terms of coefficient of variation.

4.2. Growth of Agricultural Production in West Bengal

In the post-Green Revolution period, West Bengal saw a sea change in agricultural production. The growth is characterised by a massive inter and intra-crop variation in production. Table 4.1 presents the level of production of different crops in West Bengal during 1970-71 to 1994-95 and percentage share of different districts to state's total production.

From the table it is observed that foodgrains' production in the state was 7493.7 thousand tonnes in 1970-71, which increased to 13279.0 thousand tonnes in 1994-95. Major part of food-crop has been the cereal crops mainly paddy, which is the staple food of the major inhabitants of the region. Production of cereal has increased from 7116 thousand tonnes to 13144 thousand tonnes during 1970-71 to 1994-95. The figure was 94.97 per cent of food-crop production in 1970-71 and increased to almost 99 per cent in 1994-95. The implication is that share of pulses in the total output of foodgrains has decreased during the period like the proportion of its area, as was observed in chapter-3. Production of pulses has decreased from 377.3 thousand tonnes i.e., 5.03 per cent of food-crop production in 1970-71 to only 135 thousand tonnes i.e., 1.02 per cent of foodgrains' production in 1994-95.

Among cereals, production of rice increased due to rise in production of aman and boro rice. Aman is the major rice crop in West Bengal produced in the span of July-August to December-January. Though production of aman has increased in absolute amount its proportion to total quantity of foodgrain output has decreased. Quantity of aman rice production was 4694.7 thousand tonnes i.e., roughly 63 per cent of output of foodgrain in 1970-71 and 7961.2 tonnes i.e., around 60 per cent in 1994-95. Production of boro-rice has increased significantly by almost 6 times. It was only 535.4 thousand tonnes (7.14 per cent of quantity of foodgrains) during 1970-71 and went up to 3241.5 thousand tonnes (24.41 per cent of total food-crop) at the end of the period. Production of aus had decreased marginally by around two thousand tonnes though its percentage changed from 12.14 to 6.84 in total foodgrain output during the whole period. It is notable that production of aus followed the same pattern of change as its area. Production of wheat has declined from 868.1 thousand tonnes (11.58 per cent of food-crop) to 744.5 thousand tonnes (5.6 per cent of foodgrains) during 1970-71 to 1994-95 period. Among non-food crops, production of oilseed observed an increase from merely 59.2 thousand tonnes to 415.8 thousand tonnes i.e., by 356.6 tonnes (about seven times of initial level of output). Production of jute has increased from 2683.6 thousand bales to 5569 thousand bales during the whole period i.e., it more than doubled. On the other hand production of potato increased by almost 5 times, from 929.7 thousand tonnes to 5171.6 thousand tonnes.

4.3 Growth Rate of Output of Crops/ Crop-Groups in West Bengal During 1970-71 to 1994-95

Table 4.2 displays a contrast among the growth rates of different crops or crop- groups during the whole and different sub-periods. From the table it is evident that percentage growth of output of oilseed over its initial value has been the highest, 602.36 during 1970-71 to 1993-94, whereas, that for boro rice and potato had been 505.44 and 456.27 respectively. Negative growth rate has been observed in case of pulses and wheat. Marginal decline in the production of aus in the state was due to significant decline in its production in the districts of Birbhum, West Dinajpur, Malda and Jalpaiguri that outweighed the positive growth in other districts. The change occurred in sympathy with the variation in area, in spite of a marginal growth of yield. Production of wheat has declined in the state at the rate of 14.24 per cent during 1970-71 to 1994-95 while, that of pulses has decreased at the rate of 64.22 per cent. Thus we find that the decrease in production of wheat and pulses was due to decline in area, which had taken place at a more rapid rate than the positive rate of growth of their yield. Those land-areas have been shifted in favour of potato, mustard etc., whose area has increased at the cost of the former.

Estimated trend rate of growth of production of different crops is presented in Table 4.3. The table reveals that average annual exponential rate of growth of production of food-crops in West Bengal during 1970-71 to 1994-95 was 2.63 per cent per annum. The rate was higher in the sub-period 1979-80 to 1994-95 and more rapid during 1982-83 to 1994-95 than the earlier sub-period. Lower rate of growth of production of foodgrains during 1970-71 to 1981-82 than that in 1970-71 to 1978-79 can be attributed to uneven rainfall that has often ruined the crop production in the kharif season (agricultural production in the state was highly affected due to devastating flood in 1978 and drought in 1980 in the kharif season). In all those cases area under crop were almost left unaffected excepting however production. Though the flow of irrigation has been smoothened afterwards and the flood control measures have been improved, farmers in the region especially drought-prone zones are still not in a position to tackle the severe problems created by the vagaries of nature. In 1989 and 1992 production of boro rice had been affected seriously in many areas on account of shortfall of water during March-April. This can be attributed partly to untoward weather and partly to electricity problem. Output of aus and aman during 1991 and 1994 has also been affected marginally owing to the flood in a few regions. Thus after 1986-87 the growth has been slackened as is observed from table-4.3. Annual exponential rate of growth of production of foodgrains was 3.84 per cent during 1986-87 to 1994-95, which was 1.14 and 5.13 per cent respectively during 1970-71 to 1981-82 and 1982-83 to 1994-95 sub-periods.

Within foodgrains cereal production gathered momentum after 1978-79. The annual exponential growth rate of production increased from merely 1.95 per cent during 1970-71 to 1978-79 to over 5 per cent during 1979-80 to 1994-95. The rate further increased to 5.31 per cent per annum during 1982-83 to 1994-95, but registered a fall below 4 per cent per annum when reckoned for the sub-period 1986-87 to 1994-95. Cereals' acreage has earlier been observed to have increased at the cost of pulses and so might have been for production. However, major part of cereal is occupied by rice whose major component is aman. Most of the net cropped area in the kharif season is devoted to the production of aman. But net cropped area after 1980 has not increased significantly and hence the level of output of aman rice has increased only due to the upward revision of yield from time to time. After reaching a high level in the mid-eighties it became very difficult to maintain the same pace of growth in its yield (to be observed in the next chapter).

Production of pulses has receded and the rate of decline was very rapid after mid-eighties. Annual exponential rate of decline in the production of pulses is greater than the rate of increase in output of cereal, as a whole. This can be attributed to the fact that pulses occupy a small portion, while cereal a larger portion of total area under foodgrains (as observed in chapter-3). Hence a decrease in area even at a rapid rate meant for pulses, had led to reallocation of the same in favour of cereal, the area under which however increased at a relatively smaller rate. In addition to that yield of cereals has not increased at so rapid rate that growth rate of cereals' production had outweighed the rate of decline of output of pulses.

Major part of cereal is composed of different varieties of rice and wheat. It is also reflected from the table that output of rice has increased at the cost of wheat and other inferior cereals (which are not included in the table). Production of paddy increased at only 1.68 per cent per annum during 1970-71 to 1978-79, whereas the annual exponential rate of growth was 5.4 per cent during 1979-80 to 1994-95. Production of paddy as well as its main component, aman attained a faster rate of growth after 1982-83. The trend rate of growth of paddy output during 1982-83 to 1994-95 was 5.87 per cent per annum and that of aman during 1982-83 to 1993-94 was 5.43 per cent. During post mid-eighties period growth rate was 4.35 per cent and 4.3 per cent per annum for aman and paddy as a whole, respectively.

Though production of aus decreased at an annual exponential rate of 2.62 per cent during 1970-71 to 1978-79, it has increased during 1979-80 to 1993-94 by around 5 per cent annually. The rate of growth is also increasing. This is clearly reflected from 8.7 per cent and 20.71 per cent per annum rate of growth during 1982-83 to 1993-94 and 1985-86 to 1993-94 sub-periods. Initially output had decreased despite a positive trend in area during 1970-71 to 1978-79. This was due to clearly negative trend in yield rate. While the negative trend in acreage was noticed in the immediate latter period, output of aus registered a positive trend, obviously due to rising yield at a rate higher than the decline of area under it.

Boro rice emerged as one important food as well as commercial crop over time in West Bengal. Output of it has increased at an exponential rate of 7.09 per cent per annum during 1970-71 to 1993-94 period. In this case also output witnessed an increasing rate of growth. During 1970-71 to 1978-79 sub-period production of boro (summer) rice was growing at an annual average rate of 5.67 per cent, which increased to 11.26 per cent during the sub-period 1979-80 to 1993-94.

Like area, production of wheat had increased during the early years (from 1970-71 to 1978-79) at around 4 per cent per annum. After 1978-79 it started declining by around 0.21 per cent per annum only, despite a larger rate of decrease in area allocated to its cultivation. The overall rate of decline was 1.73 per cent per year. However, in recent past (after 1986-87) despite continuous decline in its area production of wheat has increased marginally due to a rise in productivity at a rate, which more than offset the rate of fall in its acreage.

Among non-food crops, potato and oilseed grew tremendously during the entire and in all sub-periods. The only difference is that growth rate of potato was highest during the early years while that of oilseed occurred after 1982-83. This means, oilseed production found acceleration whereas that of potato observed a deceleration in rate of growth. The overall rate of growth of oilseed in terms of output was higher than that of potato and also jute.

Jute, which was the primary cash crop during the early years even before 1970, has grown in terms of output significantly at an annual average rate of 3.87 per cent throughout the entire period. But area under jute first registered a declining trend though the overall trend was barely positive. The trend rate of growth of production was 4.15 and 2.94 per cent respectively during 1970-71 to 1981-82 and 1982-83 to 1993-94 sub-period i.e., though area observed an increasing trend rate of growth, production in it was found to grow at a decreasing rate. During 1985-86 to 193-94 production has increased only at 0.69 per cent per annum, which is very insignificant.

4.4 District-wise Pattern of Agricultural Production During 1970-71 to 1994-95

From Table 4.1 it is evident that the production of foodgrains is highly concentrated in the southern region except Purulia. Almost half of the output of foodgrains comes from four major agricultural districts, namely, Burdwan, Midnapore, 24-Paraganas and Murshidabad. Proportion of state's total production of food crop has increased notably in the districts of Burdwan, Midnapore, Hooghly, Nadia and 24-Paraganas whereas the proportion has decreased in case of Birbhum, Murshidabad, and Purulia in the south and Jalpaiguri, Cooch-Behar in the north. In absolute term however, production of foodgrain has increased in all the districts but at a disproportionate rate. Cereal, the major component of foodgrain particularly, production of rice reflects same pattern of distribution and change within the districts. Absolute and proportion of rice-output has increased significantly in case of Burdwan Midnapore, Howrah, Hooghly, 24-Paraganas, Nadia in southern Bengal and Malda in the northern Bengal. In other districts, proportion of rice to total output of the state has decreased, despite a rise in production in absolute term except Jalpaiguri.

Among different kinds of rice, production of boro rice, the major summer crop has increased in all the districts significantly. However, the proportion of output in the four leading districts, Burdwan, Midnapore, Howrah and Hooghly to state's total output has decreased. This is because of the rapid growth of boro production in the erstwhile backward districts where increasingly more areas have been devoted to the cultivation of boro rice with the development of irrigation during summer time. The districts that had already access to major sources of irrigation have not been able to keep pace with the laggard districts, where irrigation development started later and at a rapid rate. Production of pulses has decreased in all the districts except Cooch-Behar and Darjeeling.

Among non-food crops, production of oilseed was earlier concentrated in the districts of Nadia, Murshidabad and West Dinajpur. Those three districts together were the source of more than 50.0 per cent of states total oilseed production in 1970-71. Locational shift in oilseed production also occurred from those districts to other districts over time. The proportion of state's total oilseed production by those three districts together, declined to around 36.0 per cent during 1993-94. The major growth in oilseed production has been observed in central and southern districts. Highest rate of growth has been observed in Burdwan. Birbhum also turned into a major oilseed producing district from its former character of pulses producer. Growth rate of production of jute during 1970-71 to 1993-94 was rather slow. This was because of the overall sluggish rate of growth of area under jute. Output of jute has increased in all the districts except Howrah, Jalpaiguri and Darjeeling despite the fact that area under it has increased marginally. Maximum rate of growth has been noticed in case of Nadia and Murshidabad.

Another important cash crop whose production has recorded an enviable rate of growth is potato. Most of the production in absolute and proportional terms came from three south-central districts, Burdwan, Hooghly and Midnapore. Their contribution to state's total output has however decreased from over 82 per cent in 1970-71 to nearly 74 per cent in 1993-94. Still now they are the major contributor to state's potato production. Hooghly, Burdwan and Midnapore were at the three successive top positions in the ranking of total potato production during early years of the period. Vast of areas in Midnapore were later brought under the cultivation of potato and the district became the second highest potato producer in the state. During the two and half decade production in the district has increased by roughly ten times to that of 1970-71.

A close look at the districtwise distribution of output of each crop over time reveals that inter-district variation in the percentage contribution to state's production has been reduced in case of aus, aman and boro rice since 1970-71. This is evident from the reduction in coefficient of variation. This result also reveals the rapidity of the growth rate of the laggard districts, which have been greater than that of the existing developed districts. Inter-district variation in production of wheat, cereal as a whole, pulses and foodgrains as a whole has declined over time. Among the non-food crops reduction of inter-district disparity has taken place in the production of oilseed during 1970-71 to 1993-94 while the case is reversed for other crops.

Inter-district and inter-crop variation in growth rate of absolute production of major crops/crop groups in West Bengal has been displayed in Table 4.2. It is also revealed from the table that growth of aus was positive in the major districts except Birbhum in the south and West-Dinajpur, Malda and Jalpaiguri in the north. Growth of wheat production was highest in Malda. It rose by 3550.0 per cent over its initial value, followed by Jalpaiguri and Darjeeling, about 900.0 per cent during this twenty-five years. It was positive in all the northern districts and the rates were higher than that of any of the southern districts. In the southern and central region significant increase in output of wheat has taken place in Burdwan (by about 90.0 per cent) and in Purulia (at 166.67 per cent). Significant decrease in production of wheat has been observed in case of Hooghly, Howrah and Birbhum. Growth of oilseed production has been the highest in the district of Burdwan followed by Hooghly, Bankura, Midnapore, Birbhum, and 24-Paraganas. Growth rate of production of potato was highest in Cooch-Behar. Next to it in the order are Jalpaiguri, Bankura, Midnapore etc. Hooghly and Burdwan were originally the major growers of potato and attained a peak level of production growth in the middle of eighties. Subsequently, more emphasis was given to the production of oilseed, particularly on mustard and hence production of potato increased but at a relatively slower rate.

District-wise pattern of exponential rate of growth shows a quite different pattern during different sub-periods. Production of foodgrains had increased significantly after 1980 in all the districts except Jalpaiguri. Though trend rate of growth was positive in all but West-Dinajpur during 1970-71 to 1978-79 it was much lower and even negative for some districts during 1970-71 to 1981-82. This was mainly due to the shortfall of production, caused by the incidence of devastating natural calamities (flood and drought) that has affected almost all the districts of West Bengal during major rice producing season within 1978 to 1981. Despite these natural calamities Burdwan, Malda and Darjeeling observed a quite substantial rate of growth of production of foodgrains in all the sub-periods. After 1982-83 all the districts of West Bengal attained high rate of growth in the production of foodgrains. More than 5 per cent per annum rate of growth was observed in Burdwan, Bankura, Midnapore, Hooghly, 24-Paraganas, Nadia, Darjeeling and Purulia.

Production of pulses has decreased throughout the whole period in all the districts except Darjeeling. During 1970-71 to 1978-79 positive trend had been noticed in Burdwan, Howrah, 24-Paraganas, West-Dinajpur, Jalpaiguri, Darjeeling and Cooch-Behar. During the period of 1979-80 to 1994-95 it was decreasing in most of the districts at a significant rate except Purulia. Very high rate of decline was observed during post-mid eighties period in Burdwan, Bankura, Howrah and Hooghly.

Production of cereal and its major contributor rice, (particularly aman rice) observed a similar pattern of trend in all the districts like that of total foodgrains. The erstwhile backward districts experienced higher growth rates in the latter periods than the districts, which had already achieved momentum.

Production of aus was found to follow a declining trend during the early years in the major districts except Hooghly, 24-Paraganas, Nadia and Murshidabad. During 1979-80 to 1993-94 it has increased in all the districts except West-Dinajpur and Malda. In spite of a fall in area in the major districts, production went through increasing trend due to the higher rate of rise in yield.

Among different varieties of paddy highest ever rate of growth in all the districts was observed in case of summer rice or boro rice. This is a clear indication of advancement of irrigation infrastructure and technology. In addition to that development of crops with short period maturity and high yielding varieties has decreased to some extent the problem of water crisis and converted the situation in many cases to a favourable one. Over 10 per cent average rate of growth per annum has been found in laggard districts like Bankura, Cooch-Behar and West-Dinajpur. Alongside Nadia also observed a tremendous rate of growth in respect of production of major crops.

Within the group of non-food crop varieties, production of oilseed has been increasing remarkably in all the districts and sub-periods despite an inter-district and inter-crop variation in growth rate. Deceleration in the rate of growth in the production of oilseed has been found in Burdwan, Birbhum and Malda while acceleration has been observed in Midnapore, Howrah, 24-Paraganas, Nadia, West-Dinajpur, Cooch-Behar and Purulia. The other important cash crop, potato, which also earns huge amount of money to the farmers, displayed a positive trend of production in all the districts. But after the immediate post-mid-eighties it suffered a decelerating tendency in the major potato growing districts. Jute, once the major money earner was observed to lose its relative importance. Though its area was not increasing significantly, production went through increasing trend in all the districts except Birbhum, Bankura and Howrah during 1970-71 to 1993-94. During 1985-86 to 1993-94 however significant rate of decline was observed in Jalpaiguri and Darjeeling. Though in most of the south Bengal districts it was negative during 1985-86 to 1993-94 sub-period, the trends were however insignificant.

4.5. Summary of Observation

From the overall analysis, it is clear that, production of oilseed as a whole (particularly of mustard), boro rice and potato has increased significantly over the years. Growth rates were accelerating up to mid-eighties, beyond which they followed a slight deceleration. Production of food-crop as a whole also followed the same trend. Growth rate of food crop production was very slow during 1970-71 to 1978-79 relatively to that of 1979-80 to 1994-95. Within foodgrains, production of wheat and pulses declined like area under them. Therefore it can be argued that production of oilseeds; potato and boro rice has increased at the cost of wheat, pulses and other inferior crops. Production of wheat was increasing during the initial years of Green Revolution and started declining after 1978-79. Rapid adjustment has taken place with the expansion of irrigation potential and other agrarian technologies. The system gradually approached towards optimum utilisation of existing irrigation capacity and other resources. Difficulty of raising area under these crops grew with the increase in area under them and so growth rates have started to decrease slightly after 1985-86. Further jump in the production of crops requires a further breakthrough in technology.

Despite highest rate of growth in production achieved by oilseed, rice remains the primary crop (in terms of total output) of the state. Though production of aus decreased during 1970-71 to 1978-79, it experienced an increasing trend during the next part of the entire period. It was due to growth in its yield as area has decreased throughout the whole period. Initially, production of wheat had increased because of the thrust given to it in the Green Revolution package. But after the generation of possibility of earning more profit from other ventures it became relatively less important. Boro rice has emerged as one important food as well as cash crop. The phenomenal rise in production of oilseeds and potato was due to both yield and area growth whereas, the growth in production of boro rice was mainly due to increase in acreage under it.

Inter-district disparity in the production of each crop was noticeable. Though the growth of production has been associated with the decline in inter-district disparity in the production of boro rice and oilseed, coefficient of variation has increased slightly in case of potato. Decline in disparity in the production of oilseeds and boro rice implies that the laggard districts have advanced faster in these fields than the existing developed districts. Production of foodgrains was highly concentrated in the developed districts of southern part. Though production of it has increased in all the districts, proportion of output to state's total production has decreased in Burdwan, Hooghly, Nadia and 24-Paraganas. Production of wheat experienced an increasing trend in most of the northern districts; it followed a negative trend in most of the southern districts. In absolute amount, production of jute has increased disproportionately in all the districts, despite an insignificant change in its acreage.

Table 4.1: District-wise Production of Different Crops in West Bengal (1970-71 to 1994-95)

Crop→	Aus*		Aman*		Boro*		Rice	
District	1970-1	1993-4	1970-1	1993-4	1970-1	1993-4	1970-1	1994-5
Burdwan	55.9	77.9	584.8	1057.0	106.6	506.7	747.3	1694.3
	(6.14)	(8.58)	(12.46)	(13.28)	(19.91)	(15.63)	(12.17)	(13.847)
Birbhum	91.5	29.8	504.5	641.8	13.7	160.8	609.7	799.0
	(1.005)	(3.28)	(10.75)	(8.062)	(2.559)	(4.961)	(9.93)	(6.53)
Bankura	40.4	80.6	457.4	701.9	4.0	130.1	511.8	975.5
	(4.44)	(8.88)	(9.956)	(8.817)	(0.747)	(4.014)	(8.335)	(7.972)
Midnapore	101.8	116.8	820.9	1321.8	160.6	658.8	1083.3	2283.8
	(11.19)	(12.86)	(17.49)	(16.60)	(30.00)	(20.32)	(17.64)	(18.67)
Howrah	2.5	4.7	68.6	108.6	30.7	146.6	101.8	218.2
	(.275)	(.518)	(1.461)	(1.364)	(5.734)	(4.523)	(1.658)	(1.783)
Hooghly	14.0	29.1	190.1	432.2	87.7	238.3	291.8	750.4
	(1.54)	(3.204)	(4.049)	(5.429)	(16.38)	(7.352)	(4.752)	(6.133)
24 Paraganas	40.1	60.8	433.0	1008.0	63.2	386.1	536.3	1475.8
	(4.407)	(6.70)	(9.223)	(12.66)	(11.80)	(11.91)	(8.734)	(12.06)
Nadia	106.3	128.2	103.4	274.7	13.5	353.0	223.2	700.6
	(11.68)	(14.16)	(2.202)	(3.45)	(2.52)	(10.89)	(3.635)	(5.726)
Murshidabad	81.8	91.9	296.5	494.1	19.5	206.2	397.8	793.2
	(8.99)	(10.12)	(6.316)	(6.206)	(3.642)	(6.361)	(6.479)	(6.483)
West Dinajpur	145.8	56.8	353.9	600.4	9.4	201.3	509.1	848.1
	(16.02)	(6.25)	(7.538)	(7.542)	(1.756)	(6.21)	(8.291)	(6.931)

Table-4.1 contd.

Crop→	Aus*		Aman*		Boro*		Rice	
District	1970-1	1993-4	1970-1	1993-4	1970-1	1993-4	1970-1	1994-5
Malda	70.1	30.7	121.8	305.1	24.8	216.2	216.7	514.7
	(7.703)	(3.38)	(2.594)	(3.832)	(4.632)	(6.67)	(3.529)	(4.206)
Jalpaiguri	70.1	62.2	221.0	255.4	0.2	4.4	291.3	271.3
	(7.703)	(6.85)	(4.707)	(3.208)	(.037)	(.136)	(4.744)	(2.217)
Darjeeling	8.1	13.4	40.6	55.2	0.2	1.2	48.9	66.1
	(.89)	(1.48)	(0.865)	(0.693)	(.037)	(.037)	(.796)	(0.54)
Cooch Behar	79.4	115.9	207.9	279.1	0.7	26.2	288.0	340.5
	(8.725)	(12.76)	(4.428)	(3.506)	(.131)	(.808)	(4.69)	(2.783)
Purulia	2.2	9.4	280.3	425.9	0.6	5.6	283.1	504.4
	(.242)	(1.035)	(5.971)	(5.35)	(.112)	(.173)	(4.611)	(4.122)
West Bengal	910	908.2	4694.7	7961.2	535.4	3241.5	6140.1	12235.9
Coeff. of Var.	68.062	65.082	66.96	66.33	129.69	85.79	63.07	71.04

Source: Government of West Bengal, Bureau of Applied Economics and Statistics, Statistical Abstracts (Various issues).

Notes: (i) The last year for those * marked crops/ crop groups is 1993-94 as the data for those crops/ crop groups were not available at district level for the year 1994-95.

(ii) Figures in the parentheses represent percentage shares of the corresponding districts.

Contd.. . . .

Table 4.1 contd.

Crop	Wheat		Cereal		Pulses		Foodgrains	
District	1970-1	1994-5	1970-1	1994-5	1970-1	1994-5	1970-1	1994-5
Burdwan	70.5	7.4	818.3	1701.8	15.9	1.2	834.2	1703.0
	(8.121)	(0.994)	(11.499)	(12.95)	(4.214)	(0.889)	(11.13)	(12.83)
Birbhum	177.4	36.0	788.6	835.8	14.9	7.1	803.5	842.9
	(20.44)	(4.835)	(11.081)	(6.359)	(3.949)	(5.259)	(10.72)	(6.348)
Bankura	17.2	17.1	530.4	993.7	6.8	0.4	537.2	994.1
	(1.981)	(2.297)	(7.453)	(7.56)	(1.802)	(0.296)	(7.169)	(7.486)
Midnapore	26.1	27.5	1110.7	2311.7	35.9	9.8	1146.6	2321.5
	(3.007)	(3.694)	(15.61)	(17.59)	(9.515)	(7.259)	(15.30)	(17.48)
Howrah	7.7	0.5	109.6	218.7	4.0	0.5	113.6	219.2
	(0.887)	(0.067)	(1.54)	(1.664)	(1.060)	(0.370)	(1.516)	(1.651)
Hooghly	53.0	1.1	344.9	751.5	8.2	0.5	353.1	752.0
	(6.105)	(0.148)	(4.847)	(5.717)	(2.173)	(0.370)	(4.712)	(5.663)
24 Paraganas	30.8	15.1	567.4	1490.9	31.3	8.2	598.7	1499.1
	(3.548)	(2.028)	(7.973)	(11.34)	(8.296)	(6.074)	(7.989)	(11.289)
Nadia	122.8	113.2	349.4	815.0	72.3	31.1	421.7	846.1
	(14.15)	(15.21)	(4.91)	(6.201)	(19.16)	(23.04)	(5.627)	(6.372)
Murshidabad	250.9	267.2	664.2	1062.7	95.2	33.1	759.4	1095.8
	(28.90)	(35.89)	(9.333)	(8.085)	(25.23)	(24.52)	(10.13)	(8.252)
West Dinajpur	50.1	60.6	567.4	920.1	23.0	15.0	590.4	935.1
	(5.771)	(8.14)	(7.973)	(7.00)	(6.096)	(11.11)	(7.879)	(7.042)

Table-4.1 contd.

Crop	Wheat		Cereal		Pulses		Foodgrains	
District	1970-1	1994-5	1970-1	1994-5	1970-1	1994-5	1970-1	1994-5
Malda	47.3	112.4	299.3	636.0	50.0	16.4	349.3	652.4
	(5.449)	(15.10)	(4.206)	(4.839)	(13.25)	(12.15)	(4.661)	(4.913)
Jalpaiguri	0.8	29.2	295.2	303.1	1.6	1.5	296.8	304.6
	(0.092)	(3.922)	(4.148)	(2.306)	(0.424)	(1.111)	(3.961)	(2.294)
Darjeeling	0.4	4.0	80.4	204.5	0.5	0.8	80.9	205.3
	(0.046)	(0.537)	(1.13)	(1.556)	(0.133)	(0.593)	(1.08)	(1.546)
Cooch Behar	11.3	37.3	300.3	378.9	4.3	4.6	304.6	383.5
	(1.302)	(5.01)	(4.22)	(2.883)	(1.14)	(3.407)	(4.065)	(2.888)
Purulia	1.8	4.8	290.0	519.6	13.3	4.8	303.3	524.4
	(0.207)	(0.645)	(4.075)	(3.953)	(3.525)	(3.556)	(4.047)	(3.949)
West Bengal	868.1	744.5	7116.4	13144.0	377.3	135.0	7493.7	13279.0
Coeff. of Var.	121.29	139.29	57.756	64.796	107.22	114.92	56.667	64.347

Source: Government of West Bengal, Bureau of Applied Economics and Statistics, Statistical Abstracts (Various issues).

Note: (i) The last year for those * marked crops/ crop groups is 1993-94 as the data for those crops/crop groups were not available at district level for the year 1994-95.

(ii) Figures in the parentheses represent percentage shares of the corresponding districts.

Contd.. . . .

Table 4.1 contd.

Crop	Oilseeds*		Jute*		Potato*	
District	1970-1	1993-4	1970-1	1993-4	1970-1	1993-4
Burdwan	1.5 (2.534)	38.0 (9.139)	116.1 (4.326)	134.5 (2.415)	256.1 (27.547)	912.6 (17.646)
Birbhum	2.4 (4.054)	30.6 (7.359)	2.9 (0.108)	5.9 (0.106)	55.8 (6.002)	190.7 (3.687)
Bankura	1.6 (2.703)	20.6 (4.954)	9.7 (0.361)	10.6 (0.19)	43.9 (4.722)	443.8 (8.581)
Midnapore	4.2 (7.095)	52.4 (12.602)	106.1 (3.954)	152.0 (2.729)	134.0 (14.413)	1288.9 (24.923)
Howrah	1.8 (3.041)	3.40 (0.818)	37.9 (1.412)	15.6 (0.28)	29.1 (3.13)	87.3 (1.688)
Hooghly	2.0 (3.378)	42.8 (10.293)	293.7 (10.944)	521.3 (9.36)	282.6 (30.397)	1630.3 (31.524)
24 Paraganas	5.4 (9.122)	49.2 (11.833)	232.0 (8.645)	466.1 (8.37)	32.4 (3.485)	112.6 (2.177)
Nadia	12.9 (21.791)	64.8 (15.584)	385.6 (14.369)	1551.8 (27.865)	3.3 (0.355)	51.6 (0.998)
Murshidabad	10.0 (16.892)	45.0 (10.823)	420.1 (15.654)	1428.9 (25.658)	38.2 (4.109)	114.4 (2.212)
West Dinajpur	7.7 (13.007)	39.8 (9.572)	310.7 (11.578)	499.0 (8.96)	17.8 (1.915)	32.5 (0.628)
Malda	4.0 (6.757)	11.0 (2.646)	120.0 (4.472)	186.1 (3.342)	4.10 (0.441)	20.4 (0.394)
Jalpaiguri	1.5 (2.534)	5.4 (1.299)	270.7 (10.087)	155.5 (2.972)	7.0 (0.753)	74.8 (1.446)

Table-4.1 concld.

Crop	Oilseeds*		Jute*		Potato	
District	1970-1	1993-4	1970-1	1993-4	1970-1	1993-4
Darjeeling	0.2	1.0	18.3	17.3	11.7	76.5
	(0.338)	(0.241)	(0.682)	(0.311)	(1.258)	(1.479)
Cooch Behar	2.3	7.8	358.8	424.4	9.3	120.4
	(3.885)	(1.876)	(13.37)	(7.621)	(1.00)	(2.328)
Purulia	1.4	4.0	1.0	--	4.9	14.8
	(2.365)	(0.962)	(0.037)		(0.527)	(0.286)
West Bengal	59.2	415.8	2683.6	5569.0	929.7	5171.6
Coeff. of Var.	89.333	74.076	82.238	121.187	141.046	143.389

Source: Government of West Bengal, Bureau of Applied Economics and Statistics, *Statistical Abstracts (Various issues).*

Note: (i) The last year for those * marked crops/crop groups is 1993-94 as the data for those crops/crop groups were not available at district level for the year 1994-95.

(ii) Figures in the parentheses represent percentage share of the corresponding district.

Table 4.2: Growth rate of Output of Different Crops During 1970-71 to 1994-95

(in percentage)

District\Crop	Aus*	Aman*	Boro*	Rice	Wheat	Cereal	Pulses	Foodgrains	Oilseeds*	Jute*	Potato
Burdwan	39.36	80.75	375.33	126.72	89.50	107.97	-92.45	104.15	2433.33	15.85	256.35
Birbhum	-67.43	27.22	1073.72	31.05	-79.71	5.99	-52.35	4.90	1175.0	103.45	241.76
Bankura	99.43	50.17	3152.5	90.60	-0.58	87.35	-94.12	85.05	1187.5	9.28	910.93
Midnapore	14.73	61.02	310.21	11.08	5.36	108.13	-72.70	102.47	1147.62	43.26	861.87
Howrah	88.00	58.31	377.52	114.34	-93.51	99.54	-87.5	92.96	88.89	-58.84	200.0
Hooghly	107.86	127.35	150.6	157.16	-97.92	117.89	-93.90	112.97	2040.0	77.49	476.89
24 Paraganas	51.62	132.79	510.92	175.18	-7.82	162.76	-73.80	150.39	811.11	100.91	247.53
Nadia	20.60	165.67	2514.81	213.89	6.50	133.26	-56.98	100.64	402.33	302.44	146.36
Murshidabad	12.35	66.64	957.44	99.40	20.96	60.00	-65.23	44.30	350.0	240.13	199.48
West Dinajpur	-61.04	69.65	2041.49	66.59	137.63	62.16	-34.78	58.38	416.88	60.61	82.58
Malda	-56.21	150.49	771.77	137.52	3550.0	112.50	-67.2	86.77	175.00	55.08	397.56
Jalpaiguri	-11.27	15.57	2100.0	-6.87	900.0	2.68	-6.25	2.63	260.0	-42.56	968.57
Darjeeling	65.43	35.96	500.0	35.17	900.0	154.35	60.00	153.77	400.0	-5.46	553.85
Cooch Behar	45.97	34.25	3642.86	18.23	230.09	26.17	6.98	25.90	239.13	18.28	1194.62
Purulia	327.27	51.94	833.33	78.17	166.67	79.17	-63.91	72.90	185.71	-	202.04
West Bengal	-0.20	69.58	505.44	99.28	-14.24	84.70	-64.22	77.20	602.36	107.52	456.27

Source: (i) Government of West Bengal, Bureau of Applied Economics and Statistics, Statistical Abstracts (Various issues).
(ii) Government of West Bengal, Directorate of Agriculture.

Note: * indicates that the period for those crops is 1970-71 to 1993-94.

Table 4.3: Exponential Rate of Growth of Production of major Crops in West Bengal (Districtwise) During 1970-71 to 1994-95 and Different Sub-periods

	Aus						Aman					
Period → District↓	70/1-78/9	79/80-93/4	70/1-81/2	82/3-93/4	85/6-93/4	70/1-93/4	70/1-78/9	79/80-93/4	70/1-81/2	82/3-93/4	85/6-93/4	70/1-93/4
Burdwan	-.03	.053*	-.0393**	.0675*	.0468*	.0088	.0542*	.0401*	.0261*	.0463*	.0459*	.0283*
	(.04)	(.01)	(.024)	(.019)	(.0226)	(.01)	(.017)	(.006)	(.009)	(.007)	(.0101)	(.0038)
Birbhum	-.213*	.13*	-.246*	.154*	.1019*	-.0432*	.0402*	.0348*	.0266*	.0486*	.0364*	.0257*
	(.05)	(.02)	(.057)	(.037)	(.055)	(.02)	(.023)	(.011)	(.0136)	(.0156)	(.0177)	(.0053)
Bankura	-.033	.107*	-.065*	.133*	.096*	.02	.0375	.0546*	.0027	.0586*	.0343*	.0248*
	(.03)	(.02)	(.023)	(.022)	(.0285)	(.013)	(.035)	(.012)	(.0203)	(.0156)	(.0106)	(.0075)
Midnapore	-.113*	.078*	-.0703*	.0923*	.1158*	.0227	.0374**	0459*	.00243	.0534*	.0291	.0207*
	(.02)	(.01)	(.017)	(.015)	(.0193)	(.006)	(.023)	(.014)	(.0113)	(.0201)	(.0259)	(.007)
Howrah	-.20	.009	-.101	-.0578*	-.1378*	.0124	-.0464	.0182*	-.0016	.0207*	.0057	.0205*
	(.17)	(.04)	(.0112)	(.048)	(.0723)	(.03)	(.086)	(.011)	(.045)	(.0137)	(.0191)	(.012)
Hooghly	.061	.041*	.0023	.045*	.0156	.0093	.0259	.0582*	.024	.0633*	.0107	.0433*
	(.07)	(.02)	(.028)	(.029)	(.0434)	(.013)	(.041)	(.0397)	(.0184)	(.0128)	(.1123)	(.016)
24-Paraganas	.02	.053*	-.0106	.0453*	.0542*	.0235*	-.0584	.0463*	-.0518	.0604*	.0682*	.0043
	(.06)	(.01)	(.025)	(.016)	(.0273)	(.01)	(.103)	(.013)	(.056)	(.016)	(.0201)	(.015)
Nadia	.026	.037*	-.0096	.0569*	.0474	.0019	.0722**	.0717*	.0591*	.101*	.100*	.0546*
	(.06)	(.02)	(.019)	(.026)	(.0456)	(.011)	(.055)	(.017)	(.0259)	(.024)	(.03)	(.01)
Murshidabad	.085	.026*	.0097	.0172	.0183	.002	-.0462	.0609*	-.025	.1001*	.108*	.0179
	(.06)	(.01)	(.029)	(.016)	(.030)	(.011)	(.0902)	(.017)	(.0495)	(.0208)	(.024)	(.0145)

Contd.. . . .

Table 4.3 contd.

West Dinajpur	-.074*	-.0342*	-.0518*	-.0498*	-.0078	-.0342*	-.0066	.0452*	.0043	.0525*	.0441*	.0284*
	(.03)	(.01)	(.021)	(.021)	(.0318)	(.007)	(.0174)	(.009)	(.0119)	(.012)	(.0213)	(.0048)
Malda	-.04**	-.0033	-.0602*	-.0269*	-.0375	-.0239*	.0156	.0355*	.044*	.0475*	.064*	.0416*
	(.03)	(.02)	(.022)	(.024)	(.0428)	(.008)	(.031)	(.011)	(.0167)	(.015)	(.026)	(.006)
Jalpaiguri	-.035	.0405*	-.0404*	.0497*	.0865*	-.0016	-.0221	.0228*	-.0124	.0321*	.0228*	.0059
	(.03)	(.01)	(.017)	(.016)	(.0207)	(.007)	(.0183)	(.009)	(.0129)	(.012)	(.015)	(.0048)
Darjeeling	-.053**	.079*	-.0354*	.0735*	.0617	.039*	-.0032	.0210*	.0032	.0238**	.0293*	.0124*
	(.03)	(.02)	(.017)	(.039)	(.0714)	(.012)	(.019)	(.009)	(.0129)	(.014)	(.015)	(.0045)
Cooch-Behar	-.002	.058*	-.0233	.0555*	.0816*	.0177*	-.0535*	.0361*	-.125	.0312*	.0196	.0247*
	(.03)	(.01)	(.018)	(.011)	(.0149)	(.007)	(.031)	(.006)	(.0215)	(.008)	(.0102)	(.006)
Purulia	-.043	.173*	-.137*	.224*	.2402*	.0023	.0158	.0579*	-.018	.0542*	.0022*	.0189*
	(.06)	(.02)	(.048)	(.0214)	(.0313)	(.02)	(.016)	(.017)	(.0195)	(.0227)	(.0096)	(.008)
West Bengal	-.026	.05	-.044*	.087*	.2071*	-.0069	.0288*	.0444*	.0121	.0543*	.0435*	.0254*
	(.03)	(.04)	(.01)	(.064)	(.1017)	(.02)	(.013)	(.009)	(.009)	(.012)	(.0102)	(.004)

Note: (i) Figures in the parentheses represent standard error, (ii) * indicates the coefficient is significant at 5% level of significance by two tailed test.

(iii) ** represents the coefficient is significant at 10% level of significance by two tailed test.

Table-4.3 contd.

Period	Boro 70/1-78/9	Boro 79/80-93/4	Boro 70/1-81/2	Boro 82/3-93/4	Boro 85/6-93/4	Boro 70/1-93/4	Rice 70/1-78/9	Rice 79/80-94/5	Rice 70/1-81/2	Rice 82/3-94/5	Rice 86/7-94/5	Rice 70/1-94/5
Burdwan	.0542	.1072*	-.0186	.0923*	.0498*	.0479*	.0367*	.0526*	.014	.0554*	.0392*	.0337*
	(.043)	(.02)	(.039)	(.0235)	(.0255)	(.012)	(.01)	(.006)	(.0105)	(.007)	(.0061)	(.004)
Birbhum	.1997*	.1216*	.057	.1231*	.0482	.0719*	.0169	.0421*	.0092	.052*	.0229*	.0252*
	(.053)	(.027)	(.068)	(.0354)	(.0457)	(.015)	(.023)	(.01)	(.0133)	(.013)	(.0134)	(.005)
Bankura	.1609*	.2488*	.0505	.2118*	.1343*	.1591*	.007	.0671*	-.008	.0707*	.0494*	.0335*
	(.049)	(.025)	(.046)	(.0343)	(.0382)	(.016)	(.018)	(.01)	(.0151)	(.013)	(.0078)	(.006)
Midnapore	.0089	.1098*	-.0084	.0923*	.0772*	.0647*	.0086	.0605*	-.0037	.063*	.0441*	.0337*
	(.035)	(.01)	(.021)	(.014)	(.0241)	(.008)	(.011)	(.008)	(.0095)	(.011)	(.0135)	(.005)
Howrah	.0391	.1597*	-.0235	.1309*	.1054*	.0865*	-.0073	.0601*	.004	.0546*	.0257*	.045*
	(.053)	(.017)	(.035)	(.0155)	(.0226)	(.013)	(.023)	(.01)	(.015)	(.0125)	(.0186)	(.0055)
Hooghly	.025	.0508*	-.123	.0543*	.0608*	.0154*	-.0071	.0454*	.0054	.0543*	.053*	.0289*
	(.035)	(.01)	(.023)	(.0135)	(.0215)	(.007)	(.029)	(.007)	(.0175)	(.0072)	(.0082)	(.005)
24-Paraganas	.0811*	.0996*	.0646*	.0782*	.0681*	.0909*	.0551*	.0551*	.0209	.0588*	.0524*	.035*
	(.026)	(.01)	(.014)	(.0103)	(.0156)	(.005)	(.015)	(.008)	(.014)	(.0107)	(.0164)	(.005)
Nadia	.1723*	.120*	.1491*	.1072*	.0725*	.1316*	.0505*	.0764*	.0473*	.0829	.048*	.062*
	(.04)	(.01)	(.0252)	(.0142)	(.0141)	(.007)	(.0215)	(.007)	(.0119)	(.0105)	(.0098)	(.004)
Murshidabad	.0998*	.1092*	.0859*	.1088*	.0642*	.0974*	.0359	.0583*	.0349*	.078*	.0588*	.0417*
	(.032)	(.01)	(.0203)	(.0183)	(.0222)	(.006)	(.027)	(.01)	(.0146)	(.0125)	(.0171)	(.0055)
West Dinajpur	.0398	.2334*	.0007	.2216*	.1792*	.1342*	-.0192	.054*	-.0093	.0584*	.0521*	.030*
	(.049)	(.017)	(.032)	(.0253)	(.0385)	(.015)	(.019)	(.005)	(.0114)	(.007)	(.0141)	(.005)
Malda	.0781*	.1103*	.0002	.0934*	.0576*	.686*	.0242*	.0525*	.002*	.0522*	.0409*	.0397*
	(.044)	(.012)	(.024)	(.018)	(.0263)	(.009)	(.013)	(.005)	(.008)	(.006)	(.0118)	(.003)

Contd....

Table 4.3 contd.

Jalpaiguri	--	--	--	.2742*	.2479*	--	-.0217	.0224*	-.0182	.0278*	.0208	.0041
				(.049)	(.0811)		(.02)	(.008)	(.013)	(.011)	(.0173)	(.005)
Darjeeling	--	--	--	--	--	--	-.1188	.0326*	-.0755**	.0362*	.0303*	-.0033
							(.10)	(.008)	(.056)	(.0107)	(.0169)	(.014)
Cooch-Behar	.1125*	.3618*	-.0447	.4165*	.310*	.1528*	-.0164	.0379*	-.009	.0341*	.0149	.0227*
	(.034)	(.052)	(.0516)	(.062)	(.0842)	(.032)	(.014)	(.007)	(.012)	(.0086)	(.0143)	(.004)
Purulia	-.0209	.1764*	-.1193*	.1618*	.2267*	.0398**	-.001	0584*	-.0198	.0553*	.0242*	.0233*
	(.088)	(.04)	(.0613)	(.0616)	(.0952)	(.025)	(.016)	(.015)	(.0195)	(.0191)	(.0099)	(.008)
West Bengal	.0567*	.1126*	.0184	.1015*	.0757*	.0709*	.0168**	.054*	.0065	.0587*	.0429*	.0324*
	(.024)	(.009)	(.0175)	(.0129)	(.0174)	(.007)	(.01)	(.006)	(.0082)	(.008)	(.0063)	(.004)

Note: (i) Figures in the parentheses represent standard error, (ii) * indicates the coefficient is significant at 5% level of significance by two tailed test.

(iii) ** represents the coefficient is significant at 10% level of significance by two tailed test.

Table-4.3 contd.

Period	Wheat						Cereal					
	70/1-78/9	79/80-94/5	70/1-81/2	82/3-94/5	85/6-94/5	70/1-94/5	70/1-78/9	79/80-94/5	70/1-81/2	82/3-94/5	86/7-94/5	70/1-94/5
Burdwan	-.0148	-.1298*	-.1115*	-.1591*	-.1535*	-.1265*	.0334*	.0503*	.008	.0531*	.0378*	.0295*
	(.022)	(.02)	(.031)	(.0255)	(.0524)	(.02)	(.009)	(.006)	(.0105)	(.0071)	(.006)	(.0038)
Birbhum	-.0409	-.040*	-.1141*	-.043*	-.0711**	-.0736*	.0053	.0372*	-.0064	.0472*	.0176	.0159*
	(.049)	(.02)	(.0391)	(.021)	(.0401)	(.011)	(.026)	(.01)	(.0153)	(.0129)	(.01175)	(.005)
Bankura	.1079*	-.0096	-.0416	-.0392*	-.0345	-.0386*	.0138	.0648*	-.0093	.0675*	.0467*	.0306*
	(.049)	(.018)	(.0483)	(.0246)	(.0441)	(.012)	(.018)	(.01)	(.0155)	(.0128)	(.0068)	(.006)
Midnapore	.0657*	-.0108	-.0597	-.0473	.05103	-.0547*	.0106	.0597*	-.0048	.0622*	.0438*	.0322*
	(.028)	(.022)	(.037)	(.034)	(.0666)	(.013)	(.011)	(.008)	(.0099)	(.011)	(.0134)	(.005)
Howrah	.0478	-.1732*	-.1151*	-.171*	-.1253	-.1725*	-.0029	.0583*	.0015	.0537*	.0252*	.0415*
	(.044)	(.042)	(.0604)	(.057)	(.1009)	(.02)	(.021)	(.01)	(.0139)	(.0124)	(.0184)	(.005)
Hooghly	-.0229	-.1811*	-.1098*	-.2136*	-.2924*	-.1545*	.011	.042*	.0028	.051*	.0485*	.0219*
	(.036)	(.033)	(.033)	(.0484)	(.0964)	(.016)	(.018)	(.006)	(.0118)	(.0068)	(.0076)	(.004)
24-Paraganas	.0498	-.0086	-.0558	-.0379*	-.0929*	-.0303*	.055*	.0537*	.0185	.0567*	.0495*	.0331*
	(.039)	(.016)	(.0374)	(.015)	(.0131)	(.009)	(.014)	(.008)	(.0141)	(.0105)	(.0159)	(.0046)
Nadia	-.0194	-.0026	-.0474*	-.0487)*	-.008	-.0041	.0251	.0615*	.0187	.0561*	.0397*	.0465*
	(.045)	(.018)	(.0256)	(.0177)	(.0233)	(.009)	(.021)	(.006)	(.0115)	(.0083)	(.0065)	(.004)
Murshidabad	.0069	.0161	-.0382**	-.0058	.0256**	-.0017	.0214	.0449*	.0098	.0522*	.0484*	.0273*
	(.019)	(.012)	(.0182)	(.012)	(.0152)	(.006)	(.019)	(.007)	(.0115)	(.0092)	(.0117)	(.004)
West Dinajpur	.1089*	-.0106	.0258	-.0374*	.0019	-.0014	-.0023	.0463*	-.0056	.0470*	.0476*	.0256*
	(.025)	(.013)	(.0288)	(.0116)	(.0137)	(.008)	(.016)	(.005)	(.0099)	(.0062)	(.0119)	(.004)
Malda	.0565*	.0648*	-.0227	.0531*	.0709*	.0261*	.0247*	.0499*	.0104	.0489*	.0438*	.0333*
	(.019)	(.012)	(.0266)	(.0094)	(.0105)	(.007)	(.013)	(.005)	(.0084)	(.0061)	(.011)	(.003)
Jalpaiguri	.6075*	.0207	.3007*	.0295	-.0151	.0729*	.0106	.0202*	.0052	.0246*	.0119	.0051
	(.062)	(.018)	(.0937)	(.0168)	(.0287)	(.027)	(.02)	(.007)	(.0127)	(.0106)	(.0164)	(.004)

Contd. . . .

Table 4.3 contd.

Darjeeling	.4426*	.0225	.2418*	.0487	.2594*	.0624*	.0356*	.0572*	.0196*	.0564*	.0334	.0402*
	(.061)	(.04)	(.067)	(.0587)	(.0669)	(.025)	(.013)	(.013)	(.0086)	(.0204)	(.0427)	(.006)
Cooch-Behar	.3474*	-.0032	.1365*	-.0051	-.051	.0208	.029	.0328*	.0087	.0307*	.0088	.0203*
	(.053)	(.023)	(.0726)	(.0181)	(.0323)	(.019)	(.017)	(.005)	(.0111)	(.0081)	(.0118)	(.003)
Purulia	.2338*	.0177	-.0322	.0035	-.0486	-.0416*	.0051	.0589*	-.02	.0548*	.0223*	.0229*
	(.074)	(.03)	(.0829)	(.0425)	(.0702)	(.022)	(.017)	(.015)	(.0198)	(.0196)	(.0097)	(.008)
West Bengal	.0399**	-.0021	-.0392	-.0169	.0171	-.0173*	.0195**	.0503*	.00254	.0531*	.0387*	.0284*
	(.024)	(.011)	(.0268)	(.0102)	(.0151)	(.0066)	(.011)	(.006)	(.0088)	(.008)	(.0058)	(.004)

Note: (i) Figures in the parentheses represent standard error, (ii) * indicates the coefficient is significant at 5% level of significance by two tailed test.
(iii) ** represents the coefficient is significant at 10% level of significance by two tailed test.

Table-4.3 contd.

Period	Pulses						Total Foodgrains					
	70/1-78/9	79/80-94/5	70/1-81/2	82/3-94/5	85/6-94/5	70/1-94/5	70/1-78/9	79/80-94/5	70/1-81/2	82/3-94/5	86/7-94/5	70/1-94/5
Burdwan	.0048	-.1529*	-.052	-.1821*	-.2142*	-.1118*	.033*	.0497*	.0073	.0525*	.0374*	.0288*
	(.035)	(.021)	(.0251)	(.0293)	(.0493)	(.012)	(.01)	(.006)	(.0106)	(.007)	(.006)	(.003)
Birbhum	-.0196	-.0564*	-.0357	-.0513*	-.0111	-.0525*	.0047	.0359*	-.0072	.0458*	.0173	.0149*
	(.031)	(.013)	(.0181)	(.0193)	(.0366)	(.006)	(.0255)	(.009)	(.015)	(.0127)	(.0117)	(.005)
Bankura	-.027	-.0886*	-.049*	-.0154*	-.1596*	-.0715*	.0134	.0643*	-.0096	.067*	.0463*	.0301*
	(.031)	(.0196)	(.018)	(.0293)	(.0555)	(.009)	(.0177)	(.009)	(.015)	(.0128)	(.0067)	(.006)
Midnapore	-.013	-.0199	-.0368*	-.0083	-.0185	-.0353*	.010	.0587*	-.0055	.0616*	.0434*	.0312*
	(.026)	(.015)	(.0174)	(.021)	(.0385)	(.007)	(.011)	(.008)	(.01)	(.011)	(.0132)	(.005)
Howrah	.111*	-.1569*	.0498*	-.2056*	-.2566*	-.0678*	.0024	.0537*	.0034	.0488*	.023	.0388*
	(.027)	(.024)	(.025)	(.0282)	(.028)	(.016)	(.019)	(.009)	(.013)	(.013)	(.0198)	(.005)
Hooghly	-.0839*	-.2031*	-.0706*	-.2241*	-.1849*	-.141*	.0097	.0413*	.0019	.0504*	.0483*	.0211*
	(.036)	(.028)	(.0211)	(.042)	(.0823)	(.014)	(.018)	(.006)	(.012)	(.007)	(.0076)	(.004)
24-Paraganas	.0061	-.0536*	-.0149	-.0533*	-.0161	-.0406*	.0372	.0521*	.0156	.0553*	.0489*	.034*
	(.02)	(.0176)	(.0147)	(.0264)	(.0438)	(.008)	(.031)	(.008)	(.019)	(.01)	(.0159)	(.005)
Nadia	-.0224	-.0175	-.0368*	-.023	-.0935*	-.0237*	.0181	.0543*	.0128	.0516*	.0322*	.0396*
	(.031)	(.013)	(.0179)	(.0189)	(.0206)	(.006)	(.018)	(.006)	(.0107)	(.0085)	(.0062)	(.003)
Murshidabad	-.0079	-.0566*	-.0479*	-.0673*	-.0266	-.0556*	.018	.0394*	.0032	.046*	.0461*	.0212*
	(.03)	(.012)	(.0211)	(.0154)	(.0247)	(.006)	(.018)	(.006)	(.0116)	(.0085)	(.0109)	(.004)
West Dinajpur	.0116	-.028*	-.0061	.0732*	.0693*	-.0306*	-.0019	.0445*	-.0057	.0458*	.0479*	.0242*
	(.025)	(.013)	(.0149)	(.0181)	(.0092)	(.006)	(.015)	(.004)	(.01)	(.006)	(.0116)	(.003)
Malda	-.0341	-.0159	-.0252*	-.0201	-.0551	-.0148*	.0181**	.0454*	.0062	.0448*	.0385*	.0293*

Contd.. . .

Table 4.3 contd.

	(.022)	(.013)	(.0127)	(.0194)	(.0384)	(.006)	(.01)	(.004)	(.007)	(.0055)	(.0096)	(.002)
Jalpaiguri	.1431*	-.0772*	.1048*	-.0671*	-.0505*	-.0209*	.0119	.0191	-.0039	.0238*	.0115	.0049
	(.038)	(.01)	(.0234)	(.0127)	(.0241)	(.011)	(.02)	(.007)	(.0125)	(.01)	(.0162)	(.004)
Darjeeling	.112*	-.0023	.0939*	.053*	.0313	.0099	.0362*	.0567*	.0203*	.0564*	.0333	.04*
	(.024)	(.02)	(.0187)	(.0176)	(.0343)	(.0098)	(.013)	(.013)	(.0085)	(.02)	(.0425)	(.005)
Cooch-Behar	.0219	.0122	-.0014	.0284*	-.00606	-.0003	.0288	.0319*	.0085	.0324*	.0244	.0186*
	(.042)	(.011)	(.0267)	(.0118)	(.0178)	(.007)	(.017)	(.007)	(.0107)	(.011)	(.0221)	(.003)
Purulia	-.0718*	.0362*	-.0635*	.0254	-.0516	-.008	.0029	.0585*	-.0213	.0543*	.0211*	.0224*
	(.041)	(.018)	(.0275)	(.0246)	(.038)	(.01)	(.017)	(.014)	(.0197)	(.019)	(.0091)	(.007)
West Bengal	-.0106	-.0338	-.0321*	-.0365*	-.045*	-.0351*	.0183**	.044*	.0114	.0513*	.0384*	.0263*
	(.019)	(.006)	(.0123)	(.0081)	(.013)	(.0034)	(.01)	(.005)	(.007)	(.008)	(.0052)	(.003)

Note: (i) Figures in the parentheses represent standard error, (ii) * indicates the coefficient is significant at 5% level of significance by two tailed test.

(iii) ** represents the coefficient is significant at 10% level of significance by two tailed test.

Table-4.3 contd.

Period	Total Oilseed 70/1-78/9	79/80-93/4	70/1-81/2	82/3-93/4	85/6-93/4	70/1-93/4	Potato 70/1-78/9	79/80-93/4	70/1-81/2	82/3-93/4	85/6-93/4	70/1-93/4
Burdwan	.258*	.0448*	.3072*	.0295	-.0029	.1648*	.1501*	.0408*	.1005*	.0301*	.0353**	.0603*
	(.027)	(.018)	(.021)	(.0255)	(.0443)	(.016)	(.0424)	(.009)	(.0179)	(.013)	(.0229)	(.008)
Birbhum	.1476*	.1054*	.1618*	.0832*	-.0378	.1365*	.0672*	.078*	.0288	.062*	.0263	.0559*
	(.062)	(.028)	(.0324)	(.0418)	(.0426)	(.013)	(.0307)	(.015)	(.0193)	(.023)	(.0367)	(.007)
Bankura	.2118*	.0795*	.1895*	.0744*	.0475**	.1235*	.121*	.1295*	.0882*	.1249*	.1111*	.1103*
	(.034)	(.014)	(.0243)	(.0227)	(.0323)	(.009)	(.032)	(.013)	(.0217)	(.019)	(.0269)	(.007)
Midnapore	.0661*	.1704*	.0932*	.1765*	.1575*	.1389*	.0954*	.1329*	.0846*	.1272*	.1193*	.1144*
	(.025)	(.013)	(.0254)	(.0164)	(.0269)	(.007)	(.0346)	(.01)	(.0179)	(.016)	(.0243)	(.006)
Howrah	-.0228	.04**	.0449	.0633*	.0291	.0395*	.1136*	.0533*	.0453	-.035	-.0294	.0585*
	(.077)	(.028)	(.0349)	(.0386)	(.0671)	(.014)	(.048)	(.022)	(.0343)	(.024)	(.0392)	(.01)
Hooghly	.1589*	.1155*	.1612*	.0947*	.0591	.1395*	.0998*	.066*	.0878*	.0575*	.0575*	.0767*
	(.051)	(.02)	(.0293)	(.0287)	(.0424)	(.01)	(.0148)	(.005)	(.0104)	(.006)	(.0104)	(.003)
24-Paraganas	.0677	.1628*	.098*	.1583*	.1058*	.1426*	.1253*	.0271*	.0813*	.0117	-.0074	.0465*
	(.063)	(.013)	(.0359)	(.0215)	(.0283)	(.01)	(.027)	(.014)	(.0223)	(.0206)	(.0314)	(.0078)
Nadia	.0308	.1305*	.0538	.1021*	.1004*	.1126*	.3995*	.0374**	.208*	.0122	.0463	.077*
	(.056)	(.013)	(.0446)	(.0134)	(.0197)	(.009)	(.028)	(.026)	(.0548)	(.0403)	(.0717)	(.019)
Murshidabad	.0887*	.0806*	.0787*	.0731*	.0388	.0784*	.1452*	.035*	.0642*	.0316*	.0296	.0321*
	(.019)	(.012)	(.0127)	(.018)	(.0272)	(.005)	(.0327)	(.009)	(.0212)	(.0144)	(.0265)	(.0079)
West Dinajpur	.0619*	.1028*	.02104*	.0659*	.0653*	.0743*	.2054*	.0097	.0899*	-.0327	-.0277	.0321*
	(.024)	(.015)	(.0167)	(.0179)	(.0322)	(.007)	(.046)	(.0214)	(.0437)	(.0272)	(.0458)	(.013)
Malda	.0011	.0726*	-.0026	.0438	-.0146	.0537*	.2987*	.0903*	.117*	.0796*	.0783*	.0661*
	(.04)	(.023)	(.0195)	(.0337)	(.0543)	(.01)	(.051)	(.0127)	(.0564)	(.0192)	(.0338)	(.0149)

Contd.. . .

Table 4.3 contd.

Jalpaiguri	.0645**	.0658*	.0635*	.0448*	.0629*	.0747*	.2827*	.1834*	.0922**	.19*	.2148*	.1056*
	(.042)	(.013)	(.0297)	(.0187)	(.0315)	(.007)	(.0506)	(.012)	(.061)	(.0173)	(.0253)	(.016)
Darjeeling	.0072	.0478*	.0993*	.0353	.0328	.0913*	.0936*	.0545*	.1156*	.0633*	.0982*	.081*
	(.045)	(.018)	(.0424)	(.0279)	(.0513)	(.011)	(.034)	(.012)	(.0097)	(.0194)	(.0311)	(.007)
Cooch-Behar	-.0098	.0725*	.0141	.074*	.0945*	.051*	.0267	.1918*	.0735	.1671*	.1765*	.111*
	(.032)	(.013)	(.0279)	(.0216)	(.0316)	(.007)	(.057)	(.018)	(.0664)	(.0261)	(.0444)	(.016)
Purulia	-.0298	.1672*	-.0775*	.1569*	.0546	.0654*	.150*	.1358*	-.0166	.068*	.0132	.0523*
	(.047)	(.026)	(.0259)	(.0413)	(.0413)	(.017)	(.046)	(.034)	(.0716)	(.0293)	(.0433)	(.018)
West Bengal	.0711*	.1024*	.0875*	.0878*	.0587*	.1032*	.1271*	.0762*	.0868*	.0675*	.0663*	.0765*
	(.007)	(.012)	(.0147)	(.0172)	(.0281)	(.005)	(.017)	(.005)	(.0128)	(.0073)	(.011)	(.0039)

Note: (i) Figures in the parentheses represent standard error, (ii) * indicates the coefficient is significant at 5% level of significance by two tailed test.

(iii) ** represents the coefficient is significant at 10% level of significance by two tailed test.

Table-4.3 contd.

	Jute					
Period	70/1-78/9	79/80-93/4	70/1-81/2	82/3-93/4	85/6-93/4	70/1-93/4
Burdwan	.0566**	-.0099	.0705*	-.0098	-.0521	.0208*
	(.033)	(.017)	(.02)	(.0236)	(.0371)	(.0088)
Birbhum	.0325	.0207	-.0171	.0056	-.0781	-.0055
	(.049)	(.038)	(.03)	(.0594)	(.0982)	(.0165)
Bankura	.0247	-.0388	.0364	-.0109	-.0826	-.0178
	(.06)	(.037)	(.039)	(.0559)	(.0822)	(.016)
Midnapore	.0618**	.0069	.0756*	.0624	-.0162	.0188
	(.041)	(.039)	(.025)	(.0562)	(.0257)	(.016)
Howrah	-.0197	-.0452*	.033	-.0367	-.0601	-.0084
	(.0429)	(.0267)	(.031)	(.0419)	(.0764)	(.012)
Hooghly	.0545*	.0138	.0332	.0401	.0941	.0062
	(.027)	(.037)	(.022)	(.0579)	(.1035)	(.014)
24-Paraganas	.0676*	-.0095	.0604*	.033	-.0315	.0119**
	(.028)	(.0157)	(.017)	(.0231)	(.0365)	(.007)
Nadia	.0511**	.054*	.0649*	.053*	.0284	.0601*
	(.036)	(.0129)	(.013)	(.02)	(.0339)	(.006)
Murshidabad	.0119	.0635*	.1351*	.0517*	.0339	.046*
	(.032)	(.0166)	(.019)	(.0252)	(.0451)	(.007)
West Dinajpur	-.0405	-.11. (10^{-6})	.0273	.0167	.0254	.0179*
	(.0419)	(.02)	(.0238)	(.0312)	(.057)	(.01)
Malda	.0318	.0128	.0576*	.0301	.0552	.0293*
	(.048)	(.0318)	(.02)	(.0498)	(.0893)	(.013)

Contd.. . . .

Table 4.3 concld.

Jalpaiguri	-.0513	-.0176	.0314	-.0239	-.0717*	.0232*
	(.053)	(.0162)	(.028)	(.0254)	(.0402)	(.011)
Darjeeling	-.0929*	.0086	-.0095	.002	-.0648*	.0256*
	(.037)	(.0187)	(.027)	(.0246)	(.0309)	(.01)
Cooch-Behar	-.0594	.0052	.0216	.01135	-.0055	.0273*
	(.0527)	(.0079)	(.034)	(.0085)	(.0132)	(.009)
Purulia	--	--	--	--	--	--
West Bengal	.0215	.0256*	.0415*	.0294	.0069	.0337
	(.024)	(.01)	(.0115)	(.016)	(.0276)	(.005)

Note: (i) Figures in the parentheses represent standard error, (ii) * indicates the coefficient is significant at 5% level of significance by two tailed test.

(iii) ** represents the coefficient is significant at 10% level of significance by two tailed test.

CHAPTER 5

INTER-DISTRICT DISPARITY OF AGRICULTURAL PRODUCTIVITY IN WEST BENGAL

5.1. Introduction

The post-Green Revolution Period of agricultural scenario of West Bengal is marked by manifold increase in agricultural production and productivity. Growth of agricultural production is conditional upon the growth of area under cultivation of each crop and its yield. Growth rate of net sown area (NSA) has declined over the years while the gross cropped area (GCA) has increased significantly during the aforesaid period. The growth of GCA was due to the increasing adoption of multiple crop production over extensive area year after year. Over the years, area under crops has changed disproportionately in different directions and not uniformly throughout the whole region. That has already been explained in chapter-3. Production of different crops has changed in different ways not only due to their disproportionate acreage variation, but also owing to the inter-crop variation in yield growth.

West Bengal has experienced a remarkable increase in agricultural productivity during 1970-71 to 1994-95. Increasing use of high yielding varieties of seeds, irrigation, modern technology and other improved farming practices have brought about a phenomenal change in agricultural productivity. Inter-crop and inter-district variation in yield growth is also notable. Spatial variation in agricultural productivity is the manifestation of differences in humidity, temperature, quality of soil, water-logging problem in general and adoption or diffusion of modern technology in particular. Institutional changes are also not insignificant. In this chapter districtwise variation in agricultural productivity has been described. It has been done because total value of output at a fixed set of prices from a particular area, depends on the yields of the crops cultivated in that area as well as on the pattern of allocation of that fixed area among the cultivable crops. Average productivity of land is therefore dependent not only on the yield rates but also on the changes in cropping pattern.[1] Thus the regional pattern of agricultural productivity (described latter) growth has some sot of relationship with the regional pattern of land allocation.

5.2. Layout

For the purpose of analysis, first of all, exponential rate of growth of yield of different crops has been estimated by using the data collected from various issues of *Statistical Abstract* and *Economic Review* of West Bengal. Estimation has been done for the whole as well as all sub-periods as was considered in the previous two chapters. Thereafter inter-district disparity of yield rates of major crops has been considered for the year 1970-71, 1978-79, 1985-86 and 1993-94. Inter-district disparity in yield of major crops is measured by the coefficient of variation. Then spatial variation in agricultural productivity is considered.

Here the term agricultural productivity is used to denote a composite unit, which is based upon the yield of different crops as well as allocation of land among the crops. So an index is constituted to describe the productivity level of any district compared to that of others. The index is expressed in the following way:

First of all, a *yield index* or *yield relative* has been calculated for different crops in different districts as follows: $K_{ij} = (Y_{ij}/Y_{io})* 100$, where Y_{ij} is the average yield of ith crop in the jth district.[2] Y_{io} represents the average yield of ith crop in the state. K_{ij} is the yield relative for ith crop in the jth district. In order to have an inter-district comparison; a *composite productivity index* is constituted for each district separately taking into account the variety of crops and their relative importance in different districts in terms of the proportion of area under each crop to total cropped area in each district. Then *composite productivity index* (CPI) for the jth district can be written as $CPI_j = \Sigma(Y_{ij}/Y_{io}).(A_{ij}/A_{io}).100$, where $A_{io} = \Sigma A_{ij}$ and A_{ij}/A_{io} = proportion of area under i^{th} crop in the jth district, j =1,2, ...15.[3] It is clear that the index will be higher in a district, where allocation of land is done more in favour of high yielding crops. After calculating the index for the year 1970-71,1978-79, 1985-86 and 1993-94 inter-district pattern of agricultural productivity over time has been analysed. The same procedure has been followed in case of food-crops and non-food crops separately.

5.3 Changes in Yield of Different Crops in West Bengal during 1970-71 to 1994-95

Estimated rate of growth of yield of different crops in West Bengal is presented in Table-5.1. It is observed that exponential rate of growth of yield of foodgrains was 2.8 per cent during 1970-71 to 1994-95, whereas the rates for cereals and pulses were 2.46 and 0.95 per cent respectively. During 1970-71 to 1978-79 yield of foodgrains as a whole, cereals and pulses had increased exponentially at the rate of 1.36, 1.33 and –0.20 per cent per annum respectively. These rates further decreased to 1.42, 0.31 and –0.72 per cent respectively during 1970-71 to 1981-82. This decrease in yield was due to natural calamities (flood and drought) that had frequently occurred during 1978-79 to 1981-82 and affected the production, mainly in the kharif season. Yield of foodgrains total, cereals and pulses has however increased at an annual average rate of 4.31, 4.08 and 1.63 per cent respectively during 1979-80 to 1994-95 and those figures were respectively 5.03, 4.20 and 0.93 per cent per annum during 1982-83 to 1994-95. Here, after 1982-83 though growth rate of yield of cereals and foodgrains had shown an increasing trend, while that for pulses was decelerating. During 1986-87 to 1994-95 annual average growth-rates were 4.73, 3.36 and 0.68 per cent.

Within cereal crops, rice experienced a significantly higher rate of growth in yield than wheat. The rate was 2.68 per cent per annum throughout the entire period in case of rice and only 0.12 per cent in case of wheat, which was insignificant. This is the indication of relatively more importance given to the leading food crop rice, rather than to wheat. The rate of yield growth in case of rice showed an increasing trend up to mid-eighties and then followed a decelerating trend. The rates were 1.37, 4.29, 4.58 per cent respectively during 1970-71 to 1978-79, 1979-80 to 1994-95 and 1982-83 to 1994-95. Average annual exponential rate of growth of yield of rice during 1986-87 to 1994-95 was 3.30 per cent. On the other hand, yield of wheat followed a negative trend during 1970-71 to 1978-79, 1970-71 to 1981-82 and 1982-83 to 1994-95 sub-period. However, it followed a positive and significant growth rate during 1986-87 to 1994-95.

Among different varieties of rice, yield of aus and aman experienced significantly positive trend rate of growth during the entire period. The rates were 2.34 and 2.29 per cent per annum, whereas the rate of yield growth in case of boro rice was only 0.513 per cent per annum during 1970-71 to 1993-94. Yield of the main rice crop aman, registered an accelerating rate of growth up to 1984-85 and then a slight deceleration. Yield of boro rice also followed a same pattern of change, but the case of aus was quite different. Its yield recorded an accelerating growth throughout the entire period. This is clear from the sub-period growth rates.

Among non-food crops, average annual exponential rate of growth of yield was the highest in the case of oilseeds. The rate of growth was 4.59 per cent per annum during 1970-71 to 1993-94, while the rates were 2.26 and 2.37 per cent respectively in case of jute and potato during the same period. The rates of growth during 1970-71 to 1978-79 were only 1.67, 0.88 and 1.35 per cent for oilseed, jute and potato. Though the rate was significant in case of oilseeds and it was insignificant for jute and potato. The rate of yield growth in case of oilseeds during 1985-86 to 1993-94 was higher than that during 1970-71 to 1978-79; but the trend during the former sub-period was not significant due to higher standard error (i.e., greater degree of fluctuation). Similarly, though yield of potato has recorded only 0.97 per cent rate of growth annually during 1982-83 to 1993-94 it was significant because of very low standard error.

5.4 Districtwise Pattern of Yield Growth of Major Crops

Inter-district variation in growth rate of yield of different crops during the post-seventies in West Bengal was notable. Yield of foodgrains has increased at significant rates in all the districts during the whole period despite the fact that the rates were significantly different. It was highest in Nadia and lowest in Jalpaiguri. During the sub-period 1970-71 to 1978-79, the trend rate of growth was negative in Howrah, West Dinajpur, Jalpaiguri and Cooch Behar and decreased during 1970-71 to 1981-82 in almost all the districts. In this period negative trend was observed in Bankura, Midnapore, Howrah, West Dinajpur, Jalpaiguri and Cooch Behar. In fact, the production of crops during kharif season was severely affected during 1978-79 to 1980-81 in most of the districts of West Bengal. The rate of growth of yield of foodgrains was significant in all the districts during 1979-80 to 1994-95. Though, during 1970-71 to 1978-79 sub-period the rate was insignificant or negative in many districts, it was positive and significant in Burdwan, 24-Paraganas, Murshidabad, Malda, Darjeeling and Purulia. Earlier, traditional technology and crude water control measures were unable to save crops from flood and drought. The development of technology and highly resistant seeds has made land more productive. During the post-mid eighties the rate of growth has decreased in the major southern districts. It has increased in Murshidabad, West Dinajpur, Malda, Jalpaiguri and Darjeeling.

Yield of total cereal registered almost a same pattern of growth in all the districts as that of foodgrains. Pulses have experienced a rising trend of yield in all the districts during 1970-71 to 1994-95. The rate of growth was insignificant in Bankura, Purulia, Howrah, Hooghly and Murshidabad in the southern West Bengal and Darjeeling in the northern Bengal. In the rest of West Bengal growth rate was significant. During 1970-71 to 1978-79 yield of pulses had decreased in Birbhum, Bankura, Midnapore, Hooghly, 24-Paraganas, Nadia in the south and West Dinajpur in the north. Though trend rate of growth was positive in other districts and significantly positive only in Darjeeling and Cooch Behar, the average trend for the state as a whole was decreasing. After 1980 it started increasing in most of the districts except Malda, Darjeeling and Cooch Behar. Since then, continuous improvement in the yield of pulses was noticed in Birbhum, Murshidabad and West Dinajpur, the three important pulses producing districts of West Bengal.

Yield of rice also follows the similar pattern of trend, like that of cereal and foodgrains total in different districts of West Bengal. This is mainly because, rice occupies the major part of cereal and also food crop of the state in terms of area and production. Within different categories of rice, aus and aman followed a significantly rising trend in their productivity in all the districts during the entire period of discussion, except in Jalpaiguri where growth rate was insignificant for aman and in Purulia trend rate of growth was insignificant in case of aus. Negative trend of yield of aus was noticed during 1970-71 to 1978-79 in all the districts except Bankura, 24-Paraganas, Nadia and Murshidabad. Rate of decline was highest in Darjeeling during that period. Range of Variation in rate of growth for yield of aus was very high during that sub-period than that in any other sub-period. However, all the districts follow an increasing trend rate of growth in yield of aus up to mid-eighties. Beyond that, the acceleration has been maintained by Murshidabad, Purulia in the south and all the northern districts. The other districts experienced a deceleration in the rate of growth after mid-eighties. This was due to the exhaustion of existing techniques of production at optimum scale that had spread over these areas during late seventies and early eighties. To maintain the pace of progress in yield, it requires further breakthrough in technology (in the field of generation of HYV seeds and supporting inputs). The districts where those technologies spread much later and irrigation development started later could maintain the pace of development beyond 1985. There the rate of growth was much lower in the early years and gradually attained momentum. During 1979-80 to

1993-94 growth rate was highest in Bankura and Nadia was far behind it. After 1982-83 Nadia came up to the top of all the districts in the growth rate of yield of aus. The pattern again changed and highest growth rate was found in West Dinajpur during 1985-86 to 1993-94.

Growth rate of yield of aman rice was highest in Murshidabad during 1970-71 to 1978-79, 1982-83 to 1993-94 and 1985-86 to 1993-94. During 1970-71 to 1993-94 and 1979-80 to 1993-94 it was highest in Nadia and during 1970-71 to 1981-82 maximum rate of growth was noticed in Malda. The rate was lowest during the early years in the district of Howrah and in Purulia during the last nine-year sub-period. Growth rate was increasing in all the districts first and recorded deceleration during post-mid-eighties. In this case also the laggard districts experienced increasing rate of growth throughout the entire period.

In case of boro rice, Burdwan is found to have an increasing trend rate of growth in yield, despite an insignificant rate of growth during 1970-71 to 1993-94. Only significant positive rate of growth during the entire period was noticed in Bankura, Midnapore, Murshidabad, Malda and Cooch Behar. The range of inter-district variation in annual growth rate during 1970-71 to 1978-79 was 6.37 per cent, which decreased to 4.84 per cent during 1985-86 to 1993-94. The same thing is true for wheat, total cereal and total foodgrains. This is the indication of more rapid adjustment and development that has taken place in the laggard districts than in the districts having an early achievement. Significant positive rate of growth in yield of wheat during the whole period has taken place in Burdwan, Birbhum, 24-Paraganas, Malda and Darjeeling. During 1970-71 to 1978-79 it was significantly positive in Howrah, 24-Paraganas, Jalpaiguri, Darjeeling and Cooch Behar. It was also significantly positive in all the districts except Burdwan, Bankura, Howrah, Hooghly, 24-Paraganas and Nadia, during 1986-87 to 1994-95. During 1970-71 to 1978-79 yield of pulses experienced a significantly positive rate of growth only in Darjeeling and Cooch Behar. It was significant during 1986-87 to 1994-95 in Birbhum, Murshidabad and West Dinajpur. There was a rapid change in rate of growth in all the districts over the years.

Among non-food crops, oilseeds as a whole experienced significant growth in yield in almost all the districts during 1970-71 to 1993-94. Average annual exponential rate of growth was the highest in the district of Nadia and lowest in Howrah. Significantly positive rate of growth was noticed in Burdwan, Murshidabad and Jalpaiguri during 1970-71 to 1978-79 while that was significantly negative in Midnapore, West

Dinajpur, Darjeeling and Purulia. After 1982-83 Burdwan and Malda recorded an overall decline in yield of oilseed while the other districts registered a significantly positive trend. During 1985-86 to 1993-94 highest trend rate of growth was found in Howrah (13.77 per cent per annum) and lowest in Burdwan (-3.84 per cent per annum).

Yield of jute was also found to have a positive trend in all the districts but the rate was not significant in the districts of Howrah and Malda during the entire period. Increasing rate of growth was observed in all the districts though the rates were different. After 1985-86 deceleration in rate of growth was found in Burdwan, Howrah, 24-Paraganas, Nadia in the south and Darjeeling, Jalpaiguri and Cooch Behar in the northern West Bengal. Potato, the other important cash crop registered a remarkable growth in yield in all the districts except Purulia throughout the entire period of discussion. The trend rate of growth was highest in Jalpaiguri and lowest in Purulia. During 1970-71 to 1978-79 the rate was negative in Birbhum and Purulia, but that was significantly positive in Burdwan, Midnapore in the southern part and in all the northern districts. During the last nine-year sub-period highest annual average rate of growth was noticed in Cooch Behar and lowest in Purulia.

Table 5.2 represents the triennia average yield of major crops/ crop groups in West Bengal. It is revealed that Burdwan, Hooghly and Birbhum were always among top five districts in terms of yield of rice, cereal, and also foodgrains. The same is true for aus and aman also. Malda, Cooch Behar and Purulia were lagging far behind the others. In respect of yield of boro rice, Nadia was at the top in 1970-73 and 1977-80 while Malda became number one in 1984-87 and 1991-94. In this case also Cooch Behar and Purulia were far below the other districts throughout all the years. The districts like Nadia, Murshidabad, West Dinajpur and Malda have shown significant improvement than the other districts. Comparing with the results obtained from table-5.1, it can be argued that the formerly backward districts has progressed at faster rate in terms of yield than the existing advanced districts. There was more scope for raising yields by removing the bottlenecks in different spheres. In case of potato and jute also Burdwan, Hooghly, Birbhum and Bankura irrespective of change in growth rate of yield, always remain ahead of others in absolute terms. Relatively faster rate of growth in yield of oilseed was noticed in Hooghly, 24-Paraganas, Nadia, West Dinajpur and Malda than the other districts. Though yield of oilseed has increased sharply during the early years, it became much slower than the other crops in the latter years.

Inter-district variation in yield of different crops has been measured in terms of the coefficient of variation. It is observed from the table-5.3 that inter-district disparity in yield has increased over the years in case of aus, aman, total rice and jute. It has decreased in case of boro-rice, wheat, pulses, potato and sugarcane. The largest inter-district variation in yield was recorded in case of potato during all the four discrete years. The coefficient of variation was 44.9, 40.76, 39.08 and 39.14 per cent respectively in 1970-71, 1978-79, 1985-86 and 1993-94. The lowest variation was noticed in case of pulses for all those years. The coefficient of variation was 12.84, 10.04, 9.6 and 11.83 per cent respectively during 1970-71, 1978-79, 1985-86 and 1993-94. Sharp decline in inter-district disparity in yield was found in case of boro rice.

Table-5.4 shows the divergent trend in productivity growth of different crops during 1970-71 to 1993-94. For West Bengal as a whole highest rate of growth of yield was noticed for oilseed (187.4 per cent) and lowest for wheat (2.8 per cent). Percentage rate of growth of yield of rice, pulses, jute and potato were 86.08, 24.42, 68.17 and 72.48 respectively. Among the districts highest percentage increase in case of rice was recorded in Nadia (194.76), wheat in Darjeeling (38.31), pulses in Birbhum (67.02), oilseed and jute in Nadia (351.1 and 106.37) and potato in Darjeeling (142.42). In case of rice it was observed that aus, aman and boro rice registered highest yield growth rate in the districts of Howrah (150.35), Nadia (175.11) and Cooch Behar (70.11) respectively.

Finally the Composite Productivity Index (CPI) calculated for different districts is displayed in table-5.5. The results reveal a high degree of inter-district variation in composite agricultural productivity per hectare. The index with respect to all crops ranges from 56.19 to 124.77 per cent during 1970-71, 63.67 to 122.51 during 1978-79, 50.75 to 126.34 in 1985-86 and 46.19 to 129.05 during 1993-94. The inter-district variation is thus found to increase over the years as is also clear from the rising coefficient of variation. From the table it is noticed that Burdwan and Hooghly, the two leading agricultural districts of West Bengal always remain at the top two positions. Burdwan, Hooghly, Birbhum and Bankura were always among the top five districts throughout the entire period. Darjeeling, West Dinajpur and Cooch Behar were always among the bottom five districts in the relative rankings.

The range of variation of index for food crops was from 82.27 to 122.93, 81.61 to 123.64, 74.81 to 129.03 and 65.07 to 131.62 per cent during 1970-71, 1978-79, 1985-86 and 1993-94 respectively. Similar indices for non-food crops varied from 60.04 to 145.67, 56.07 to 137.27, 66.35 to 122.61 and 53.82 to 123.15 per cent during 1970-71, 1978-79, 1985-86 and 1993-94 respectively. It is clear from the range and coefficient of variation that inter-district variation in yield for food crop, non-food crop and with respect to all crops as a whole have a increased over time. The variation was much greater for non-food crops than for food crops. Remarkable achievement in composite productivity has been found in case of Nadia, which has jumped over many other districts. Malda and 24-Paraganas have also improved their ranking relegating some other districts downwards. However the general pattern is that most of the frontier districts always remain at the front and the lower order districts always remain at the lower rung except a few changes in order. It is clear from the coefficient of correlation between the ranks of different years as is given inTable-5.5.

5.5 Main Findings

The foregoing analysis revealed the divergent pattern of yield growth among the districts and crops over the years. Inter-district variations in CPI have increased. However, disparities in yield have decreased for boro rice, wheat, pulses, potato and sugarcane, while it has experienced an opposite trend in case of other crops. Productivity of different crops has increased differently in different districts according to the suitability to agro-climatic condition of the respective regions and variations in adoption of technology, expansion of irrigation, which will be explained in chapter-8 elaborately. Rising composite productivity is not only due to increase in yield of crops in general but also due to shift of area from low-yielding crops to high yielding crops. Specification and selection of cropping pattern also have an important bearing on productivity of land and farm income along with the yield of individual crops.

NOTES

1 If the set of prices changes then the same cropping pattern gives rise to different agricultural productivity.

2 Kaur P. and Sethi K. (1994), "Inter-district Variation in Agricultural Productivity in Punjab", *Agricultural Situation in India*, June, p. 167.

3 De U.K., (1998), "Regional Disparity in Agricultural Productivity in the State of West Bengal", *Productivity*, Oct.-Dec., pp. 508-515.

REFERENCES

1. Bhalla G. S. and Alagh Y. K., (1979), *Performance of Indian Agriculture, A District-wise Study*, Sterling Publication Pvt. Ltd., New Delhi.
2. Bhatia N. S., (1981), "State-wise Variation in Growth of Food Production in India", *Agricultural Situation in India*, Ministry of Agriculture, August.
3. Bhalla G. S. and Tyagi D. S., (1989), "Patterns in Indian Agricultural Development- A District Level Study", ISID.
4. De Utpal Kumar, (1998), "Regional Disparity in Agricultural Productivity in the State of West Bengal", *Productivity*, Oct.-Dec., pp. 508-515.
5. Kaur P. and Sethi K. (1994), "Inter-district Variation in Agricultural Productivity in Punjab", *Agricultural Situation in India*, June, p. 167.
6. Nanavati A. and Patel B. C., (1994), "Inter-district Variation in Agricultural Productivity in Gujarat", *Productivity*, Vol. 35, No. 2, July-Sept.
7. Government of West Bengal, Bureau of Applied Economics and Statistics (BAES), *Economic Review*, Various Issues.
8. Government of West Bengal, *Statistical Abstract*, Various Issues.

Table 5.1: Estimated Exponential Rate of Growth of Yield of Major Crops in West Bengal (Districtwise)

	Aus						Aman					
Period	70/1-78/9	79/80-93/4	70/1-81/2	82/3-93/4	85/6-93/4	70/1-93/4	70/1-78/9	79/80-93/4	70/1-81/2	82/3-93/4	86/7-93/4	70/1-93/4
Burdwan	-.0423*	.0299*	-.0094	.0353*	.0325*	.016*	.0522*	.0412*	.0283*	.0444*	.042*	.03*
Birbhum	-.0085	.0494*	-.0012	.0563*	.0589*	.0281*	.0113	.0389*	.0074	.0488*	.03*	.0213*
Bankura	.0172	.0685*	.0043	.0691*	.0532*	.0398*	.0051	.0489*	-.0051	.0511*	.0249*	.0207*
Midnapore	-.0548*	.0532*	-.0217	.059*	.0469*	.0282*	.014*	.0467*	.0005	.0521*	.0268	.0219*
Howrah	.0345	.037*	.0189	.0274*	-.0039	.0399*	-.0964	.0146	-.0165	.0092	.0013	.0197**
Hooghly	.0439*	.0278*	.0350*	.0263*	.0148	.0259*	-.012	.0342*	.0124	.0413*	.0346*	.025*
24-Paraganas	.0001	.0483*	.017	.0477*	.0453*	.038*	.0514*	.0476*	.0149	.0594*	.0629*	.0253*
Nadia	.0064	.0546*	.0227*	.0754*	.0484*	.0325*	.0137	.0542*	.0312	.0659*	.059*	.044*
Murshidabad	.0244	.0304*	.0245*	.0466*	.0551*	.0184*	.0568*	.0499*	.0301	.074*	.0651*	.0308*
West Dinajpur	-.0662*	.0674*	-.0408*	.0753*	.0989*	.0274*	.0096	.0374*	.0028	.0421*	.0409*	.0222*
Malda	-.0493*	.0422*	-.0258**	.0426*	.0682*	.0187*	.0343*	.027*	.0352*	.036*	.0456*	.0303*
Jalpaiguri	-.0607*	.0509*	-.0489*	.0571*	.067*	.0141*	-.0152	.0206*	-.0111	.0315*	.0321*	.0045
Darjeeling	-.1027*	.0552*	-.0642*	.0592*	.086*	.0183*	.0193	.0173*	.009	.0225*	.0337*	.0108*
Cooch-Behar	-.0464*	.0682*	-.0315*	.0709*	.096*	.0253*	-.021	.02*	-.0084	.0172*	.0095	.0117*
Purulia	-.0479	.066*	-.0557**	.0488*	.0622*	.0109	.0052	.0402*	-.01	.0324**	-.0115	.0147*
West Bengal	-.0402*	.0536*	-.0182*	.0623*	.063*	.0234*	.0187	.0404*	.0085	.0468*	.0354*	.0229*

Notes: (i) * indicates the coefficient is significant at 5% level of significance by two tailed test.
(ii) ** indicates the coefficient is significant at 10% level of significance by two tailed test.

	Boro						Rice					
Period	70/1-78/9	79/80-93/4	70/1-81/2	82/3-93/4	85/6-93/4	70/1-93/4	70/1-78/9	79/80-94/5	70/1-81/2	82/3-94/5	86/7-94/5	70/1-94/5
Burdwan	-.0174	.0209*	-.0261*	.0232*	.0254*	.001	.0376*	.039*	.0156**	.04*	.0254*	.0272*
Birbhum	-.0107	.0238*	-.0228*	.0211*	.0072	.0032	.0128	.0376*	.0063	.0437*	.0134	.023*
Bankura	.0248	.0468*	-.013	.0391*	.0134	.0214*	.0087	.051*	-.0033	.0512*	.0299*	.028*
Midnapore	.012	.0067	.0103	.0122**	-.0012	.0088*	.0098	.0479*	-.0004	.0493*	.0281*	.028*
Howrah	.0139	.0144*	-.0037	.012*	-.0042	.0044	-.0283	.0295*	-.0039	.0218*	.0069	.0267*
Hooghly	.0121	.0059	-.046	.0113	.0178	-.003	.0024	.0303*	.0066	.0346*	.032*	.021*
24-Paraganas	.0091	.0073*	-.0012	.0091*	-.0085*	.0016	.0495*	.0454*	.0179	.0489*	.0402*	.028*
Nadia	.0122	.0124*	-.0074	.0139	.0183	.003	.0327*	.0511*	.0383*	.0529*	.0378*	.0469*
Murshidabad	.0241	.0187*	.0162	.0265*	.0142*	.0175*	.0407*	.0466*	.0281*	.061*	.0507*	.032*
West Dinajpur	-.048*	.0343*	-.0404*	.0277*	.0272	.006	-.011	.051*	-.0082	.055*	.0539*	.028*
Malda	-.0149	.0224*	-.0041	.0015	.0193	.0194*	.0044	.0395*	.0172*	.04*	.0477*	.0338*
Jalpaiguri	NA	NA	NA	-.0137	-.0212	NA	-.0284**	.025*	-.0196*	.0319*	.0332*	.006
Darjeeling	NA	NA	NA	NA	NA	NA	-.002	.0219*	-.0023	.0276*	.0506*	.0089*
Cooch-Behar	-.0102*	.0007	.0284*	-.0172*	-.0084	.0231*	-.0303	.0313	-.0143	.0287*	.0234*	.0173*
Purulia	-.0389	.0148	-.0306	-.0106	-.0026	-.0009	.1037	.0396*	.0523	.0327*	.0118	.035*
West Bengal	.00253	.0135*	-.0063	.0139*	.0072	.00513	.0137	.0429*	.0059	.0458*	.033*	.0268*

Notes: (i) * indicates the coefficient is significant at 5% level of significance by two tailed test.
(ii) ** indicates the coefficient is significant at 10% level of significance by two tailed test.
(iii) NA means not available.

Contd. . . . .

Table-5.1 Contd.

Period	Wheat						Total Cereal					
	70/1-78/9	79/80-94/5	70/1-81/2	82/3-94/5	85/6-94/5	70/1-94/5	70/1-78/9	79/80-94/5	70/1-81/2	82/3-94/5	86/7-94/5	70/1-94/5
Burdwan	-.0249	-.0018	-.0295*	-.0189	.0059	.0083*	.033*	.0391*	.0121	.0396*	.0257*	.026*
Birbhum	-.0139	.0199*	-.0228*	.0106**	.0372*	.006*	.007	.0366*	.0005	.0415*	.0146*	.0207*
Bankura	-.0118	.0202*	-.0324*	-.0024	.0145	.0047	.0099	.0503*	-.0046	.0494*	.0294*	.0271*
Midnapore	-.028*	.0147**	-.0374*	.0041	.0415*	-.0066	.0098	.0476*	-.0015	.0488*	.0281*	.0272*
Howrah	.0443*	-.042*	.0135	-.0656*	-.061*	-.0185*	-.0224	.0291*	-.0033	.0214*	.0069	.0256*
Hooghly	-.014*	.0029	-.0236*	-.0104	.0122	-.0052	-.0004	.0285*	.0029	.0316*	.0278*	.0187*
24-Paraganas	.032*	.0172*	-.0072	-.0067	.0115	.0085*	.0489*	.0446*	.0163	.0474*	.039*	.0275*
Nadia	-.0195**	-.0017	-.0271*	-.0303*	-.0007	-.0017	.0138	.0405*	.0173*	.0338*	.0317*	.0354*
Murshidabad	.0257**	.0131	-.0094	-.0065	.0306*	.0056	.023**	.0393*	.0079	.0524*	.1114*	.0197*
West Dinajpur	-.0309*	.018**	-.0261**	.005	.0587*	.0044	-.004	.0466*	-.0069	.0472*	.0531*	.0258*
Malda	.0072	.0144	-.009	-.0054	.0451*	.0095*	.0132	.0368*	.0167*	.0345*	.0466*	.0313*
Jalpaiguri	.0639*	-.0045	.028**	-.0093	.0424*	.0003	-.0152	.0233*	-.0148	.029*	.0289**	.0059**
Darjeeling	.104*	-.0005	.064*	.0014	.0828*	.0141*	.026*	.0531*	.0094	.0538*	.0557	.0331*
Cooch-Behar	.0492*	.0018	.0088	.004	.0315**	-.0053	-.0039	.0274*	-.0046	.0273*	.0238*	.0145*
Purulia	-.0013	.0152	-.0092	.0075	.0722*	.0068	.0071	.0395*	-.0101	.0332*	.0154**	.0177*
West Bengal	-.0117	.0098	-.0235*	-.0086	.0312*	.0012	.0133	.0408*	.0031	.042*	.0336	.0246*

Notes: (i) * indicates the coefficient is significant at 5% level of significance by two tailed test.
(ii) ** indicates the coefficient is significant at 10% level of significance by two tailed test.
(iii) NA means not available.

Table-5.1 Contd.

	Pulses						Total Foodgrains					
Period	70/1-78/9	79/80-94/5	70/1-81/2	82/3-94/5	85/6-94/5	70/1-94/5	70/1-78/9	79/80-94/5	70/1-81/2	82/3-94/5	86/7-94/5	70/1-94/5
Burdwan	.0033	.0185*	-.0076	.0058	.0023	.0112*	.0331*	.0406*	.0128	.0409*	.0268*	.0274*
Birbhum	-.0217	.0278*	.0055	.0304*	.0444*	.0223*	.006	.0388*	.0021	.0434*	.0163*	.0232*
Bankura	-.0142	.0083	-.0116*	.0035	.002	.0034	.0099	.0509*	-.0041	.05*	.0303*	.0277*
Midnapore	-.022	.0526*	-.0296	.0487*	.037	.021*	.0088	.0493*	-.0018*	.0499*	.0292*	.0285*
Howrah	.017	.008	.0084	.0035	.0008	.0072	-.0238	.0348*	-.0051	.0279*	.0118	.0277*
Hooghly	-.0118	.0205*	-.0134	.0235**	-.0179	.0056	.002	.0322*	.0045	.0359*	.0326*	.021*
24-Paraganas	-.0004	.0066	.0009	-.0039	.0249	.0085	.0472*	.0459*	.0163	.048*	.0398*	.0288*
Nadia	-.0084	.0156**	-.0122	.0053	-.0191	.0095*	.0147	.0459*	.0173*	.0383*	.0385*	.0389*
Murshidabad	.0022	.0206*	-.0251**	.0158**	.0354*	.001	.0217*	.0438*	.007	.0475*	.0499*	.0263*
West Dinajpur	-.0114	.0173*	-.0081	.0233*	.0413*	.0065*	-.005	.0475*	-.007	.0478*	.0521*	.0265*
Malda	.0184	-.0076	.0378*	-.0193*	-.0285	.0186*	.0203*	.0379*	.0179*	.0324*	.0443*	.0335*
Jalpaiguri	.0238	.0146**	.0259*	.0227*	.001	.0147*	-.0164	.0241*	-.0154	.0297*	.0285**	.0064**
Darjeeling	.0965*	-.0134**	.0614*	.0021	-.0316	.002	.0266*	.0525*	.0098	.0529*	.0542*	.0329*
Cooch-Behar	.0127*	-.0002	.0249*	-.0088	.0012	.0141*	-.0032	.0267*	-.0035	.0245*	.0116	.0154*
Purulia	.0017	.0192**	-.0158	.0045	-.0056	.0047	.0046*	.0392*	-.0113	.0327*	.0175*	.0172*
West Bengal	-.002	.0163*	-.0072	.0093	.0068	.0095*	.0136*	.0431*	.0142*	.0503*	.0473*	.0282*

Notes: (i) * indicates the coefficient is significant at 5% level of significance by two tailed test.
(ii) ** indicates the coefficient is significant at 10% level of significance by two tailed test.
(iii) NA means not available.

Contd.. . . .

Table-5.1 Contd.

Period	Total Oilseed						Jute					
	70/1-78/9	79/80-93/4	70/1-81/2	82/3-93/4	85/6-93/4	70/1-93/4	70/1-78/9	79/80-93/4	70/1-81/2	82/3-93/4	86/7-93/4	70/1-93/4
Burdwan	.096*	.0053	.0756*	-.0057	-.0384**	.0334*	.0095	.0302*	.0223*	.0317*	.0278*	.0283*
Birbhum	.0201	.0489*	.0336	.0556*	-.024	.0444*	-.0337	.0323*	.0019	.0262*	.0376*	.0275*
Bankura	-.0111	.0382*	.0205	.0295	-.0031	.0441*	-.0158	.0398*	.0006	.034*	.0572*	.0293*
Midnapore	-.0444*	.0613*	-.02	.0485*	.0162	.036*	.0146	.0308*	.0286*	.0331*	.0443*	.0295*
Howrah	-.0224	.0215	.0164	.0572	.1397*	.0104	-.059*	.0106	-.022	-.0012	.0051	.0112
Hooghly	.0447	.0534*	.031	.0471*	-.0101	.0446*	-.0047	.0268*	.0053	.0256*	.0201	.0181*
24-Paraganas	.0374	.0742*	.0278	.0671*	.0421	.057*	.0118	.0297*	.0094	.0298*	.0212*	.0175*
Nadia	.0283	.0563*	.0556*	.0514*	.0616**	.0655*	.0235	.0448*	.0159	.0435*	.0313*	.0315*
Murshidabad	.069*	.0436*	.0417*	.0407*	.0278	.037*	.0075	.0421*	-.0029	.0308*	.0346	.025*
West Dinajpur	-.0283**	.0839*	-.0338*	.069*	.0596*	.0391*	-.0019	.0313*	.0014	.0399*	.0508**	.0221*
Malda	.061	.024**	.0142	-.001	-.0168	.0345*	.0143	.0321*	.0084	.0349*	.0515	.0083
Jalpaiguri	.0713*	.042*	.0749*	.0461*	.0592*	.0505*	-.0081	-.0091	.0071	-.0167	-.0383	.0092**
Darjeeling	-.0992*	.0149**	.0186	.024*	.0286**	.0307*	-.046*	.022*	-.0247	.0074	-.0165	.0203*
Cooch-Behar	-.0149	.0683*	-.0125	.0797*	.0923*	.022*	-.0102	.0051	.0081	.0073	-.0058	.012*
Purulia	-.0517*	.0518*	-.0201	.0306	-.0302	.0281*	NA	NA	NA	NA	NA	NA
West Bengal	.0167*	.048*	.0289*	.0384*	.0243	.0459*	.0088	.0322*	.0084	.0295*	.0216	.0226*

Notes: (i) * indicates the coefficient is significant at 5% level of significance by two tailed test.
(ii) ** indicates the coefficient is significant at 10% level of significance by two tailed test.
(iii) NA means not available.

Table-5.1 Contd.

	Potato					
Period	70/1-78/9	79/80-93/4	70/1-81/2	82/3-93/4	85/6-93/4	70/1-93/4
Burdwan	.032*	.0146*	.0328*	.009	.0174	0.221*
Birbhum	-.126	.0534*	-0.093*	0.425*	0479*	0.332*
Bankura	-.0068	.330*	.0106	.0026*	.0210*	0298*
Midnapore	.0402*	.0289	.0366*	.0159*	.0036	.0383*
Howrah	.0221	.0207*	.0356*	0.177*	.0158	.0336*
Hooghly	.0076	.0063	.0177*	-.006	-.0118	0.157*
24-Paraganas	.001	.0182	.0099	.0061	-0.173	.0223*
Nadia	.031	.0282*	.0051	.0179	0.191	.0164*
Murshidabad	.0133	0.359*	-.0065	.0336*	0.291*	.0106**
West Dinajpur	.0709*	.0174	.0159	-.385*	-0.479	.0153**
Malda	.1048*	.0527*	-0.46*	.041*	0.481*	.0337*
Jalpaiguri	.599*	.0561*	.0302	-0531*	.0841*	.0325*
Darjeeling	.0463	0.195**	-0548	0.182	0522**	.0385*
Cooch-Behar	.0857	.0676*	.0336**	0.582*	.0947*	.0373*
Purulia	-.0746	-0.57*	.0121	-083*	-.0803*	-.0061
West Bengal	.0135	.0183*	.0236*	.0097*	0.118*	.0237*

Notes: (i) * indicates the coefficient is significant at 5% level of significance by two tailed test.
(ii) ** indicates the coefficient is significant at 10% level of significance by two tailed test.
(iii) NA means not available.

Table 5.2: Yield of Different Crops/Crop Groups in West Bengal in the Selected Years (Districtwise) (kgs./ha)

Crop→	Aus				Aman				Boro			
District	1970-73	1977-80	1984-87	1991-94	1970-73	1977-80	1984-87	1991-94	1970-73	1977-80	1984-87	1991-94
Burdwan	1985.7 (1)	1644.3 (1)	1954 (3)	2469.7 (3)	1301.3 (3)	1860 (1)	1907.3 (1)	2549.7 (1)	3178 (2)	2744.7 (8)	2576.7 (12)	3154.7 (4)
Birbhum	1596.3 (2)	1604.7 (2)	1773.7 (4)	2639 (1)	1458.3 (1)	1668.3 (3)	1722.7 (3)	2202 (4)	3166.7 (3)	2873.3 (6)	2742 (9)	2968.3 (9)
Bankura	1079.7 (9)	1162.7 (5)	1575.7 (6)	2330.3 (5)	1354 (2)	1343.7 (4)	1656.3 (4)	2084.3 (6)	2086.7 (12)	2380.3 (9)	2521.7 (14)	3052 (5)
Midnapore	1209 (6)	899.3 (9)	1190.3 (8)	1719.7 (8)	1064.7 (11)	1123.3 (9)	1384.7 (10)	1808.3 (8)	2765.7 (7)	2809.7 (7)	2839 (5)	2881 (11)
Howrah	1069.3 (10)	1019.7 (6)	2136 (1)	2044.3 (6)	1091.3 (9)	892.3 (15)	1466.3 (8)	1504.7 (12)	2689.3 (8)	2985.7 (2)	2837.3 (6)	3006.3 (7)
Hooghly	1247 (5)	1561 (3)	2106 (2)	2355 (4)	1285 (4)	1304.3 (5)	1839.7 (2)	2255.7 (2)	2909 (5)	2945.3 (4)	2707.3 (10)	2971 (8)
24-Paraganas	1335 (3)	1352.7 (4)	1758 (5)	2524 (2)	969.7 (13)	1291.3 (6)	1214.3 (13)	1825.7 (7)	3000.3 (4)	2974 (3)	2919.3 (3)	2950.7 (10)
Nadia	905.7 (13)	995 (7)	1250.7 (7)	1820.3 (7)	863 (15)	1116 (10)	1623.3 (5)	2156.7 (5)	3277.3 (1)	3204 (1)	2840.3 (4)	3203.3 (2)
Murshidabad	819.3 (15)	981 (8)	1110 (9)	1437.3 (10)	1125.3 (8)	1734.3 (2)	1490.7 (7)	2247.7 (3)	2611.7 (9)	2929 (5)	2821.7 (8)	3160.3 (3)
West Dinajpur	1146 (7)	717.3 (10)	892.3 (10)	1692.3 (9)	972 (12)	1045.3 (11)	1244.7 (12)	1508.3 (11)	2803.7 (6)	2067.3 (10)	2582.3 (11)	3050 (6)
Malda	926.7 (12)	686 (11)	886 (11)	1342.7 (12)	906 (14)	1199.3 (7)	1429.7 (9)	1691 (9)	2580 (11)	2023.7 (11)	3320 (1)	3240.3 (1)
Jalpaiguri	1107.7 (8)	653.7 (12)	718.3 (13)	1232.3 (14)	1188.7 (5)	1015 (13)	1046.7 (15)	1335.3 (14)	1833.3 (13)	NA	3065.3 (2)	2568 (12)
Darjeeling	1237.7 (4)	588.3 (13)	835.3 (12)	1386.7 (11)	1074.7 (10)	1175.7 (8)	1314.3 (11)	1529.3 (10)	1833.3 (14)	NA	NA	2030.3 (15)
Cooch-Behar	837.67 (14)	533 (15)	712 (14)	1310.7 (13)	1155.7 (6)	991 (14)	1186 (14)	1256.7 (15)	1727.7 (15)	1621.3 (13)	2825.7 (7)	2445 (13)
Purulia	960 (11)	545.7 (14)	680.7 (15)	1050.7 (15)	1137.3 (7)	1033.3 (12)	1508.3 (6)	1473 (13)	2600 (10)	1940.3 (12)	2559.3 (13)	2278.7 (14)
West Bengal	1104	864.7	1093	1676.3	1140	1285.7	1460.7	1879.7	2904.7	2798.7	2838	3052.3

Sources: (i) Government of West Bengal, Bureau of Applied Econo.nics and Statistics, *Statistical Abstract (Various issues).*
(ii) Government of West Bengal, Bureau of Applied Economics and Statistics, *Economic Review (Various issues).*

Note: (i) Figures in the parenthesee represent rankings.
(ii) NA implies not available.

Contd....

Table-5.2 Contd.

Crop→	Rice				Wheat				Cereal			
District/Year	1970-73	1977-80	1984-87	1991-94	1970-73	1977-80	1984-87	1991-94	1970-73	1977-80	1984-87	1991-94
Burdwan	1523 (2)	1963 (1)	2032 (1)	2698 (1)	2418 (2)	1869 (8)	2080 (7)	1845 (12)	1570 (3)	1954 (1)	2033 (2)	2694 (1)
Birbhum	1518 (3)	1749 (2)	1825 (4)	2282 (4)	2041 (6)	1794 (9)	2043 (9)	2324 (3)	1598 (2)	1750 (2)	1818 (5)	2279 (5)
Bankura	1324 (5)	1345 (6)	1697 (6)	2205 (6)	1950 (8)	1598 (14)	2188 (4)	2215 (5)	1341 (5)	1360 (7)	1707 (8)	2200 (7)
Midnapore	1200 (6)	1226 (8)	1563 (9)	2044 (9)	2356 (3)	1670 (10)	1876 (12)	2060 (10)	1216 (8)	1236 (9)	1566 (10)	2044 (9)
Howrah	1325 (4)	1209 (9)	1797 (5)	1904 (11)	1493 (13)	1872 (7)	2095 (6)	1166 (15)	1331 (6)	1240 (8)	1800 (6)	1902 (11)
Hooghly	1629 (1)	1642 (3)	2029 (2)	2455 (3)	2253 (14)	1877 (6)	2064 (8)	2072 (8)	1685 (1)	1657 (3)	2029 (3)	2454 (2)
24-Paraganas	1069 (12)	1407 (5)	1433 (11)	2019 (10)	1971 (7)	2059 (1)	2474 (2)	2417 (1)	1093 (11)	1423 (6)	1450 (12)	2023 (10)
Nadia	989 (15)	1326 (7)	1951 (3)	2475 (2)	2426 (1)	2002 (3)	2647 (1)	2143 (7)	1280 (7)	1438 (5)	2101 (1)	2417 (4)
Murshidabad	1110 (9)	1537 (4)	1565 (8)	2261 (5)	1878 (10)	2043 (2)	2307 (3)	2331 (2)	1380 (4)	1652 (4)	1739 (7)	2269 (6)
West Dinajpur	1037 (14)	973 (13)	1241 (12)	1787 (7)	2213 (5)	1632 (11)	1899 (11)	2243 (4)	1088 (13)	1037 (12)	1292 (13)	1812 (12)
Malda	1081 (11)	1134 (10)	1616 (7)	2083 (8)	1880 (9)	1896 (5)	2143 (5)	2214 (6)	1091 (12)	1199 (10)	1635 (9)	2047 (8)
Jalpaiguri	1168 (7)	907 (14)	971 (15)	1235 (15)	1226 (14)	1546 (15)	1550 (14)	1590 (14)	1162 (9)	973 (15)	1005 (15)	1251 (15)
Darjeeling	1097 (10)	1051 (11)	1217 (13)	1482 (13)	933 (15)	1606 (13)	1383 (15)	1870 (11)	1020 (15)	1189 (11)	1872 (4)	2425 (3)
Cooch-Behar	1051 (13)	828 (15)	1078 (14)	1302 (14)	1558 (12)	1992 (4)	1688 (13)	1603 (13)	1061 (14)	994 (14)	1072 (14)	1319 (14)
Purulia	1138 (8)	1029 (12)	1505 (10)	1559 (12)	1737 (11)	1626 (12)	1929 (10)	2061 (9)	1123 (10)	1032 (13)	1478 (11)	1553 (13)
West Bengal	1223	1328	1568	2064	2154	1858	2185	2168	1276	1367	1605	2071

Sources: (i) Government of West Bengal, Bureau of Applied Economics and Statistics, *Statistical Abstract (Various issues).*
(ii) Government of West Bengal, Bureau of Applied Economics and Statistics, *Economic Review (Various issues).*

Note: (i) Figures in the parentheses represent rankings.
(ii) NA implies not available.

Table-5.2 Contd.

Crop→	Pulses				Foodgrains				Oilseeds			
District	1970-73	1977-80	1984-87	1991-94	1970-73	1977-80	1984-87	1991-94	1970-73	1977-80	1984-87	1991-94
Burdwan	524 (4)	512 (7)	591 (5)	649 (4)	1525 (2)	1894 (1)	2004 (1)	2688 (1)	371 (9)	658 (2)	775 (3)	683 (10)
Birbhum	466 (11)	434 (14)	518 (10)	773 (3)	1504 (3)	1651 (2)	1760 (5)	2243 (4)	322 (14)	472 (5)	684 (6)	734 (6)
Bankura	497 (10)	452 (12)	520 (9)	539 (13)	1318 (4)	1337 (6)	1689 (6)	2191 (5)	388 (6)	425 (8)	752 (5)	693 (8)
Midnapore	524 (5)	446 (13)	487 (13)	786 (2)	1176 (7)	1189 (8)	1528 (9)	2022 (8)	565 (2)	447 (6)	539 (10)	915 (3)
Howrah	531 (3)	547 (5)	529 (8)	594 (8)	1274 (5)	1162 (10)	1660 (7)	1889 (10)	597 (1)	692 (1)	434 (13)	801 (5)
Hooghly	506 (7)	463 (10)	503 (11)	523 (14)	1627 (1)	1615 (3)	1998 (2)	2450 (2)	472 (3)	597 (3)	921 (1)	997 (1)
24-Paraganas	501 (8)	517 (6)	581 (6)	580 (10)	1051 (11)	1356 (5)	1406 (12)	1986 (9)	431 (4)	438 (7)	754 (4)	993 (2)
Nadia	550 (2)	565 (4)	631 (3)	597 (6)	1063 (10)	1203 (7)	1785 (4)	2158 (6)	336 (13)	393 (9)	805 (2)	888 (4)
Murshidabad	644 (1)	648 (2)	647 (2)	816 (1)	1200 (6)	1420 (4)	1548 (8)	2140 (7)	353 (11)	498 (4)	559 (8)	730 (7)
West Dinajpur	509 (6)	467 (9)	470 (15)	595 (7)	1045 (12)	988 (13	1253 (13)	1753 (12)	381 (8)	286 (14)	427 (14)	670 (11)
Malda	499 (9)	583 (3)	731 (1)	619 (5)	943 (15)	1089 (11)	1505 (10)	1858 (11)	354 (10)	375 (10)	552 (9)	527 (15)
Jalpaiguri	417 (14)	452 (11)	489 (12)	563 (11)	1149 (8)	953 (15)	993 (15)	1243 (15)	191 (15)	335 (12)	443 (12)	689 (9)
Darjeeling	413 (15)	731 (1)	533 (7)	546 (12)	1010 (14)	1179 (9)	1854 (3)	2382 (3)	383 (7)	355 (11)	492 (11)	555 (13)
Cooch-Behar	454 (13)	496 (8)	605 (4)	585 (9)	1037 (13)	975 (14)	1126 (14)	1297 (14)	351 (12)	288 (13)	284 (15)	588 (12)
Purulia	458 (12)	371 (15)	477 (14)	491 (15)	1094 (9)	990 (12)	1421 (11)	1498 (13)	408 (5)	272 (15)	578 (7)	546 (14)
West Bengal	539	538	593	650	1203	1292	1541	2214	354	396	618	784

Sources: (i) Government of West Bengal, Bureau of Applied Economics and Statistics, *Statistical Abstract (Various issues).*

(ii) Government of West Bengal, Bureau of Applied Economics and Statistics, *Economic Review (Various issues).*

Note: (i) Figures in the parentheses represent rankings.

(ii) NA implies not available.

Contd.. . . .

Table-5.2 Concld.

Crop→	Potato				Jute			
District	1970-73	1977-80	1984-87	1991-94	1970-73	1977-80	1984-87	1991-94
Burdwan	15800 (2)	20626 (1)	22729 (3)	25350 (2)	1714 (6)	1655 (3)	2185 (4)	2923 (4)
Birbhum	12523 (9)	11528 (10)	15286 (9)	21290 (6)	1768 (4)	1435 (7)	2279 (3)	2928 (3)
Bankura	15206 (4)	17413 (4)	21789 (4)	25798 (1)	1727 (5)	1644 (4)	2109 (7)	3056 (1)
Midnapore	12016 (10)	15412 (5)	21661 (5)	22878 (5)	1521 (8)	1665 (2)	2147 (5)	2930 (2)
Howrah	15090 (5)	18262 (3)	24153 (2)	24772 (4)	1833 (2)	1423 (8)	2134 (6)	2292 (9)
Hooghly	18172 (1)	20599 (2)	27288 (1)	24820 (3)	1944 (1)	1930 (1)	2392 (1)	2828 (5)
24-Paraganas	12702 (7)	12812 (9)	16487 (7)	15636 (9)	1557 (7)	1562 (5)	1793 (10)	2310 (7)
Nadia	13500 (6)	15303 (6)	15787 (8)	17560 (8)	1309 (10)	1465 (6)	1999 (9)	2511 (6)
Murshidabad	12560 (8)	13428 (8)	14524 (10)	19038 (7)	1329 (9)	1352 (9)	2000 (8)	2307 (8)
West Dinajpur	4543 (15)	5766 (15)	7208 (13)	5453 (15)	976 (15)	950 (13)	1019 (15)	1375 (11)
Malda	4673 (12)	7715 (11)	8306 (12)	11206 (13)	1033 (14)	1126 (11)	1292 (12)	1679 (10)
Jalpaiguri	4689 (11)	6461 (14)	6769 (15)	11726 (11)	1183 (11)	1142 (10)	1187 (14)	1108 (14)
Darjeeling	4610 (13)	6730 (12)	8679 (11)	10849 (14)	1055 (13)	856 (14)	1324 (11)	1298 (12)
Cooch-Behar	4577 (14)	6637 (13)	7001 (14)	12434 (10)	1107 (12)	1111 (12)	1213 (13)	1219 (13)
Purulia	15428 (3)	13711 (7)	21538 (6)	11296 (12)	1800 (3)	NA	2364 (2)	NA
West Bengal	13790	16232	20490	21923	1290	1344	1667	2020

Sources: (i) Government of West Bengal, Bureau of Applied Economics and Statistics, *Statistical Abstract (Various issues)*.
(ii) Government of West Bengal, Bureau of Applied Economics and Statistics, *Economic Review (Various issues)*.

Note: (i) Figures in the parentheses represent rankings.
(ii) NA implies not available.

Table 5.3 Variation in Yield of Different Crops among the Disctrics of west Bengal: 1970-71 to 1993-94 (kgs/hectare)

Crop	Year	Highest	Lowest	Average	Coeff. of Var(%)
Aus	1978-79	1613.24	569.63	884.55	32.307
	1978-79	1833.53	695.76	1088.99	32.53
	1985-86	2050.83	823.45	1311.85	34.09
	1993-94	2482.45	905.06	1630.90	37.25
Aman	1970.71	1257.64	767.39	1220.70	15.52
	1978-79	1590.81	1004.86	1216.13	15.42
	1985-86	1962.55	1097.18	1426.05	17.77
	1993-94	2494.89	1137.40	1719.18	22.21
Boro*	1970-71	2881.31	1568.69	2341.44	19.09*
	1978-79	2939.52	1557.57	2483.39	15.46*
	1985-86	3001.90	1547.89	2624.18	13.87
	1993-94	331.57	1536.91	2807.07	14.86
Rice	1970-71	1380.22	720.54	1019.75	19.79
	1978-79	1713.00	951.84	1253.88	18.90
	1985-86	2069.37	1043.15	1509.26	19.96
	1993-94	2568.30	1094.44	1874.97	23.02
Wheat	1970-71	2275.60	1248.87	1874.83	14.17
	1978-79	2244.86	1398.00	1882.20	11.43
	1985-86	2218.31	1543.02	1894.97	11.43
	1993-94	2334.38	1347.49	1916.69	13.92
Pulses	1970-71	657.21	396.62	475.74	12.84
	1978-79	662.49	442.13	513.03	10.04
	1985-86	667.14	456.92	550.24	9.60
	1993-94	733.33	474.42	597.67	11.83
Oilseed	1970-71	485.89	204.80	319.89	22.66
	1978-79	561.27	309.82	431.70	17.74
	1985-86	762.80	382.22	566.09	18.38
	1993-94	1089.86	455.78	779.72	24.05
Jutte**	1970-71	1795.43	750.69	1269.14	21.96
	1978-79	2075.17	895.87	1503.69	23.38
	1985-86	2355.48	1045.76	1749.71	25.75
	1993-94	2809.89	1248.00	2087.88	29.34

contd.

Table-5.3 Concld.

Crop	Year	Highest	Lowest	Average	Coeff. of Var(%)
Potato	1970-71	18807.29	4324.27	10620.19	44.90
	1978-79	21324.25	5571.39	12691.76	40.76
	1985-86	23801.41	6201.21	14953.29	39.08
	1993-94	27911.67	7008.65	18189.95	39.14
Sugarcane	1970-71	6797.00	2910.00	4987.13	23.114
	1978-79	6297.00	3900.00	5104.13	15.20
	1985-86	7618.00	4094.00	5558.19	18.13
	1993-94	7654.33	3480.33	5570.38	17.001

Source: Same as 5.2

Note: * and ** represent the number of observations 13 and 14 respectively.

Table 5.4: Percentage Change in Productivity of Different Crops During 1970-71 to 1993-94 (Districtwise)

District	Aus	Aman	Boro	Rice	Wheat	Pulses	Oilseed	Jute	Potato
Burdwan	44.48	98.38	2.37	86.08	-17.38	29.38	115.59	91.73	66.25
Birbhum	90.41	60.30	7.64	69.72	14.80	67.02	177.66	88.23	114.60
Bankura	149.78	60.98	63.59	90.41	11.42	8.14	176.03	96.19	98.46
Midnapore	90.41	65.48	22.43	90.41	-14.08	62.09	128.88	97.87	112.27
Howrah	150.35	57.32	10.65	86.08	-33.90	18.02	27.02	29.38	116.58
Hooghly	81.43	77.71	-6.45	62.09	-11.27	13.79	178.94	51.63	43.49
24-Paraganas	139.65	78.94	3.75	90.41	21.59	21.59	271.0	49.56	67.01
Nadia	111.17	175.11	7.14	194.76	-3.83	24.42	351.1	106.37	45.82
Murshidabad	52.68	103.07	49.56	108.76	13.75	2.33	134.20	77.71	27.61
West Dinajpur	87.80	66.63	14.80	90.41	10.65	16.13	145.79	66.25	42.18
Malda	53.74	100.75	56.24	118.58	24.42	48.83	121.12	21.03	117.08
Jalpaiguri	38.31	10.91	NA	14.80	0.69	40.23	222.67	23.57	111.17
Darjeeling	51.29	28.20	NA	23.00	38.31	4.81	102.61	59.51	142.42
Cooch-Behar	77.72	30.88	70.11	48.87	-11.48	38.31	65.87	31.78	135.82
Purulia	28.79	40.23	-2.03	123.67	16.93	11.42	90.85	NA	-13.09
West Bengal	71.29	69.45	12.58	86.08	2.8	24.42	187.40	68.17	72.48

Sources: (i) Government of West Bengal, Bureau of Applied Economics and Statistics, *Statistical Abstract* (Various issues).
(ii) Government of West Bengal, Bureau of Applied Economics and Statistics, *Economic Review* (Various issues).

Note: NA means not available.

Table 5.5: Composite Productivity Index

District	For All Crops				For Food Crops				For Non-Food Crops			
	1970-71	1978-79	1985-86	1993-94	1970-71	1978-79	1985-86	1993-94	1970-71	1978-79	1985-86	1993-94
1	2	3	4	5	6	7	8	9	10	11	12	13
Burdwan	124.77 (1)	122.51 (1)	126.34 (1)	129.05 (1)	122.93 (1)	123.64 (1)	129.03 (1)	131.62 (1)	126.08 (3)	125.44 (2)	122.61 (1)	113.46 (4)
Birbhum	116.73 (3)	113.42 (3)	115.96 (3)	114.46 (3)	119.41 (2)	116.22 (2)	119.28 (2)	117.75 (2)	88.091 (11)	87.77 (10)	95.57 (9)	94.35 (8)
Bankura	109.59 (4)	107.58 (4)	107.53 (4)	109.13 (5)	112.23 (4)	110.29 (4)	110.90 (3)	111.19 (5)	99.24 (8)	98.70 (8)	97.96 (8)	98.81 (7)
Midnapore	93.16 (7)	93.85 (8)	97.76 (7)	96.10 (8)	93.70 (9)	93.81 (7)	97.24 (6)	95.03 (9)	106.55 (6)	108.15 (5)	112.42 (2)	107.614 (5)
Howrah	95.78 (6)	94.47 (7)	91.93 (9)	93.33 (10)	93.31 (11)	90.92 (10)	90.62 (9)	91.34 (10)	131.49 (2)	114.36 (3)	105.35 (7)	91.273 (9)
Hooghly	119.50 (2)	119.71 (2)	120.64 (2)	117.93 (2)	115.20 (3)	114.73 (3)	83.60 (12)	115.41 (3)	145.67 (1)	137.27 (1)	107.65 (5)	123.15 (1)
24-Paraganas	90.05 (9)	93.31 (9)	94.90 (8)	97.95 (7)	89.55 (12)	91.45 (9)	93.05 (7)	96.08 (8)	115.03 (4)	113.74 (4)	111.84 (4)	114.14 (3)
Nadia	89.02 (10)	97.57 (6)	106.02 (5)	113.61 (4)	93.53 (10)	102.30 (6)	104.43 (5)	111.478 (4)	92.58 (10)	103.34 (7)	112.26 (3)	122.24 (2)
Murshidabad	101.60 (5)	101.05 (5)	104.78 (6)	107.57 (6)	106.45 (5)	105.32 (5)	106.94 (4)	110.50 (6)	107.89 (5)	106.08 (6)	106.02 (6)	103.69 (6)
West Dinajpur	76.12 (12)	77.46 (14)	76.58 (12)	79.89 (11)	82.27 (15)	83.78 (13)	83.21 (13)	83.36 (11)	69.77 (14)	68.27 (14)	67.69 (14)	67.31 (11)
Malda	75.76 (13)	81.104 (11)	84.68 (10)	94.54 (9)	84.91 (14)	87.45 (12)	92.12 (8)	100.99 (7)	98.48 (9)	87.34 (11)	80.89 (10)	72.50 (10)
Jalpaiguri	90.80 (8)	77.98 (13)	70.46 (14)	64.52 (14)	94.49 (8)	81.67 (14)	74.80 (15)	65.57 (15)	83.13 (13)	73.85 (13)	71.11 (12)	64.023 (12)
Darjeeling	56.19 (15)	63.67 (15)	50.75 (15)	46.19 (15)	99.26 (6)	87.84 (11)	84.51 (11)	76.87 (13)	60.04 (15)	56.67 (15)	66.35 (15)	53.96 (14)
Cooch-Behar	84.23 (11)	78.95 (12)	74.86 (13)	71.81 (13)	85.87 (13)	81.61 (15)	77.65 (14)	74.59 (14)	85.345 (12)	74.87 (12)	71.03 (13)	62.785 (13)
Purulia	66.56 (14)	87.87 (10)	82.64 (11)	77.62 (12)	98.41 (7)	92.26 (8)	88.29 (10)	81.84 (12)	104.083 (7)	92.86 (9)	80.504 (11)	53.823 (15)
Coef. of Var.	20.43	17.32	21.36	23.17	12.536	13.456	15.715	18.56	21.868	22.266	19.721	26.908
Rank Correlation	R_{23} = .89, R_{24} = .83. R_{25} = .79, R_{34} = .97, R_{35} = .93, R_{45} = .986				R_{67} = .814, R_{68} = .518, R_{69} = .89, R_{78} = .80, R_{79} = .89, R_{89} = .80				$R_{10,11}$ = .96, $R_{10,12}$ = .76, $R_{10,13}$ = .636, $R_{11,12}$ = .882, $R_{11,13}$ = .79, $R_{12,13}$ = .882			

Sources: (i) Government of West Bengal, Bureau of Applied Economics and Statistics, *Statistical Abstract (Various issues).*
(ii) Government of West Bengal, Bureau of Applied Economics and Statistics, *Economic Review (Various issues).*

Notes: (i) R_{ij} means rank correlation between i^{th} and j^{th} column.
(ii) Figures in the parentheses represent rankings.

CHAPTER 6

IMPACT OF CROP DIVERSIFICATION ON AGRICULTURAL PRODUCTION

6.1. Introduction

Change in cropping pattern is one of the major aspects of changing agricultural scenario of West Bengal. In the earlier analysis, it has been observed that the cropping pattern has been undergoing continuous changes in terms of acreage allocation or production composition since 1970-71. The diversification in acreage allocation or production composition has been characterised by a major shift of area from other crops to boro rice, potato and mustard or increase in component of boro rice, potato and mustard to total agricultural production compared to the other crops.

Now, total agricultural production in value terms of any geographical region in any year is the sum of the output in value terms of different crops produced in that region during that particular year. Output of any individual crop in value terms again depends on acreage distributed for growing that crop, yield and price of that crop. If prices are assumed to be constant, value of output of each crop changes on account of variation in area and yield level. Therefore, total agricultural production of any given region varies due to changes in *gross cropped area* (GCA) (sum of area under all the crops, grown in the region), yield of each crop and reallocation of total area for the production of each crop assuming, prices to be constant. Changes in agricultural output due to reallocation of land resources to different crops, when total area under cultivation, yield of every crop and prices remain constant, represent the effect of crop diversification or changing cropping pattern on agricultural production.

Decomposition of agricultural production growth in West Bengal, into the contributions of changes in area, yield and cropping pattern is a further revelation of dynamic growth process. Simple disaggregated growth rates of output of individual crops into area and productivity components of the state level are presented in Table 6.1[1].

From the table it is clear that, output of potato, oilseed and boro rice has increased significantly throughout the whole period and in all sub-periods. Components of production growth, area and yield display different patterns of change for different crops and in different sub-periods. In other words, the growth of agricultural production is marked by inter-crop and intra-crop variation in area and yield growth. Rise in total agricultural output (in value terms) which displayed an increasing trend at exponential rate of 2.96 per cent per annum during 1970-71 to 1993-94 had been due to growth of GCA which has increased by only 0.38 per cent per annum and significantly due to rise in productivity, whose annual exponential growth rate was 2.58 per cent. Here aggregate output of the region can be expressed as $Q_t = A_t . \alpha_t$, where Q_t , A_t and α_t are output (in value terms), gross cropped area (GCA) and composite productivity (in value terms) at time t[2]. Composite productivity depends on both, yield of the respective crops and acreage distribution to each crop i.e., yield and cropping pattern. In West Bengal growth rate of agricultural production has been largely affected by productivity growth, which is composed of the yield and cropping pattern component.

The productivity component of aggregate output growth is attributable to changes in yield and cropping pattern. The former measures the impact of changes in output per unit of area of individual crops on total output while, the latter captures the shifts of acreage from crops with relatively low values of output per unit of area to higher value crops. Yield of individual crops has increased manifold (from Table 6.1) during the post-Green Revolution period. Impact of yield growth on individual crops' production and thus on total agricultural production has been remarkable. Along with that cropping pattern can be viewed as another important factor affecting agricultural production.

6.2. Major

Change in cropping pattern is an inseparable part of agricultural growth process. Irrespective of agricultural production it has multiple impacts on rural economy. The major impacts of changes in cropping pattern are on the (i) growth of agricultural production, (ii) employment of labour and optimum use of human resources, (iii) stabilisation of farm income over the seasons and (iv) conservation and enhancement of natural resources. Though this chapter pertains to the evaluation of the effect of crop diversification (changes in cropping pattern) on the agricultural production of the state during 1970-71 to 1993-94, it will not be irrelevant to spend a few words on each of the components of the aforesaid set of impacts.

(i) One of the major problems facing the agricultural economy of the state is the dominance of the small and marginal farmers. In terms of number as well as cultivated area, they constitute a significant part of the state's agricultural sector. Approximately 91.4 per cent of the operational holdings in West Bengal are below two hectares according to 1990-91 agricultural Census Report.[3] They constitute nearly 33.6 per cent of total cultivated area. Majority of small and marginal farmers is poor. A change in cropping pattern may help rising production value of each farm and the output of a region (state). So it is imperative on the part of the farmers to introduce a new cropping pattern in view of rising income from their limited holdings. Crop diversification or changing cropping pattern can thus lead to an improvement of their standard of living with a major impact on, especially the small and marginal farmers, whose income are highly dependent on their farm revenue. At the macro level it thus enhances the total returns from agriculture of the state. This is thus one of the major considerations that goad public policies in the direction capable of generating the desirable outcome[4].

(ii) Another important problem of the economy like the other developing economies is the existence of unemployment or underemployment of working population. A number of earlier studies have shown that there was a severe problem of seasonal unemployment (owing to low intensity of cultivation before the emergence of and in the early part of Green Revolution) and under-employment in large parts of the state. The intensive cultivation (introduction of multiple cropping[5] and very short period crops) has reduced the temporal variation and brought more regularity in the demand for labour in the agricultural sector. Now the slack season has been appreciably shortened and agricultural labourer remain active almost throughout all the seasons of the year. As a result, seasonal fluctuation of agricultural wage has been reduced significantly. During 1970-71 coefficient of variation in daily wage of farm worker (from monthly data collected from agricultural wages in India) in West Bengal was around 8 per cent (in case of field labourer) and reduced to 5.7 per cent during 1993-94[6].

(iii) The severe problem of instability of farm income associated with the price fluctuation again suggests the need for a judicious choice of crop-mix. The farmers on their own would try and may arrive at an optimum crop-mix, which would enable them to spread out the risks and ensure a steady flow of income over the year.

(iv) Besides these, in several circumstances crop diversification becomes essential to restore the degraded natural resource base or to enhance the value of natural resources. In several instances a new cropping pattern has been introduced to retain or enhance the value of natural resources, primarily land and water. In eastern India, particularly in West Bengal introduction of wheat in the early periods of Green Revolution in a predominantly rice regime to utilise residual moisture in the production of wheat is one of the several instances. The introduction of wheat in that system was expedited to economise on the irrigation requirements[7]. Non-judicious choice of crop-mix in Punjab exacerbates the problem of waterlogging and salinity and raises the issue of long-term sustainability of agricultural production and farm income (Gill, 1992). In West Bengal, introduction of very short period varieties of rice seed to save water and grow more crops with limited water as well as to convert semi-arid zone into a favourable rice zone is another good example of maintenance and conservation of resources. Admittedly, there are other technological and economic factors, which have prompted different crop-combinations in different parts of the state. But the objectives of optimising the use of resources especially water and at the same time saving land from waterlogging and salinity problem have important implications for the farm economy of the corresponding regions.

These are the major impacts of changes in cropping pattern, which again have a feedback effect on cropping pattern of the respective region. Since long, many studies have been undertaken to discuss the effects of changing cropping pattern or crop diversification on agricultural production in different regions. A brief review of those earlier attempts is presented below.

6.3 Review of Some Earlier Studies Relating to Impact of Changes in cropping pattern

Some earlier studies have aimed at examining the effect of changes in cropping pattern on the growth of agricultural production over time. Although some attempts were made earlier to explain agricultural growth in terms of the area and yield components[8], the first systematic study came from Minhas and Vaidyanathan[9]. Their analysis includes, besides area and yields components, a component on cropping pattern and the interaction of yield and cropping pattern. They have assessed the contribution of the above factors by using an additive scheme of decomposition. According to that scheme absolute changes in value of gross agricultural output can be described as

$$Q_t - Q_0 = A_t \ \Sigma C_{it} \ Y_{it} \ P_i - A_0 \ \Sigma C_{i0} \ Y_{i0} \ P_i \ ,$$

$$\text{or,} \quad Q_t - Q_0 = (A_t - A_0) \ \Sigma C_{i0} \ Y_{i0} P_i + A_t \ \Sigma (C_{it} - C_{i0}) \ Y_{i0} P_i$$

$$+ A_t \ \Sigma C_{i0} \ (Y_{it} - Y_{i0}) P_i + A_t \ \Sigma (C_{it} - C_{i0}) \ (Y_{it} - Y_{i0}) P_i \quad (1)$$

Where Q_t = value of gross agricultural output at constant prices (P_i) during period t. A_t = *gross cropped area* during period t, $C_{it} = (A_{it}/A_t)$ = proportion of area under ith crop (C_{it}) to the *gross cropped area* during period t. Y_{it} = physical output per acre of crop i during period t.

The first three components on the right hand side of the equation represent respectively the contribution of change in area, cropping pattern and yield to absolute change in the value of gross agricultural output. The last term shows the interaction effect of change in yield and cropping pattern on the growth of output. In the above scheme the component elements are so chosen that their contributions to output growth be determined by more or less independent set of factors. They have analysed the contribution of different components to total output growth during 1951-54 to 1958-61 in 14 states and also for 268 districts belonging to 13 states. Later Minhas gave a seven-component additive version[10], which was subsequently used by Mishra[11], Sondhi and Singh[12]. Dharm Narain's work[13] is an extension of the study of Minhas and Vaidyanathan. He decomposed the growth of productivity in agriculture into three factors, namely changes in cropping pattern, locational shifts of area under individual crops and pure yield effect. He concluded that the growth of agricultural productivity in India during the fifties was mainly due to the first two factors, that is cropping pattern effect and locational shift effect. During the sixties, however, the pure yield effect was found to have a major influence on growth of productivity, which was a result of technological change.

Vidya Sagar (1977) has decomposed the change in the value of gross agricultural output at prevalent prices into three major components: area, productivity and price and their interactions[14]. The productivity component is a composite of crop-structural components viz. cropping pattern, price structure and yield structure and their interactions[15].

C. G. Ranade (1980) has examined the effect of cropping pattern, fertiliser and irrigation simultaneously upon agricultural production during 1962-65 to 1970-73, across 54 agroclimatic regions belonging to 14 major states in India[16]. He has used an index of cropping pattern, similar to that of Dharm Narain in order to explain the pure cropping pattern shift effect. But unlike Dharm Narain he has used all India average yields and prices of different crops during 1970-73 instead of base year yield and prices. He found a positive relationship between cropping pattern index and agricultural productivity.

Boyce (1987) has decomposed the variation in agricultural output of West Bengal into the contribution of changes in area, yield and cropping pattern [17]. For the purpose of analysis he has used the multiplicative index of Minhas and Parikh (1966)[18]. He has estimated and split up the output growth into the effects of area, yield and cropping pattern for the thirty-two year period (1949 to 1980) as a whole and two sub-periods 1949-64 and 1965-80 separately. The cropping pattern component has been estimated by two alternative ways. One is residual method, where area and yield growth rates are subtracted from the output growth rate (alternatively pure yield growth is subtracted from productivity growth) and other is the direct method where, cropping pattern growth is estimated directly[19]. The results obtained by him are quoted here in Table-6.2.

The results in the table indicate that in West Bengal it is pure yield increase, rather than cropping pattern changes, that has been the major sources of productivity growth. Cropping pattern plays a greater role in the second sub-period, when the rate of yield increase is higher as the interaction phenomenon would lead one to expect. Moreover, from the district-wise analysis he observed that the two productivity components, yield and cropping pattern together exceed the area component in the fastest growing central districts. The yield-cropping pattern interaction component was positive in all cases (Boyce 1987, p.277).

Dhindsa and Sharma (1995) had used the seven factor additive model as suggested by Minhas and Parikh for analysing the effect of cropping pattern change on agricultural output in Punjab during 1965-66 to 1990-91. In the present analysis also for its simplicity the same type of methodology is adopted to analyse the impact of changes in Cropping pattern on the growth of agricultural output in West Bengal[20].

6.4. Component Analysis of Changes in Agricultural Output

In order to employ the seven factor additive model as suggested by Minhas, first of all, output of major crops has been computed from the log linear trend equations and aggregated together to arrive at the estimated total value of output of the state. Value of each crop-output at each point of time is calculated by multiplying the estimated output with constant base year price (triennia average of 1969,70 and 71). Then changes in agricultural output during 1970-71 to 1993-94 has been computed and split up according to the source of variation. The same sort of analysis has also been made for the two sub-periods 1970-71 to 1981-82 and 1982-83 to 1993-94. The model used in this analysis is presented below.

Total change in agricultural output over the time period can be divided into various components as follows:[21]

$$Q_t - Q_0 = A_t \ \Sigma C_{it} Y_{it} P_i - A_0 \ \Sigma C_{i0} Y_{i0} P_i ,$$

Or

$$\begin{aligned} \Delta Q = Q_t - Q_0 &= (A_t - A_0) \ \Sigma C_{i0} Y_{i0} P_i + A_0 \ \Sigma C_{i0} (Y_{it} - Y_{i0}) P_i \\ &+ A_0 \ \Sigma (C_{it} - C_{i0}) Y_{i0} P_i + (A_t - A_0) \ \Sigma (C_{it} - C_{i0}) Y_{i0} P_i \\ &+ (A_t - A_0) \Sigma C_{i0} (Y_{it} - Y_{i0}) P_i + A_0 \ \Sigma (C_{it} - C_{i0}) (Y_{it} - Y_{i0}) \\ & P_i + (A_t - A_0) \ \Sigma C_{it} - C_{i0}) (Y_{it} - Y_{i0}) P_i \end{aligned}$$

Where $Q_0 = A_0 \ \Sigma C_{i0} Y_{i0} P_i$ and $Q_t = A_t \Sigma C_{it} Y_{it} P_i$ represent total value of agricultural output {at constant prices (P_i)} of the region in the base and final period respectively. A_0 and A_t are *gross cropped areas* in the base and final period respectively. $C_{i0} = (A_{i0}/A_0)$, $C_{it} = (A_{it}/A_t)$ and Y_{i0}, Y_{it} represent respectively the proportion of area under i[th] crop to *gross cropped area* in the base and final period and yield of ith crop in the base and final year. P_is are the prices (triennia average of harvest prices) of crops in the base period. The first three components on the right hand side represent the direct effect of area, yield and cropping pattern. The next three are the interaction effects of area and cropping pattern, area and yield, cropping pattern and yield. The last one is the interaction of all these three area, yield and cropping pattern[22].

6.5 Analysis of Results Obtained on the Basis of Component Method

From Table 6.3 it is seen that during 1970-71 to 1993-94, 57.57 per cent of the growth in agricultural production has been contributed by yield growth, 18.58 per cent by cropping pattern changes and only 9.34 per cent of output growth has been due to acreage growth. The interaction effects together provide only 14.51 per cent of total change in agricultural output, of which contribution of area-yield and yield-cropping pattern interaction effects are 5.26 and 6.92 per cent respectively.

Relative contribution of different components changed significantly during the two sub-periods. Though during 1970-71 to 1981-82, cropping pattern and area-cropping pattern interaction effects were negative they turned to be positive in the immediately next period (1982-83 to 1993-94). The effect of area growth was very high (47.53 per cent) during 1970-71 to 1981-82 but reduced to almost one-fourth during 1982-83 to 1993-94. The effect of cropping pattern change during this period is almost identical to that of area and yield-cropping pattern interaction component. Yield-cropping pattern interaction effect has been reduced to less than half from 24.04 per cent during 1970-71 to 1981-82 period to 11.60 per cent during the following half.

The above component analysis revealed that most of the increase in output has been brought about by the yield growth. Though in the early stage of Green Revolution (during 1970-71 to 1981-82) impact of acreage growth was much stronger, it was later over taken by yield growth and yield-cropping pattern interaction component together. During 1982-83 to 1993-94 however, yield, cropping pattern and their interaction component together contributed about 77 per cent of aggregate variation of total crop production. The results of the component analysis support the earlier conclusion of increasing difficulty involved with the area expansion rather than yield and cropping pattern adjustment. Earlier it was found that expansion of irrigation and development of technology has made possible the expansion of acreage in the early period of Green Revolution when huge amount of land was available for cultivation especially during off-monsoon seasons. But deceleration of acreage growth started after the optimum utilisation of available sources of irrigation have been completed with consequent stress, shifted on to cropping pattern growth.

The increase in effect of changes in cropping pattern during 1982-83 to 1993-94 compared to that in the earlier period is an indicator of sizeable shift of area in favour of high yielding and higher priced crops. Earlier it has been found that cropping pattern in the state has changed largely in favour of crops having higher initial yield in value terms like boro rice, potato and major oilseeds including mustard. On the other hand area under relatively lower value crops like pulses, jowar, bazra, ragi etc. has decreased substantially in proportion to *gross cropped area*. Moreover, positive value of yield-cropping pattern interaction component is indicative of a sizeable shifts of area in favour of crops, whose yield has increased. But the result reveals that this interaction effect has decreased during 1982-83 to 1993-94 sub-period than in earlier one. This implies a slower movement of area towards the crops whose yield level increased over time.

6.6. An Alternative Component Analysis

It is well known that, in order to measure the changes in output (in value terms) over a period of time, four responsible factors namely, (i) changes in *gross cropped area* (A), (ii) changes in yield rates (Y), (iii) changes in cropping pattern (C) and (iv) changes in the prices of crops (P) are generally taken into consideration[23]. Total change in output over a period can be written as

$$Q_t - Q_0 = \Delta Q_{(A.C.Y.P)} = \Sigma A_{it} Y_{it} P_{it} - \Sigma A_{i0} Y_{i0} P_{i0}$$

where P_{i0} and P_{it} are the prices of ith crop in the base and final period. A_{i0} and A_{it} are area under ith crop in the base and final period respectively. $\Delta Q_{(A.C.Y.P)}$ represents the changes in output due to changes in above mentioned four factors. The other symbols are used in the same sense as used in former analysis. This methodology is followed because it is necessary and easily possible to eliminate the effects of other factors from the total change for isolating the cropping pattern effect.

From the total change in output, effect of changes in yield rates and prices can be eliminated by multiplying the areas in the final period with the respective yield rates and prices as in the base period and then subtracting from it the total production (value) in the base period. Therefore, $\Delta Q_{(A.C)} = \Sigma A_{it} Y_{i0} P_{i0} - \Sigma A_{i0} Y_{i0} P_{i0}$. From this again the effect of change in *gross cropped area* can further be eliminated, assuming that the increase or decrease in area under the crops has changed in the same proportion as that of *total cropped area*. Therefore, the effect of cropping pattern changes alone, will be

$$\Delta Q_{(A.C)} - \Delta Q_{(A)} = \Delta Q_{(C)} = \Sigma A_{it} Y_{i0} P_{i0} - \Sigma A_{i0} Y_{i0} P_{i0} (A_t / A_0) \quad \Delta Q_{(C)}$$

represents the effects of area changes of different crops occurred due to substitution effect, on total value of output. The same sort of analysis was earlier followed by National Council of Applied Economic Research (NCAER, 1966) in order to explain the impact of cropping pattern change in Punjab. The results obtained by using this method are explained below.

6.7 Analysis of Changes in Output due to Changes in Cropping Pattern Following the Alternative Component Analysis

On the basis of this methodology the changes in output (in value terms) due to cropping pattern changes alone has been measured. The results obtained are presented in Table 6.4.

It has been found that in absolute terms, total value of agricultural crop production due to changes in cropping pattern has increased by Rs 205.83 crores over a period of 24 years (from 1970-71 to 1993-94)[24]. This can be viewed as the net impact of changes in proportion of area under each crop or substitution of crops. From the inter-crop comparison of the impact of acreage substitution it has been found that the largest contribution in this respect has come from boro rice. The second highest contribution in the descending order was of potato. The increase in total returns due to boro rice and potato were Rs 246.616 crores and Rs 115.402 crores respectively. Other crops that appreciably contributed to this total change have been mustard and jute. Maximum nagative change in return came from adverse change in acreage under pulses (-Rs 70.048 crores). Other crops that caused decline in total returns are aus (-Rs 41.96 crores), wheat (-Rs 33.355 crores) and sugarcane (-Rs 22.323 crores) etc.

6.8. Overall Observations

From the above discussion it is revealed that, though intensive cultivation embedded in intensive use of inputs and technological change has made a significant contribution to total change in agricultural production, through increased yield rate, contribution of changes in cropping pattern is by no means negligible. Increase in yield is important from the point of view of increasing returns from agriculture in any region and equally important is the choice of combination of crops or cropping pattern at any given situation to maximise revenue from agricultural activities not only in the current situation but also for its sustainability in future. Any particular cropping pattern is not optimum and maximum remunerative in all situations. With the changing circumstances judicious choice of crop-mix also alters. An inter-district analysis in order to make inter-district comparison may also be done, which would strengthen the conclusion reached above.

NOTES

1 Sastri earlier made the same sort of analysis in case of wheat. For reference: Sastri A.V. K (1960), "Relative Contribution of Area and Yield to Increased Production of Wheat During the First Plan", *Agricultural Situation in India*, Vol.XV, No.5, August. pp. 481-486.

2 Since $Q_t = A_t \cdot \gamma_t$, $\frac{\dot{Q}}{Q} = \frac{\dot{A}}{A} + \frac{\dot{\gamma}}{\gamma}$ i.e., growth rate of output is the sum of acreage and productivity growth rates.

3 Source: Agricultural Census of West Bengal, 1990-91, conducted by Land and Land Reforms Department and Evaluation Wing, Directorate of Agriculture, Government of West Bengal.

4 One of the objectives of the Government is to maximise total income of the state as well as to maintain supply-demand equality in each crop market. So Government policies are framed to encourage the production of deficient crops as well as to discourage the production of some other crops whose supply exceeds demand. Policies are also introduced to divert demand from any crop/crops to other (substitutes) and to encourage research activities to generate improved varieties of desired crops, which have some excess demand along with the objective of maximising agricultural earning from the fixed supply of land.

5 Introduction of multiple cropping leads to increase in intensity of cultivation.

6 The coefficient of variation of daily wage is calculated from the monthly data obtained from *Agricultural Wages in India, 1969-70, 1971-72 and 1993-94*; published by Directorate of Economics and Statistics, Ministry of Agriculture, Government of India.

7 VyasV.S. (1996), op. cit., p-639.

8 Sastri (1960), op. cit.

9 Minhas B.S. and Vaidyanathan A. (1965), " Growth of Crop Output in India, 1951-54 to 1958-61, An Analysis by Component Elements", *Journal of the Indian Society of Agricultural Statistics*, Vol. XVII, No.2 Dec. pp. 230-252.

10 Minhas B. S.(1966), " Rapporteur's Report on Measurement of Agricultural Growth", *Indian Journal of Agricultural Economics*, Vol. XXI, No.4, Oct.-Dec.

11 Mishra V. N. (1971), " Growth of Crop Output in Gujarat: A Component Analysis", *Anvesak*, Vol.1, No. 1, June, pp. 1-15.

12 Sondhi R. and Singh K., (1975), " Component Analysis of Food Grain Economy of India", *Journal of Social and Economic Studies*, Vol. III, No.2, Sept.

13 Narain Dharm, (1965), *Impact of Price Movements on Areas Under Selected Crops in India: 1900-1939*, Cambridge University Press.

14 Sagar Vidya (1980), " Decomposition of Growth Trends and Certain Related Issues", *Indian Journal of Agricultural Economics*, Vol.35, No.2, April-June, pp. 42-59.

15 Introduction of price variation was a good thinking, because, even if the other components remain unchanged still a particular region may devote its resources for the production of some crops for which the region has competitive price advantage, though those crops are not required for self use. The people of that region can purchase the commodity/ commodities needed for their use from other regions if there is no hindrance of commercial transaction and they also can maximise the value of total agricultural output.

16 Ranade C. G. (1980), "Impact of Cropping Pattern on Agricultural Production", *Indian Journal of Agricultural Economics*, Vol.35, No.2, April-June.

17 Boyce J.K. (1987), op. cit., Appendix A.5, pp. 273-277.

18 Minhas and Parikh (1966) op. cit.

19 Cropping Pattern Component is estimated from equation: $\text{Ln } c_t = a_c + b_c t$, where $C_t = \Sigma c_{it} y_{in} p_i$ with y_{in} = final year yield of ith crop as estimated from the equation $\text{Ln } y = a_y + b_y.t$.

20 Vidya Sagar (1980) has argued in the context of a multiplicative scheme demonstrated by Minhas, that the results obtained by the end points method do not differ from the one obtained by using the entire time series data. In this case the component growth rates are additive. For reference: Vidya Sagar (1980), "Decomposition of Growth Trends and Certain Related Issues", *Indian Journal of Agricultural Economics*, Vol.35, No.2, April-June, pp.42-60.

21 Since the emphasis is given on crop diversification and its impact on agricultural output, the variation in prices has not been introduced. In an extended version Vidya Sagar has introduced pure price effect and the effects of interaction of price changes with other factors as separate components along with the others included in the additive model. For reference, Sagar V. (1980), op. cit.

22 Here the word interaction need not be confounded with the term used in the statistical analysis of 'experimental design'. It indicates the impact of joint movements in the two-factors/three factors on the overall production increase. It has a resemblance to 'covariance' between the two. For example, a positive yield-cropping pattern interaction component would imply that the crop structure has shifted in favour of those crops, which show higher growth of yield. If pure cropping pattern effect were positive then it would mean a shift of acreage in favour of crops having high initial productivity.

23 This methodology has earlier been considered by NCAER (1966).

24 This is calculated at the base year (1970-71) constant prices.

REFERENCES

1. Gill K. S. (1992), " Diversification of Agriculture in Punjab: Progress and Possibilities", *Agricultural Situation in India*, Vol.17, No.5, August.

2. Government of India, Ministry of Agriculture, Directorate of Economics and Statistics, *Agricultural Wages in India, (Various issues)*.

3. Minhas B.S. and Vaidyanathan A. (1965), " Growth of Crop Output in India, 1951-54 to 1958-61, An Analysis by Component Elements", *Journal of the Indian Society of Agricultural Statistics*, Vol. XVII, No.2 Dec. pp. 230-252.

4. Minhas B. S. (1966), " Rapporteur's Report on Measurement of Agricultural Growth", *Indian Journal of Agricultural Economics*, Vol. XXI, No.4, Oct.-

Dec.

5. Mishra V. N. (1971), " Growth of Crop Output in Gujarat: A Component Analysis", *Anvesak*, Vol.1, No. 1, June, pp. 1-15.
6. Narain Dharm, (1965), *Impact of Price Movements on Areas Under Selected Crops in India: 1900-1939*, Cambridge University Press.
7. Narain Dharm, (1977), " Growth of Productivity in Indian Agriculture", *Indian Journal of Agricultural Economics*, Vol. XXXII, No.1, Jan.-Mar., pp.1-44.
8. Ranade C. G. (1980), " Impact of Cropping Pattern on Agricultural Production", *Indian Journal of Agricultural Economics*, Vol.35, No.2, April-June.
9. Sagar Vidya (1980), " Decomposition of Growth Trends and Certain Related Issues", *Indian Journal of Agricultural Economics*, Vol.35, No.2, April-June, pp. 42-59.
10. Sastri A.V. K (1960), " Relative Contribution of Area and Yield to Increased Production of Wheat During the First Plan", *Agricultural Situation in India*, Vol.XV, No.5, August. Pp. 481-486.
11. Sondhi R. and Singh K., (1975), " Component Analysis of Food Grain Economy of India", *Journal of Social and Economic Studies*, Vol. III, No.2, Sept.
12. Vyas V. S. (1996), "Diversification in Agriculture: Concept, Rationale and Approaches", *Indian Journal of Agricultural Economics*, Vol. 51, No.4, Oct.- Dec., pp.636-643.

Table 6.1: Contribution of Rate of Area and Yield Growth on the Rate of Growth of Output of Different Crops in West Bengal during 1970-71 to 1993-94 (exponential rate of growth)

Crop/Crop Group	1970-71 to 1993-94*			1970-71 to 1981-82			1982-83 to 1993-94**		
	Production	Area	Yield	Production	Area	Yield	Production	Area	Yield
Aus	.0045	-.0207	.0252	-.0439	-.0258	-.0181	.087	-.0154	.0623
Aman	.0253	.0024	.0229	.0121	.0036	.0085	.0543	.0077	.0468
Boro	.0709	.0658	.0051	.0184	.0247	-.0063	.1015	.0861	.0139
Wheat	-.0173	-.0186	.0012	-.0392	-.0158	-.0235	-.0169	-.0084	.0086
Pulses	-.0351	-.044	.0095	-.0321	-.0247	.0072	-.0365	-.0493	.0093
Jute	.0337	.0111	.0226	.0414	.033	.0084	.0293	-.0019	.03
Potato	.0765	.0529	.0237	.0868	.0632	.0236	.0675	.0581	.0097
Mustard	.122	.0774	.0444	.0692	.0234	.0458	.0991	.094	.0316
Oilseed	.104	.0581	.0459	.0871	.0581	.0289	.0878	.0494	.0384
Sugarcane	-.0453	-.0531	.0069	-.0344	-.0477	.0133	.0341	-.043	.0086

Note: *and ** indicate that the periods are 1970-71 to 1994-95 and 1982-83 to 1994-95 for wheat and pulses. For other crops data were not available for 1994-95.

Sources: (i) Government of West Bengal, Bureau of Applied Economics and Statistics, *Statistical Abstracts, (Various issues)*.

(ii) Government of West Bengal, Bureau of Applied Economics and Statistics, *Economic Review, (Various issues)*.

Table 6.2: Decomposition of Agricultural Output Growth by Alternative Methods, West Bengal, 1949-80 and Sub-periods (Percentage shares are given in parentheses)

Method of Estimation of Cropping Pattern Component	Growth Rates[a]			
	Output[b]	Area[c]	Yield[d]	Cropping Pattern
1949-80				
Omitted	1.74	.845 (48.6)	.895 (51.4)	---
Residual[e]	1.74	.845 (48.6)	.604 (34.7)	.291 (16.7)
Direct[f]	1.74	.845 (48.6)	.604 (34.7)	.284 (16.3)
1949-64				
Omitted	1.671	.777 (46.5)	.893 (53.5)	---
Residual	1.671	.777 (46.5)	.882 (52.8)	.011 (0.7)
Direct	1.671	.777 (46.5)	.882 (52.8)	-.073 (-4.4)
1965-80				
Omitted	2.74	.844 (30.8)	1.897 (69.2)	---
Residual	2.74	.844 (30.8)	1.324 (48.3)	.572 (20.91)
Direct	2.74	.844 (30.8)	1.324 (48.3)	.660 (24.1)

Notes: a. Growth rates = b*100

b. Estimating equation: $\text{Ln } Q = a_Q + b_Q.t$; Q_t = value of output at constant prices, t= 1, 2,.....n.

c. Estimating equation: $\text{Ln } A = a_A + b_A.t$; where A = gross cropped area.

d. Estimating equation:

$\text{Ln } \alpha = a\alpha + b\alpha.t$;

where

$\alpha_t = Q_t/A_t = \Sigma C_{it} Y_{it} P_i$,

Y_{it} = yield of ith crop at time t,

P_I = price of ith crop at base year,

C_{it} = the base year share of ith crop in gross cropped area, as estimated from equation: $\text{Ln } C = a_C + b_C.t$.

e. Cropping pattern component $b_C \mp b_Q - b_A - b_r$.

f. Cropping pattern component is estimated from equation:

$\text{Ln } C = a_C + b_C.t$,

where

$C_t = \Sigma C_{it} Y_{in} P$ with Y_{in} = final year yield of ith crop as estimated from the equation: $\text{Ln } \tilde{a} = a\alpha + b\alpha.t$.

Table 6.3: Relative Contribution of Various Components to the Growth of Total Crop Output in West Bengal (in Percentage)

Effects	1970-71 to 1993-94	1970-71 to 1981-82	1982-83 to 1993-94
Individual Effect			
Area	9.34	47.53	12.76
Yield	57.57	29.64	52.33
Cropping Pattern	18.58	-3.36	12.70
Sub-total	85.49	73.81	77.79
Interaction Effects			
Area and Cropping Pattern	1.70	-0.14	1.76
Area and Yield	5.26	1.27	7.24
Yield and Cropping Pattern	6.92	24.04	11.60
Area, Yield and Cropping Pattern	0.63	1.03	1.61
Sub-total	14.51	26.2	22.21
Grand total	100.00	100.00	100.00

Table 6.4 Contribution of Various Crops in Total Returns due to Cropping Pattern Changes in West Bengal: 1970-71 to 1993-94 (Rs. Crores)

Crop Group	Crop			
	Value in 1970-71 $= \Sigma A_{i0}\ Y_{i0}\ P_{i0}$	Value in 1993-94at constant base year prices and yields $= \Sigma A_{i0}\ Y_{i0}\ P_{i}$	Value in 1970-71 multiplied by $A_t\ /A_0$ $= (A_t\ /A_0).\ \Sigma A_{i0}\ Y_{i0}\ P_{io}$	Change in return due to change in Cropping Pattern $= \Sigma A_{it}\ Y_{i0}\ P_{i0} - \Sigma A_{i0}\ Y_{i0}\ P_{i0}\ (A_t\ /A_0)$
Aus	89.26	55.449	97.412	-41.963 (-.204)
Aman	555.211	586.72	605.92	-19.20 (-.093)
Boro	71.43	324.57	77.954	246.616 (1.198)
Wheat	75.913	49.491	82.846	-33.355 (-.162)
Pulses	96.241	34.983	105.031	-70.048 (-.34)
Jute	68.096	87.901	74.315	13.586 (.066)
Potato	50.51	170.525	55.123	115.402 (.5607)
Mustard	3.537	20.978	3.86	17.118 (.083)
Sugarcane	28.027	8.264	30.587	-22.32 (-.108)
Total	1038.225	1338.881	1133.048	205.833 (1.00)

Note: Figures in the parentheses represent proportion to total change.

CHAPTER 7

DETERMINANTS OF CROP DIVERSIFICATION

7.1 Basic Argument

This chapter deals with the analysis of important causes behind the undergoing pattern of diversification of crops in West Bengal during the post-Green Revolution period, as has been explained in chapter-3. Broadly speaking, the diversification in any particular geographical area is based on the changing social, economic, technological, geographical[1] and institutional structure of that region. Specificity of requirement of different factors in case of different crops and their availability on time as well as the system of agriculture (subsistence i.e., for self-consumption or commercial i.e., for making money) are the key factors in determining acreage allocation. Major underlying factors which are conceived to be of great importance in determining the allocation of land resources among competing crops[2] are prices[3] and yields of different crops, level of irrigation, availability and variation of other agricultural inputs (pattern of agricultural implements, varieties of seeds, synthetic fertiliser etc.) and geographical characteristics of the respective region. On the basis of their nature of influence the factors can be grouped into two broad categories.

On the one hand increase in price and productivity of any crop relative to that of others, provided other things remain unchanged, may tempt the farmers to allocate resources for producing that in preference to others and vice-versa. Therefore, high relative price and productivity of any crop at the existing state of technology, given other conditions of agricultural production (in other words, high relative profitability) may create an affinity of the farmers towards that crop and vice-versa. These factors may be designated in view of their provocative and attractive forces, as the *forward stimulating factors or pull factors*. They are so christened because though the farmers at the existing state of technology and other production conditions, can avail themselves of alternative available opportunities, their choice for some particular crops is dictated by the *relative pull or attractive force* of the said factors (like relative price, yield or proceeds per acre[4] of the competing crops).

On the other hand, there are other factors like rainfall, irrigation, improvement and availability of technology[5] etc. at relatively cheaper cost which generate conditions congenial for the farmers to produce some crops which, without the aforesaid facilities could hardly be feasible[6]. Thus, a change in these factors may be associated with a change in the cropping pattern. These factors may be identified as the *backward motivating factors or push factors*, since they enable the farmers to produce the crops. Specific crop has specific time and quantum of requirement of these factors, due to the particular biological nature of the production process of different crops. Adequate and timely appearance of these factors in different seasons push forward the farmers to allocate land or expand production of crops specifically, sensitive to those specific factors.

Here actually the distinction between these two types of encouraging factors is made only to mark the nature of influence that they exert on the farmers' cropping decision. A question may arise regarding the relative superiority or importance of these two types of factors in determining cropping pattern of any region. The answer is definitely based on the condition or state of the society to which the farmers belong[7]. Importance of *backward motivating factors or push factors* like irrigation, favourable climate etc. are felt in all situations provided there is a desire for the production of crops whether, food or non-food. In a system of traditional agriculture, production of crops was primarily organised for self-consumption and so the cropping decision of the farmer is prompted mainly by his family requirements. But allocation of land in different use in that system was directed by the availability of those respective factors depending on the sensitivity of alternative consumption crops to the respective factors. Even in a system of commercialised agriculture, cultivation of crops is contingent upon these factors. However, in this system price, yield and profitability enter as decisive factors which when change, instigate an inter-crop area shift in a particular region bestowed with alternative opportunities and no dearth of the essential inputs.

Dharm Narain (1965) has distinguished between production for self-consumption and production for market, while explaining the *supply response to price*. He made the conclusion that allocation of area for the production of crops for *self-consumption* responds significantly to rainfall (broadly weather) rather than price changes, while cash crops respond more to price than the weather components (specifically rainfall)[8].

It is of course true that, profitability influenced through changes in productivity or yield is partly dependent upon the supporting force of these input factors. Conversely, attractive price and profitability of some crops relative to that of the others may encourage the modification and innovation of technical implements needed to remove the conditions hostile to the production of those crops. For example, increase in relative profitability of potato has led to expansion of potato cultivation on the land (which would otherwise have been used for producing other relatively lower value crops[9], or remain fallow during that season) where it was not possible earlier, with the help of manual labour[10]. This shift of area from other crops to potato or extension of potato cultivation on new land has become practicable after the modification and innovation of technology (application of increaşing number of tractors, power tiller etc.) and growth of suitable, highly resistant seeds.

But attempts (stimulated by high relative price of some crops) to remove all the conditions, hostile to the production of some desirable crops (e.g. hostile agro-climatic and legal conditions) through the evolution and innovation of superior technology may be infructuous in some cases. For example, in spite of high price of tea, farmers in the southern West Bengal cannot cultivate tea due to adverse agro-climatic condition[11]. However, in the tea growing region like Darjeeling substitution of land in favour of tea may take place at the cost of area under other sowable crops and is not hampered due to the aforesaid reasons. Similarly, in spite of high price, opium cultivation cannot be practised owing to the legal prohibition.

In the short run, changing price may not bring about a significant change in acreage under crops. This is due to the particular biological nature of agricultural production. If price changes in the post cultivation or harvest period of any crop, it would not have any impact on its acreage during the same season/year. However, it may have effect in the next year (next crop rotation) when the particular season will recur. Sometimes, due to substitutability in consumption a change in price of some crop may influence the area under other crop/crops that follows the former in the same crop rotation. For example, an increase in price of aman rice/mustard may cause shift in area under boro rice/til, since, aman and boro rice are substitutable in consumption, as are mustard and til. But the preparation time and other facilities like, irrigation may limit the possibility of expansion. Moreover, if both boro rice and til were to expand simultaneously (as they are cultivated during the same season) a tussle between them would begin. It is also true that the impact of rising price in this case is not so prompt as that of decrease in price. This is because the cultivator can easily reduce area under any crop if he desires than when he wants to expand. However, the market forces (price and profitability) have the ultimate bearing on the changing *cropping pattern* in a region endowed with full flow of productive resources (push factors) and an well established market structure[12]. High relative price and so profitability[13] of any crop has the motive force that evokes the farmers to come forward to generate means for the growth of that crop. If price of opium soars high, farmers would take the risk of disobeying law and undertake its production in a clandestine fashion.

From the foregoing analysis it is clear that both the two types of factors have the potentiality to influence the *cropping pattern* of any region. They are interwoven in a well-knit system of agriculture through direct and indirect impulse on farmers' decision. But their motivation changes along with the development of the society. Spatial difference also matters in differential role of alternative factors in the determination of crop diversification in agriculture.

Existence of alternative opportunities however creates a conflict of allocation of land resources to alternative crops when there is limited availability of land. In the traditionally backward society, the farmers, specifically small and marginal farmers usually allot a major part of their land holding for the production of means for their self-use. With the development of marketing system or growing commecialisation, farmers increasingly switch over to some specific crops[14]. Production in this system is maintained mainly for earning profit. In this system of capitalist farming it is possible to collect the means of requirement from the market in exchange of money that had earlier been obtained in exchange of goods produced by the individual farmers. Most of the agricultural regions in West Bengal has already attained nearly a full-fledged multiple cropping system[15] and a cropping pattern movement has already set in, highly in favour of boro rice, potato, mustard and high yielding varieties of each crop[16].

7.2. Review of Some Former Studies

Attempts to examine the causes behind the cropping pattern change are not adequate. Most of the earlier studies designed to analyse the impact of different factors on the acreage growth under different crops, have recognised all types of factors, noted above. But many of them have put emphasis either on market forces (pull factors) or push factors in isolation. Relative prices are much recognised attracting force that plays a crucial role in the determination of acreage of different crops of any region. Mark Nerlove (1958) was the first man to provide a systematic analysis of price responsiveness of farmers in acreage allocation towards various crops[17]. Before him a few scattered studies were made to determine the supply response of farmers to price changes of certain crops in different areas. The prominent among them were those of J. D. Black (1924)[18], B. B. Smith (1925)[19], L. H. Bean (1929)[20], J. M. Cassels (1933)[21] and R. M. Walsh (1944)[22]. Most of those studies suggest that farmers respond very little to price variation in planning their acreage and output[23]. They have used simple statistical tools for their explanation. R. M. Walsh (1944) ran a series of regressions of cotton acreage in U.S.A. on (i) composite price of cotton and cottonseed; (ii) price of cotton and (iii) price of cottonseed lagged one year and deflated by an index of prices paid by the farmers[24]. He found the coefficient to be significantly larger for the period 1925-33 than that in 1910-24 and price of cottonseed appeared to be non-significant in acreage determination, while the price of cotton was. Walsh took the above index as an indicator of production cost although many of the items included in the index are consumption goods purchased by the farmers. Though he noted a close inverse relation between cotton and corn acreage growth between 1910 and 1933, he failed to find a significant coefficient for corn price lagged one year in his multiple regressions which include both cotton and corn prices.

In all those analyses of supply response to price, the use of acreage as an approximation of planned output may not be a good procedure. As both acreage and yield determine output, it can be approximated by acreage only if yield is expected to be constant. But it can not be a reasonable assumption because in the long run, technological change is very likely to cause an improvement in yield[25]. So expected yield should have also been taken into account, which was later considered by Nerlove. Moreover, prospective yield has some kind of motivating force, which would in the long run affect the acreage planning of farmers. Only a few of the earlier researchers have explicitly introduced prices of other crops in their estimation of acreage allocation among the competing crops. Long run shifts in acreage from one crop to another, for whatever reason, change the relative importance of different crops. As prices of crops, which compete for area, may play a relevant role in this inter-crop acreage shift, prices of competing crops could always be explicitly introduced in the explanation of acreage diversification.

In his pathbreaking analysis, Nerlove has explained the price responsiveness of farmers in terms of a *partial stock adjustment model* (a dynamic model) which later has been used by many agricultural economists in their explanation of *cropping pattern* change. He also used Hick's (1946) method of *cobweb* in the analysis of dynamic adjustment of acreage in the long run[26]. In his earlier approach he has distinguished between the actual and expected normal price[27]. Expected normal price was found to be more important factor in determining long run equilibrium acreage in contrast with the actual price level. Prices in his econometric approach were assumed to be independent data and farmers were the price takers and they adjust acreage distribution in response to the variation of prices and their expectations regarding future values. The farmers however, cannot adjust area allocation immediately. There is always a time lag between the price variation and the consequent adjustment measures taken by the farmers on their cropping decision. The extent of time lag for adjustment depends on the nature of the commodity and the *adjustment bottlenecks* (specificity of input bottlenecks) which again depends on the time needed to make up the lack in the input requirements. Thus he had introduced an *adjustment factor* in the same way as the *coefficient of expectation* introduced in his model[28]. In spite of all these, prices remained as the chief factors in his analysis of acreage growth under corn, cotton and wheat in U.S.A.

Dharm Narain (1965) in his pioneering work has observed that the shifts in *cropping pattern* are traceable to changes in the relative prices of crops, expansion of irrigation and changes in technology, all of which alter the relative profitability of crops in ways which affect different regions differently[29]. In his explanation of impact of price movements on areas under crops, he made a distinction between the *production for self-consumption* and *production for market*. Production for self-consumption in his system means the production of foodgrains and production of commercial crops indicates the production of non-food crops. He also made the hypothesis that proportion of area under commercial crops increases with the size of the land holding. This statement finds support from the argument that the small farmers allocate major portion of their holdings for the production of food crops to meet their own (family) consumption need while the large farmers could afford a large portion of their area for non-food crops. So a large farmer can be assumed to be more commercial minded than a smaller one because he has a larger surplus to sell. However, the proportion of area under cash crops, though increases do not increase sharply with the size of the holdings[30]. In his study rainfall, broadly weather, is found to have a leading role in determining the area to be allocated for growing foodgrains, whereas, the prices (market forces) are the leading determinants of area under commercial crops. Moreover, price relatively to weather becomes a feebler consideration when different food crops compete among themselves for area. Whereas, price acquires the prime consideration when foodgrains as a whole compete with the cash crops.

Most of the aforesaid studies, in order to explain the price responsiveness, have often used the deflated price of crops. Different analysts have used different indices for the adjustment of price[31]. In Walsh's study, it was the index of goods and services, which the farmer buys. Rationale of using this index derives from an effort to arrive at "real" price i.e., the *purchasing power* of the nominal price the farmer gets[32]. But the basket purchased by farmer contains the goods for his direct consumption as well as the inputs or implements for the production of commodities. If the portion of direct consumption goods constitute a very negligible part of total expenditure then the argument will have some relevance. This is because the portion of his purchase that goes to inputs and implements will affect the cost of cultivation and so when the price is deflated by the aforesaid index the changing cost is scraped out of the profit function. The influence of price of commodity he produces as well as yields remains the then only determining factor. On the other hand, if the consumption goods constitute a major part of the purchasing basket then a upward variation in price of those commodities will raise the cost of living and will force the farmer to exert more pressure on land for earning more (in that case also, if it is not possible to expand net or gross area under cultivation a substitution of land from lower value crops to higher value crops may take place). The adjustment of price by this index in that case results in wiping out the effect of changes in cost of living. This is most likely that, small farmers spend relatively more on goods for direct consumption whereas, the big one spends more on means for production. So the case would be different foı the two types of farmers.

Another argument which may be advanced against it is that, any rational farmer in a modern agricultural system always tries to maximise his net agricultural income from his limited holding, whatever be the expenditure on the goods he buys. Along with that, the general increase in price of his purchasing basket which contains both consumption goods as well as inputs would force him to strive to earn more (as the case noted above). He then may try to expand area under cultivation if possible or may take recourse to inter-crop acreage substitution. In fact, if the cultivator is purely commercial, it is the changing relationship between the prices or in principle the comparative profits of different crops that are likely to provide the stimulus to change in area under individual crops. Where relative profitability is involved, any correction for changes in costs, which is uniformly applied to different crops, is meaningless. Since the cost components of different crops are different and so the incidence of variations in constellation of factor prices on various crops will be different. So deflation of all prices by a general term can not be the right method. Thus, price of each competing crop should have a distinct adjustment factor, which are very difficult to calculate. Moreover, if the farmer compares relative price of competing crops in explaining the relative area allocation, then deflation of each price by a common denominator does not matter much.

Some of the former analysts have used the general index of wholesale prices to deflate the price, who seeks to remove the effects of forces which, influence prices in general, so that 'corrected' price may reveal changes specific to the particular item under study. The use of this general index of agricultural prices rests on the belief that a general decline in the prices obtainable for the several crops the farmer grows, or can grow, would not by itself induce him to contract his total sown area. A fall in his earning notwithstanding, he will endeavour to make the most of his resources by concentrating on crops which are relatively more profitable.

In the context of per unit prices one may consider cost per unit of output instead of cost per unit of area. But the former varies with every variation in yield and these variations can not be assumed to be too small. In the present analysis this will be considered by taking into account the proceeds per hectare (price times yield per hectare). This variable i.e., relative proceed is a pertinent indicator of relative profitability where relative changes in cost is not significant between crops. Then it can also be found out whether the farmer responds more to proceeds in preference to price.

The deflation of price by general index of agricultural prices also suffers from some kind of drawbacks. It is true that (as is appeared in Raj et al.) the prices, relevant to the farmer's sowing decisions are the prices of a crop relative to that of crops, which compete for area with it. All the agricultural crops cannot be directly competitive for area with any particular crop. Only the crops that can be grown during the same season (say mustard, wheat, rabi pulses etc.) will be competitive to any crop (say potato). So in case of deflating the price, one needs to consider the prices of those competitive crops. In practice, however, a difficulty arises from the fact that competing crops can not always be placed into well-demarcated groups and these groups do not form rigid categories. In this case Dharm Narain has prescribed for using the general index of agricultural prices[33]. The above argument is also not perfectly true, because the seasons of some crops grown successively are overlapping. So, due to the overlapping harvesting and sowing season, cultivation of any crop can affect the cost-benefit of its successor. In that way they can be partially competitive. This question will be considered in the latter part of this chapter also.

The choice of the above index also involves another kind of problem. Since price of the crop, which is to be rectified, is also involved in the general index of agricultural prices, a part of its own variation will be out of consideration. The crop which has greater weightage in the index will suffer relatively more than the others. Therefore, it is better to use explicitly the price of competing crops[34]. If the method is however, applied to a large area then number of competing crops may be very large and it would be very difficult to include the prices of all of them. In this case it would be wise to follow the same method in a small region where, the number of competing crops will be limited and it will not be very difficult to consider them in the analysis[35].

Another basic argument, which may be placed against Dharm Narain's division of food crop and commercial crop, is that no such accurate demarcation is possible. In a well-developed system of agriculture accompanied by a good market structure, crops may be grown on a commercial basis. Market can play an important role in the determination of acreage of competing crops. There may be a simultaneous relationship between acreage and price. Any crop, even food crop, can turn into commercial crop if it is produced mainly for earning money, in spite of the fact that food crops are essential for daily consumption. This is because; the migration of foodgrains from a surplus zone to deficient zone is always possible through the market. In a well-developed system, any crop can be obtained in exchange of others where, money plays an important role of medium of exchange.

Let us consider the other former analyses of crop diversification. According to Sarker (1988), "variations in acreage and output have significantly interacted with jute-paddy price ratio with a one period time lag in broad conformity with the cobweb model"[36]. Gulati (1994) has argued that the growth of oilseeds during the decade of eighties in India was due to policy induced increase in administered prices of major oilseeds relative to the other crops and hence its relative profitability[37].

Vyas (1996) has argued that the significant changes in cropping pattern in India could be explained in terms of a change in relative prices[38]. In post-mid-nineteen eighties, oilseeds in both kharif and rabi seasons as well as potato in rabi season and boro rice during summer have grown much faster at the expense of less profitable crops (coarse cereals) in several parts of the country. The high level of price responsiveness often leads to a great deal of disturbance and more so if the economy is an open economy, which is more susceptible to international price fluctuation than that in domestic price as evidenced by some previous studies (Nayyar and Sen, 1994)[39].

Price responsiveness is however one aspect of the impact of the market forces on the cropping pattern change. Equally important are the market infrastructure and the institutional arrangements. If the transport and communication system is weak and there exists problem of imperfect information, cropping pattern is bound to differ from what it ought be, since the precision of the expectation formed regarding future is contingent upon the appropriateness of the actual information available. The delivery system of inputs and credit are also other important factors in determining cropping pattern decisions of the farmers.

On the other hand, Narayanamoorthy (1997) argued that factors like irrigation facility, soil condition, price policies of the government, demand for agricultural commodities etc. together determine the crop diversification[40]. Singhal and Gauraha (1997) also, while explaining the crop diversity in Madhya Pradesh found that the factors responsible for crop diversification during 1979-80 to 1993-94 were mainly rainfall and irrigation[41]. Chemical fertiliser and number of tractors have not been found as determinants of crop diversification in most of the districts of Chhattisgarh Region in Madhya Pradesh. Singh, Rai and Karwasra (1997) have studied regional variations in agricultural performance in India and found irrigation and yield have substantial impact on acreage growth of different crops in West Bengal and other states[42].

S.D.Sawant (1997) has commented on the farmers' response to the policy induced improvements in the technologies and market environment for the commercial crops[43]. Simultaneously, he has expected the diversification to continue in favour of commercial crops in both the irrigated and rain-fed areas of the western, southern and central regions excluding Uttar Pradesh. This would happen even in the absence of further hikes in their relative prices provided, continuous upgradation of technology and significant improvements in their marketing conditions are guaranteed in these regions. Ramesh Chand (1996) has also explained the impact of infrastructural, institutional and socio-economic factors on crop diversification in western Himalayan Region of Himachal Pradesh.[44]. He found irrigation as the significant factor responsible for diversification. Bhalla and Singh (1996) also found factors, like variations in the level of infrastructure and technology as responsible for changing cropping pattern in West Bengal during 1962-65 to1992-95[45]. To quote Dhindsa and Sharma,

> The decisions of the cultivators in respect of allocation of resources to different crop enterprises feasible in a region are based on social, technological, institutional, ecological and economic factors. Impact of changes in these factors can be felt only when the existing cropping pattern undergoes a change[46].

7.3 A Brief View of Nature and Causes of Crop Diversification in West Bengal

The diversification of crop in West Bengal during 1970-71 to 1994-95 in terms of variation in composition of acreage allocation among the crops has been discussed elaborately in chapter-3. Here a brief review of the earlier discussion is presented for further proceeding. In West Bengal diversification of crop has during the post-Green Revolution period largely taken place in favour of boro rice, potato, oilseed as a whole (especially mustard) and marginally in favour of jute. Though in the early years of post-Green Revolution period, area had moved in favour of wheat, it later turned gradually from wheat to other rabi crops (say), potato and mustard (from table-3.1, 3.3 and 3.6). This can be attributed to the importance, attached to food crops' production in order to tackle the scarcity of food supply in the country (and state as well) in the immediate post-Green Revolution period[47]. But after having obtained self-sufficiency in foodgrains production, agriculture became increasingly commercialised. This fundamental change seems to have been possible primarily due to the drastic expansion of irrigation. The technological change that has taken place in the field of irrigation has a remarkable impact on productivity and cropping intensity growth. In most of the areas with good irrigation facility (where regular flow of water in and out of the field is properly maintained throughout the year) cropping pattern has become more diversified. This is clearly observed later (in chapter-8) from Table 8.2A and 8.2B that show the extent of growth of irrigation in different districts in conformity with the differential cropping pattern change.

The changing agro-climatic conditions and the technology available for various crops seem to be the other determinants of the nature and pace of crop diversification in West Bengal. Certain soils and water regimes are suitable only for certain type of crops. Similarly, some of the physical and geographical characteristics (e.g., drainage condition, elevation and slopes) as well as climatic factors (e.g., rainfall and its distribution over time and space in a year, maximum and minimum temperature, humidity, intensity of sunlight etc.) are the other factors that bring spatial differences in cropping pattern. However, it is very difficult to incorporate all of them into an econometric framework due to non-availability or nature of data (some are not available and some are not systematically available).

In spite of several impediments, sometimes efforts are made to adjust or modify these natural and physical conditions with appropriate technology (that has been mentioned earlier) to introduce a new cropping pattern favouring some crops, when the cultivators are dictated by attractive price and profitability (in anticipation, if they are successful) of those crops coupled with proper information. Sometimes these efforts are however found to be quite infructuous and economically non-viable. In a few circumstances the endeavours become successful. For example, the evolution of rice varieties with shorter gestation period has enabled the farmers to grow rice even in the semi-arid region (regular water supply is essential for paddy crop), even in the critical summer time. Moreover, the emergence of seeds, which have more drought resistance power, pest resistance capacity etc., has converted the situation more advantageous to some crops. In West Bengal, technological changes of this nature have mostly led to more specification and concentration rather than diversification, and this is vindicated when we notice remarkable growth of some specific crops. Not only that, different varieties of each crop have been arriving in the field. But it is very difficult to isolate the high yielding varieties involved with (say) aus, aman etc.

from the secondary data available from several sources, as they are not furnished separately at the district level and for all crops. A first hand survey at micro level would explain the matter in a much better fashion.

7.4 Econometric Analysis of Acreage Growth of Boro rice, Potato and Oilseed

7.4.1. Regression method

In this section impact of major factors like, irrigation, rainfall, chemical fertiliser, yield and price etc. on the acreage change of some crops that have witnessed a significant growth will be explained in terms of multiplicative regression analysis. The three crops/crop group boro rice, potato and oilseed (especially mustard) have been considered only because of the burgeoning growth of these crops relatively to the others in the cropping scenario of West Bengal throughout the entire period except a few sudden disorder. Before going into the details of *modus operandi* some important points (related to our discussion) should be noted.

(i) During the earlier part of the period under consideration, many plots used to remain unploughed throughout the year, especially during off-monsoon seasons[48]. The advance of technology in different fields has enabled the cultivators to expand their net area under cultivation not only in a particular season but also in all the seasons of the year[49]. Areas under the major crops have changed not only due to substitution of other crops but also due to the expansion of cultivation to areas where formerly, hardly any crop was grown. Favourable climate, particularly, rainfall in the pre-sown time, facility of irrigation, availability of chemical fertiliser and development of new implements seem to have enhanced the expansion possibility from time to time. In the early periods, irrigation was mainly maintained in the aman season. Much of it was supplemental irrigation, used to insure against breaks in the monsoon[50]. Very limited irrigation was available during dry season when irrigation was essential. So development in the field of irrigation no doubt strengthened the cultivation of dry season crops.

(ii) Another point to reckon with is that, many plots in the early years used to remain under water and were not cultivable in the rainy season. But the development of water control measures (flood control) converted them to cropable during rainy season also.

(iii) Another important point is that, any crop may gain in area due to substitution in one place and may lose area to other crops in another place simultaneously. The possibility of this kind of change is more likely when one considers a large area like, West Bengal. In this case it is better to pursue the analysis for a smaller area, like a district. But the possibility of occurrence of the aforesaid problem can not be completely ruled out.

(iv) Yield of crops especially, the expected yields have an important role where crops compete among themselves for a particular plot. But due to agro-climatic reason, absolute and relative yields of crops differ across the region and the same land behaves differently for different crops. Moreover, inter-crop competition for area changes across the region as well as from year to year. So it is very difficult to have a particular set of crops which are competitive to some other crop or set of crops in all circumstances. In a large area number of crops compete for area with a crop is very large and thus it is very difficult to manage all of them. Number of competitive crops will be limited and manageable, if the analysis covers a small region. The minimum area for which comprehensive data on major variables are available is a district. So the regression analysis is performed for the district of Burdwan, which is reckoned with as a good agricultural district called the granary of West Bengal.

First of all, the impact of factors like irrigation, rainfall, chemical fertiliser and yield on the acreage growth of crops, which have witnessed a significant growth during the post-Green Revolution period, will be considered[51]. Later, the price factor will also be included to trace the motivational influence of price on acreage growth.

Now the identification of yield, which is to be taken into account for the regression analysis, involves a problem. Nerlove has considered the expected yield, which is approximated in advance of undertaking the production process[52]. It however depends on the capability of farmers to adjust with the uncertain behaviour and uneven oscillation of yields due to the vagaries of nature. The process is not so simple as there is plot to plot and temporal variation of yields, which merit consideration. It therefore seems meaningless to consider it in the absence of a basis for expecting a common tendency in the behaviour of per hectare yields of different crops[53]. Dharm Narain also recognised the matter and finally adopted the actual yields.

However, the farmers in each region are found to have a common tendency to use the inputs in a more or less balanced proportion, which is expected to yield maximum (for that technology) per unit of land. Sometimes different groups are found in each cluster of farmers to use inputs in different proportion, though the proportion remains same within each group and so a common expectation of yield within each group is formed though it differs from region to region due to agro-climatic variations. Data on yield of crops for each district available from statistical abstracts represent the average yield of the district and may be assumed to reflect the average of expected yield of all the cultivators of the district[54]. The value however changes over time with the process of development and accordingly there is a revision of expectation. In the present study therefore, actual yield of the region is explicitly introduced in the regression analysis.

For the purpose of analysis, equations of the form

$$Ln\ A_{it} = b_0 + b_1 LnR_t + b_2 LnI_t + b_3 LnC_t + b_4 LnY_{it} + U_{0t} \quad (1)$$

have been fitted; where A_i represents acreage of ith crop in different years, R is the level of rainfall measured in millimetre, I is the area under irrigation, C represents consumption of chemical fartiliser, y, the yield of the particular crop. b_js are the elasticities of acreage growth with respect to jth explanatory variable and U_{0i} is the conventional random disturbance term. A dummy variable will also be introduced to represent the effect of land reform measures undertaken by the government of West Bengal. Then, the stochastic form will be

$$Ln\ A_{it} = b_0 + b_1 LnR_t + b_2 LnI_t + b_3 LnC_t + b_4 LnY_{it} + b_5 D_t + U_{1t} \quad (2)$$

Where, D takes value 0 in a pre-land reform year and 1 in the post-land reform years started with 1979[55]. Here the inception of land reform year is supposed to coincide with the time when collection and distribution of vested land to the landless people started in West Bengal[56]. The constant term is supposed to reflect a joint influence of high yielding seeds, mechanisation etc., which have not been explicitly introduced. These have not been included because of non-availability of complete series of data and to avoid the complexity involved with the regression.

A question may arise regarding the use of rainfall, irrigation, chemical fertiliser and yield simultaneously in the regression equation, which often seem to be closely related. It is really difficult to form a consistent model in this type of analysis in agriculture. True, there is a complementarity between the use of chemical fertiliser and the level of irrigation and the two along with rainfall can impress the yield level. So there is a problem of multicollinearity; though the relationship is not a perfect one as yield also depends on some other factors like, variety of seed, weather conditions etc. (the multiple correlation coefficient of yield of each of potato, boro rice or mustard and rainfall, irrigation, chemical fertiliser is not one) which are not included here. The specification of relationship among the explanatory variables is a very difficult one. Moreover, dropping of any one of these variables may lead to specification bias. Hence imperfect multicollinearity is tolerated in the regression analysis to explain the variation in acreage caused by the aforesaid explanatory variables.

The regression is performed on the data collected for the district of Burdwan and then inferences are drawn on other districts or regions on the basis of the results obtained in this particular case. The regression is run on a shifting basis. First of all, one explanatory variable is introduced. Then, number of explanatory variables is increased to observe the change in explained variation of acreage growth under crop after the introduction of additional explanatory variables and the significance of the coefficient is examined. The estimated equations fitted are presented below:[57]

<u>For area under boro rice (A_b):</u>

1. $\text{Ln } A_b = -20.73 + 4.427 \text{ LnI*}, \quad \underline{R^2 = 0.566}$

   (0.826)

2. $\text{Ln } A_b = 0.72 + 0.454 \text{ LnY}_b, \quad \underline{R^2 = 0.0112}$

   (0.91)

3. $\text{Ln } A_b = -21.55 + 0.244 \text{ LnR} + 4.27 \text{ LnI*}, \quad \underline{R^2 = 0.584}$

   $(0.256) \quad (0.845)$

4. $\text{Ln } A_b = -20.2 + 3.70 \text{ LnI*} + 0.34 \text{ LnC*}, \quad \underline{R^2 = 0.765}$

   $(0.646) \quad (0.08)$

5. $\text{Ln } A_b = -20.23 + 0.012 \text{ LnR} + 3.7 \text{ LnI*} + 0.338 \text{ LnC**}, \quad \underline{R^2 = 0.765}$

   $(0.206) \quad (0.667) \quad (0.086)$

6. $\text{Ln } A_b = -25.54 + 3.703 \text{ LnI*} + 0.348 \text{ LnC*} + 0.661 \text{ LnY}_b\text{**}, \quad \underline{R^2 = 0.79}$

   $(0.628) \quad (0.0786) \quad (0.44)$

7. $\text{Ln } A_b = -25.58 - .0606 \text{ LnR} + 3.727 \text{ LnI*} + .3556 \text{ LnC**} + .694 \text{ LnY}_b,$

   $(.206) \quad (.648) \quad (.085) \quad (.468)$

   $\underline{R^2 = 0.79}$

8. $Ln\ A_b = -16.52 - .274\ LnR + 4.007\ LnI^{*} + .438\ LnC^{*} + .72\ LnY_b + 1.163\ D^{**}$
(.2527) (.839) (.194) (.335) (.67),
$R^2 = 0.816$

For area under potato (A_p):

9. $Ln\ A_p = -3.59 + 1.21\ Ln\ I^{***}$, $R^2 = 0.098$
(.78)

10. $Ln\ A_p = -1.54 + .455\ LnC^{*}$, $R^2 = 0.89$
(.034)

11. $Ln\ A_p = -6.61 + 1.19\ LnY_p^{*}$, $R^2 = 0.685$
(.172)

12. $Ln\ A_p = -2.89 + .254\ LnI + .447\ LnC^{*}$, $R^2 = 0.893$
(.287) (.0358)

13. $Ln\ A_p = -3.45 + .3823\ LnC + .269\ LnY_p^{**}$, $R^2 = .9007$
(.0566) (.169)

14. $Ln\ A_p = -6.696 + .473\ LnI^{**} + .338\ LnC^{*} + .372\ LnY_p^{*}$, $R^2 = .915$
(.284) (.06) (.173)

15. $Ln\ A_p = -5.82 - .1358\ LnR^{**} + .504\ LnI^{**} + .366\ LnC^{*} + .334\ LnY_p^{*}$,
(.0795) (.272) (.0599) (.167)
$R^2 = .924$

16. $Ln\ A_p = -5.6 - .114\ LnR + .336\ LnI + .427\ LnC^{*} + .333\ LnY_p^{*} - .0914\ D$,
(.084) (.34) (.095) (.169) (.1096)
$R^2 = .927$

For area under oilseeds (A_o):

17. $Ln\ A_o = 4.89 + 1.424\ LnI$, $R^2 = 0.014$
(2.55)

18. $Ln\ A_o = -14.71 + .276\ LnY_o$, $R^2 = 0.723$
(.364)

19. $Ln\ A_o = -11.7 + 1.4114\ LnC^{*}$, $R^2 = 0.881$
(.1104)

20. $Ln\ A_o = -2.57 - 1.72 LnI + 1.47\ LnC^{*}$, $R^2 = 0.90$
(.862) (.1075)

21. $\text{Ln } A_o = -13.7 + 1.106 \text{ LnC}^* + .804 \text{ LnY}_o^*,$ $\quad \underline{R^2 = 0.902}$

(.179) (.387)

22. $\text{Ln } A_o = -8.61 + 1.101 \text{ LnR} + .704 \text{ LnI},$ $\quad \underline{R^2 = 0.101}$

(0.77) (2.54)

23. $\text{Ln } A_o = -13.4 - 1.29 \text{ LnI}^{**} + 1.176 \text{ LnC}^* + 1.707 \text{ LnY}_o^*,$ $\quad \underline{R^2 = 0.949}$

(0.81) (.1766) (.369)

24. $\text{Ln } A_o = -15.38 + .298 \text{ LnR} - 1.323 \text{ LnI}^{**} + 1.06 \text{ LnC}^* + 1.89 \text{ LnY}_o^*,$

(.273) (.814) (.2023) (.405)

$\underline{R^2 = 0.952}$

25. $\text{Ln } A_o = -9.845 + .058 \text{ LnR} + 1.072 \text{ D}^* + .464 \text{ LnI} + .418 \cdot \text{LnC}^* + .757 \text{ LnY}_o^*$

(.213) (.253) (.753) (.215) (.3006),

$\underline{R^2 = 0.9603}$

<u>Considering the specific case of area under mustard (A_m):</u>

26. $\text{Ln } A_m = 6.335 - .671 \text{ LnI},$ $\quad \underline{R^2 = 0.0021}$

(3.09)

27. $\text{Ln } A_m = -11.72 + 1.354 \text{ LnC}^*,$ $\quad \underline{R^2 = 0.56}$

(.2567)

28. $\text{Ln } A_m = -11.36 + 2.161 \text{ LnY}_m^*,$ $\quad \underline{R^2 = 0.6363}$

(.3479)

29. $\text{Ln } A_m = -12.8 + 0.53 \text{ LnC}^{***} + 1.52 \text{ LnY}_m^*,$ $\quad \underline{R^2 = 0.67}$

(.392) (.586)

30. $\text{Ln } A_m = 8.67 - 3.84 \text{ LnI}^{***} + 1.48 \text{ LnC}^*,$ $\quad \underline{R^2 = 0.623}$

(2.02) (.252)

31. $\text{Ln } A_m = -7.07 + 0.447 \text{ LnR} - 4.018 \text{ LnI}^{**} + 1.428 \text{ LnC}^*,$ $\quad \underline{R^2 = 0.633}$

(.635) (2.0576) (.266)

32. $\text{Ln } A_m = 3.313 - 3.011 \text{ LnI} + .725 \text{ LnC}^{**} + 1.34 \text{ LnY}_m^*,$ $\quad \underline{R^2 = 0.704}$

(1.87) (.397) (0.57)

33. $\text{Ln } A_m = 2.712 + .2114 \text{ LnR} - 3.12 \text{ LnI}^{***} + .722 \text{ LnC}^{**} + 1.301 \text{ LnY}_m^*$

(.593) (1.934) (.406) (.598)

$\underline{R^2 = 0.706}$

34. $\text{Ln } A_m = 2.311 + .426 \text{ D} + .1402 \text{ LnR} - 2.456 \text{ LnI} + .532 \text{ LnC} + 1.13 \text{ LnY}_m$

(.98) (.628) (2.5) (.6031) (.73)

$\underline{R^2 = 0.709}$

From the above estimates it has been observed that, irrigation and chemical fertiliser have substantial positive impact on the acreage growth of boro rice. Chemical fertiliser and yield growth has led to acceleration in acreage of potato and oilseeds, especially mustard. In case of boro rice, yield and dummy variable (that represents the influence of land reform measures) coefficients are also found to be positive and significant but not to the extent as that of irrigation and chemical fertiliser[58]. Irrigation is the leading determinant (input) in case of boro rice because it is grown in summer time and regular water supply is essential for rice cultivation. Formerly, tanks and canals were the principal sources of irrigation and the capacity was at a very low level. The system was primarily maintained to ensure water during aman season when much of the capacity was used as supplementary irrigation, insuring against breaks in the monsoon. The growth of irrigation infrastructure here is associated with a shift in the composition of dry season crops, particularly with a rising share of area under boro rice.

But the effect of irrigation is not seen to be much stronger in case of potato, oilseeds and even negative in case of mustard. The actual situation is however not like so. The reason is that, potato and mustard are winter crops and during winter one can not depend on rainfall. Thus irrigation is essential. What happened actually is that, here area under canal irrigation (provided by government canals) has been considered from which still now, hardly a few places in West Bengal get irrigation during winter. The major part of areas in winter and summer have been covered by minor irrigation dominated by shallow tube-well, deep tube-well, submersible pumps, tanks etc. owned mainly by private people along with a few under government ownership. With the expansion of sphere of these sources cultivation of potato, mustard has increased especially after 1982-83. But continuous data on these sources are not available and so they are not included in the list of explanatory variables of present discussion (mentioned earlier). If they had been included, the coefficients would most likely have been strengthened. In the next chapter, whatever data are available will be utilised to show the spatial variation of cultivation of those crops in relation to the growth of these sources of irrigation. Again coefficient of irrigation displays a noticeable change after the addition of other variables say, chemical fertiliser, yield and even rainfall. Equation 20, 23 and 24 (in case of oilseed) show that the coefficient turned from positive to negative. This is particularly due to the nature of relationship among the explanatory variables, which is later exposed in terms of a two-way correlation table.

Though coefficient of dummy variable is significantly positive in case of oilseed as a whole, it is insignificant in case of mustard and even negative in case of potato. The low value and dubious fluctuation of coefficient would raise question about the efficiency of land reform measures in mobilising lands from other uses to these crops[59]. The distribution of vested land to the landless peasants and measures to protect occupancy right of sharecroppers through operation barga, have yielded ambiguous results in different parts as is evident from several studies[60]. There is much doubt about the contribution of the beneficiaries to the process of undergoing diversification. Most of the evaluation studies are conducted on the basis of the performances of the beneficiaries of the programmes. The diversification is actually associated with the spread of new technology and adoption of new technology by the beneficiaries is mainly dependent upon their financial strength[61]. But the government support measures are not adequate (Raychaudhuri and Sen, 1996)[62] and the channels through which the government helps are distributed are not so reliable. However, the beneficiaries may have benefited in different ways from substantial changes that have occurred in different fields of technology (especially irrigation) and inputs' market which push them forward to cultivate those crops. But, just by looking at the performances of the beneficiaries one can not single out the impact of land reforms because the improvement in this respect may be the result of advancement of other things. A comparison should be made between the cropping pattern change on the farms under the beneficiaries and of the same category (small and marginal) non-beneficiaries to ascertain the efficiency of land reform measures.

On the other hand, it is however true that the development of agriculture in certain cases is associated with a decline in sharecropping (Bardhan, 1976; Bardhan and Rudra, 1977)[63]. The fact is that the relationship between bargadars and jotedars or big land- owners has deteriorated and the latter are no longer ready to co-operate with the former in a friendly way[64]. The rural landowners are constantly under a threat of having their land forfeited, if it is not cultivated or leased out to sharecroppers. Hence the landowners take the initiative on their own to protect their properties as well as raise their resources. The big landholders are more commercials minded and thus can adopt the new technology for the cultivation of those newly emerging commercial crops. The growth-oriented change in cropping pattern in West Bengal (especially in Burdwan) thus may be largely due to major shift in irrigation rather than land reform measures[65]. However, the programme would have accelerated the process of diversification more than what it had done if the beneficiaries were extended full support from all sides of the society.

In no case rainfall shows significant effect on the variation of acreage. This may be due to the fact that the data used here relates to rainfall of the whole year, which is not evenly distributed over throughout the year. For the sowing of any crop quantity of rainfall in the pre-sowing period is most effective. If rainfall were very scanty in the germination period then cultivation would be adversely affected. Sowing of crop does not appear to be difficult in the area where irrigation is available but if rain disappears for a long time, then productivity and production will be greatly affected. This is because; maintenance of irrigation then becomes very difficult, as it is partly dependent on rainfall. Rainfall of any season can highly influence the irrigation capacity of the next season. Too much rainfall in the pre-sowing time may also adversely affect the area of cultivation of a crop.

*7.4.2. **Introduction of Price Factor***

In the above analysis it is observed that, major part of variation or growth of acreage under boro rice, potato and oilseed, especially mustard has been explained by irrigation (broadly water control), chemical fertiliser and yield. But a part of the total variation, still remain unexplained. In reality, expansion of irrigation capacity and availability as well as use of chemical fertiliser has led to the expansion of cultivation to the erstwhile uncultivated land and at the same time has accelerated the substitution of land from less profitable use to a high profitable one. In addition to the aforesaid factors, prices of the crops and their substitutes (in the sense that they can be grown on the same plot at the cost of the formers) may have some kind of influence on acreage allocation for the production of those crops. In the earlier regression analysis, yield of any crop has been considered as one of the decisive factors of area allocation under that crop. However, yield of the competitive crops would also affect the acreage under any crop. In this section, influence of prices of crops in acreage determination will be analysed. Alongside the yield of competitive crops will also be taken into account.

Price of any crop is expected to be positively correlated with its own area. Now the question arises: what is the pertinent price of a crop, the variation of which we expect to be positively correlated with those of its area? As earlier, it merits mention that the price relevant to the acreage allocation decision of the farmer usually supposed to be the expected price and not the actual current price. However in the model for the sake of simplicity we substitute the unknown observations (expected prices) with the actual observations (actual prices). But now, another question arises as to the identification of the actual price that helps the formation of expectation and the expected duration of lag between the change in price and the change in area.

There is usually observed considerable lag between the decision in respect of utilisation of land and the fruition of that decision into output, due to the particular nature of agricultural production process. In principle, the price, which motivates production decision, should neither be the price at the beginning of the production process (just prior to the sowing time) nor should it be the price at the end. The former does not determine profits as it generally undergoes changes during the process. Even if the price variation that has occurred just before the sowing decision of the farmer, is assumed to remain unaltered, he can hardly take it into account as there may not be available sufficient time for the preparation of land which can be reallocated to suitable remunerative combinations. Price at the end of the period is unborn when production is initiated. Nerlove has used a series of past prices with weights declining over time in his lag adjustment model from which the acreage variation is estimated. In practice however the immediate previous results are believed usually to play a predominant role in determining expectations[66] and farmers even in advanced countries have found to respond to actual prices. Thus the use of these latter "although not strictly in accord with the theoretical definition of supply price, ought in fact to yield results that are nonetheless significant"[67]. Nerlove's method though more scientific and consistent, can not be applied here primarily since the channels through which price information is disseminated are not so well developed in the countryside of a developing economy like West Bengal as in advanced countries[68]. Moreover, Nerlove has explained acreage variation with an emphasis on the substitution between competing crops which is more appropriate in a situation of pure commercial structure and where there is no slack in the system of agricultural production or production conditions remain unchanged. In the present case area under any crop has been changing significantly due to substitution as well as expansion of total area under cultivation and there are several sorts of changes (cost of production, market structure, government policies) which ought to be taken into account for the adjustment of prices. However, it is very difficult to take care of all of them as they are subject to continuous change. In addition to that, farmers in most of the regions are mostly influenced by the pioneering role of a few innovators, who take the risk of introducing a new technology in the production of crops. Sometimes a few farmers are forced to withdraw their decisions of cultivating some crops because of non-matching decisions by their neighbours, which would otherwise create several problems (problem of harvest, transportation and marketing etc.). Interaction with some cultivators in Burdwan suggests that most of them hardly bother to consider the prices of a few previous years (even that of past two years). Changes in prices also depends on the other uncertain features, like government policies on export, import, support prices all of which may change during the gestation period and hence it is very difficult to form expectation in advance. Under these circumstances it seems pertinent to use the prices of crops of the preceding year. In addition to that, yield of substitute crops should be included along with the yield of the crop under consideration as they also have an impact on the allocative decision of the farmer.

In view of the above arguments, prices of the crop itself, that of other relevant crops lagged one year and yield of the competitive crops are introduced in the present extended version of the former model. For the discussion three extended versions of the stochastic form are considered here. These are:

$$\text{Ln } A_{it} = a_0 + a_1 \text{LnR}_t + a_2 \text{LnI}_t + a_3 \text{LnC}_t + a_4 \text{LnY}_{it} + a_5 \text{LnP}_{i-1} + a_6 \text{LnY}_{jt} + a_7 \text{Ln } P_{j-1} + a_8 D_t + U_{2t} \quad (3)$$

$$\text{Ln } A_{it} = a_0 + a_1 \text{LnR}_t + a_2 \text{LnI}_t + a_3 \text{LnC}_t + a_4 \text{LnT}_{it} + a_5 \text{LnT}_{jt} + a_6 D_t + U_{3t} \quad (4)$$

$$\text{Ln } A_{it} = a_0 + a_1 \text{LnR}_t + a_2 \text{LnI}_t + a_3 \text{LnC}_t + a_4 \text{Ln } (P_{i-1} Y_{it} / P_{j-1} Y_{jt}) + a_6 D_t + U_{4t} \quad (5)$$

Here P_{i-1} and P_{j-1} represent respectively price of ith crop and j[th] crop lagged one year. Suffix j is used to denote the crop or crops that can be grown during the same season on the same field on which i[th] crop is cultivated, U_i s are the random disturbance terms. a_6 and a_7 in equation-3 are the cross yield and price elasticities of area under i[th] crop with respect to yield and price of jth crop. Similarly $T_i = (P_{i-1}.Y_i)$ and $T_j = (P_{j-1}.Y_j)$ are the proceeds per hectare of ith and j[th] crop evaluated at the previous year's prices. a_4 and a_5 in equation-4 represent direct and cross elasticities of area under i[th] crop with respect to proceeds per hectare of ith and j[th] crop respectively. Equation-5 where proceeds in ratio form are included is considered on the presumption that, farmers would still continue to produce i^{th} crop if relative revenue is increased, irrespective of the direction of price movement. This is done to know whether the cultivators are much concerned with the relative revenue of crop, irrespective of the cost. It is however true that; variation in yield is associated with a change in cost per unit of area. The implicit assumption is that the cost of production per unit of area either has not changed or even if it has happened, had affected all the crops in a similar fashion or the farmers had taken it at a discount.

Major competitor of boro rice in Burdwan is til. But the data on price and yield of til are not available for a major part of the period. Though price could be substituted by the price of its substitutes in use (consumption) say, mustard, the method can hardly be applied for yield. Hence it is kept out of consideration. On the other hand potato, mustard and wheat are the principal competitors during rabi season in the district. So price and yield of all of them are taken into consideration in the regression analysis for area under any one of them. Relative area of any two competitive crops can also be expressed as function of only relative price in order to fit a cobweb type of equation. The results of the regression conducted in these extended forms are presented below.

<u>For boro rice</u>:

At first considering only price as explanatory variable, we get

35. $Ln\ A_b = .454 + \underset{(.149)}{.695}\ LnP_{b-1}{}^{*}$, $\underline{R^2 = 0.50}$

Including yield along with price, we get

36. $Ln\ A_b = -5.37 + \underset{(.149)}{0.71}\ LnP_{b-1}{}^{*} + \underset{(0.65)}{.724}\ LnY_b$, $\underline{R^2 = 0.525}$

Considering gross remuneration (T_b) as explanatory variable,

37. $Ln\ A_b = -5.264 + \underset{(.144)}{0.71}\ LnT_b{}^{*}$, $\underline{R^2 = 0.525}$

Regressing on all the explanatory variables we get,

38. $Ln\ A_b = -24.44 + \underset{(.27)}{.156}\ LnR + \underset{(.99)}{3.53}\ LnI^{*} + \underset{(.674)}{.714}\ LnY_b$
$+ \underset{(.26)}{.68}\ LnP_{b-1}{}^{*} - \underset{(.274)}{.17}\ LnC + \underset{(.403)}{.067}\ D$, $\underline{R^2 = 0.856}$

Excluding dummy variable,

39. $Ln\ A_b = -23.57 + \underset{(.1945)}{.186}\ LnR + \underset{(.562)}{3.39}\ LnI^{*} + \underset{(.397)}{.625}\ LnY_b{}^{**}$

$+ .693\ LnP_{b-1}^{*} - .138\ LnC$
(0.24) (.185), $\underline{R^2 = .856}$

Eliminating rainfall again,

40. $Ln\ A_b = -23.98 + 3.501\ LnI^{*} + .716\ LnY_b^{**} + .593\ LnP_{b-1}^{*} - .047\ LnC$
(0.55) (.384) (.215)
(.159), $\underline{R^2 = 0.85}$

Taking $P_{b-1}.Y_b = T_b$ as a single variable (expected proceed per hectare, evaluated at the previous year's price) we received,

41. $Ln\ A_b = -23.99 + .174\ LnR + 3.41\ LnI^{*} + 6.74\ LnT_b^{*} - .123\ LnC,$
(.172) (.542) (.194)
(.15)

In case of potato the new forms are

42. $Ln\ A_p = 1.102 + .481\ LnP_{p-1}^{*},\quad \underline{R^2 = .444}$
(.115)

Including yield along with price, we get

43. $Ln\ A_p = -7.53 + 0.278\ LnP_{p-1}^{*} + .956\ LnY_p^{*},\quad \underline{R^2 = .807}$
(.076) (0.152)

44. $Ln\ A_p = -3.48 + 0.466\ LnT_p^{*},\quad \underline{R^2 = .698}$
(.065)

Considering all observations :

45. $Ln\ A_p = -6.093 - 0.114\ LnR + .208\ LnI + .427\ LnC^{*} + .003\ LnP_{p-1} + .355\ LnY_p^{***}$
(.094) (.355) (.129)
(.097) (.213)
$- .019\ LnP_{m-1} + .205\ LnY_m - .006\ LnP_{w-1} - .0123\ LnY_w - .244\ D_t$
(.109) (0.11) (.117) (.157)
(.137), $\underline{R^2 = 0.94}$

Excluding chemical fertiliser and dummy variable:

46. $Ln\ A_p = -8.935 - .129\ LnR + .82\ LnI^{*} + .083\ LnP_{p-1} + .671\ LnY_p^{*} + .1077\ LnP_{m-1}$
(.111) (.347) (.1196)
(.2376) (.1209)
$+ .2176\ LnY_m^{**} - .0214\ LnP_{w-1} + .0702\ LnY_w$
(.1009) (.1469) (.1904), $\underline{R^2 = 0.914}$

47. $Ln\ A_p = -6.89 + .54\ LnI^{***} + .303\ LnC^{*} + .0073\ LnP_{p-1} +$
(1.65) (.1356) (.108)
$.4187\ LnY_p^{**} - .015\ LnP_{m-1}$
(.2427) (.1237)
$+ .0688\ LnY_m - .0294\ LnP_{w-1} - .069\ LnY_w$
(.1028) (.1328) (.166), $\underline{R^2 = 0.919}$

48. $Ln\ A_p = -8.768 + .767\ LnI^{*} + .055\ LnP_{p-1} + .673\ LnY_p^{*}$
(.348) (.1183) (.24)
$+ .1155\ LnP_{m-1} + .1874\ LnY_m^{**}$
(.1155) (.098)
$-.016\ LnP_{w-1} - .1424\ LnY_w$
(.1484) (.1817), $\underline{R^2} = \underline{.892}$

Considering only I, P_{p-1} and Y_p as explanatory variables:

49. $Ln\ A_p = -12.06 + 0.77\ LnI^{*} + 0.22\ LnP_{p-1}^{*} + 1.003\ LnY_p^{*}$
(.373) (.007) (.143),
$\underline{R^2} = \underline{0.84}$

Including C to it gives

50. $Ln\ A_p = -6.63 + 0.477\ LnI^{***} + 0.35\ LnC^{*} - 0.0146\ LnP_{p-1}$
(.0292) (.0881) (.0827)
$+ 0.358\ LnY_p^{**}$
(.1956) $\underline{R^2} = \underline{.916}$

51. $Ln\ A_p = -1.813 - .121\ LnR + .087\ LnI + .493\ LnC^{*} - .0284\ LnT_p$
(.097) (.378) (.130) (.0916)
$+ .081\ LnT_m - .02 LnT_w - .159\ D_t,$
(.1038) (.084) (.1447) $\underline{R^2} = \underline{.916}$

52. $Ln\ A_p = -1.58 + .105\ LnT_p + .24\ LnT_m^{*} + .0266\ LnT_w$
(.1306) (.072) (.111) $\underline{R^2} = \underline{.808}$

53. $Ln\ A_p = -2.216 - .157\ LnR + .338\ LnI + .446\ LnC^{*}$
(.0888) (.294) (.0625)
$- .026\ Ln\ (T_p/T_m) + .013\ Ln\ (T_p/T_w)$
(.069) (.074), $\underline{R^2} = \underline{.909}$

54. $Ln\ A_p = -2.78 + .278\ LnI + .428\ LnC^{*} - .027\ Ln\ (T_p/T_m)$
(.3077) (.065) (.0726)
$+ .0097\ Ln\ (T_p/T_w)$
(.0779), $\underline{R^2} = \underline{.893}$

55. $Ln\ A_p = 3.53 - .377\ Ln\ (T_p/T_m)^{*} + .294\ Ln\ (T_p/T_w)$
(.092) (.123), $\underline{R^2} = \underline{.6002}$

In case of mustard taking price or price and yield of crops as explanatory variables we get,

55. $Ln\ A_p = 3.53 - .377\ Ln\ (T_p/T_m)^* + .294\ Ln\ (T_p/T_w)$
(.092) (.123), $R^2 = .6002$

In case of mustard taking price or price and yield of crops as explanatory variables we get,

56. $Ln\ A_m = -5.64 + 1.378\ LnP_{m-1}^*$
(.336), $R^2 = .433$

57 $Ln\ A_m = -11.47 + 0.44\ LnP_{m-1} + 1.77\ LnY_m^*$
(.366) (.472), $R^2 = .66$

58. $Ln\ A_m = -9.89 + 1.004\ LnT_m^*$
(0.17), $R^2 = .612$

Considering R, I, C, P_{m-1} and Y_m

59. $Ln\ A_m = 2.8 + .216\ LnR - 3.11\ LnI + 0.66\ LnC$
(.66) (1.99) (.738)
$+ .0682\ LnP_{m-1} + 1.32\ LnY_m^*$
(.668) (.63), $R^2 = .71$

60. $Ln\ A_m = -12.94 + .07\ LnR + .426\ LnC + .11\ LnP_{m-1}$
(.626) (0.75) (.692)
$+ 1.53\ LnY_m^*$
(.638), $R^2 = .666$

Considering the price and yield of competitive (potato and wheat) crops it gives

61. $Ln\ A_m = 3.174 - .295\ LnR - 2.72\ LnI + .809\ LnC$
(.77) (2.9) (1.054)
$+ .668\ LnP_{p-1} - .689\ LnY_p$
(.796) (1.74)
$-.251\ Ln\ P_{m-1} + .936\ LnY_m^* - .263\ LnP_{w-1} + 1.128\ LnY_w$
(.892) (.896) (.956) (1.28)
$+ .752\ D_t$
(1.12), $R^2 = .748$

The modified form is,

62. $Ln\ A_m = 6.01 + .386\ LnR - 3.53\ LnI + .437\ LnC + .738\ LnT_m$
(.6216) (2.039) (.749) (.523),
$R^2 = .667$

63. $Ln\ A_m = 4.98 + .178\ LnR - 2.1\ LnI + .118\ LnC + .397\ LnT_p$
(.697) (2.712) (.93) (.744)
$+ .422\ LnT_m - .361\ LnT_w + .91\ D_t$
(.657) (.601) (1.037), $R^2 = 0.69$

66. $\text{Ln } A_m = 3.345 + .196 \text{ Ln } (T_m/T_p) + 1.119 \text{ Ln } (T_m/T_w)^*$
$$(.696) \qquad (.49), \qquad \underline{R^2 = 0.55}$$

It is evident from the above estimated equations that the farmers are highly influenced by last year's price of the crop which is to be chosen for cultivation. The total proceeds per hectare $\{T_i = (P_{i-1}.Y_i)\}$ of any crop has a direct impact on the acreage of the crop even if any one of price and yield effect is not much significant. All these results are obtained only when own price and yield or proceeds per hectare is considered as explanatory variable. From the composition of equations 38, 39, 40 and 41 in case of area under boro rice, irrigation is found to be the mainspring behind the expansion of boro cultivation. Upward movement of expected gross remuneration per hectare (evaluated at previous year's price) through a rise in price has also imparted its force on the farmers to opt for that crop. This is clear from equations 35 to 41 where, coefficients of price and gross remuneration are found to be highly significant. However, the yield of boro rice has not been observed to change significantly during this period, though it has noticed a remarkable improvement during the decade of eighty[69]. From equations 42, 43, 44, 49 and 50 it is realised that irrigation, and chemical fertiliser are the leading inputs for potato and simultaneously the yield and price of both are found to have an attractive influence on the farmers' choice. In case of mustard direct turnover (expected proceed per hectare) effect is much strong when it is introduced as a single explanatory variable in the model. Its coefficient becomes insignificant if the same for competitors is included in the multiple regression analysis. The cross (indirect) effects of price and yield are found to result in ambiguity when different equations with alternative sets of explanatory variables are compared. Though impact of changes in price and yield of wheat on area under potato is negative, the effect of variation in those of mustard on potato is completely opposite (though not significant) which seems to be inconsistent with the rational economic behaviour. If an increase in price and yield of mustard brings an expansion of area under it, with area kept the same; acreage of potato can not increase[70]. The relative proceeds (per hectare relative yield in value terms) also exhibit the same type of result.

An explanation may be put forward in respect of the above argument and results which are seemingly contradictory. In the early years of development much of land used to remain uncropped during winter and summer seasons and thus was open to the cultivators. With the expansion of capacity of irrigation it became easier to bring those plots under cultivation during rabi season and also in summer time. Initially, during seventies, when changes came, wheat observed an impressive growth relative to the others. This was due to the government's special programme on food production, high yielding varieties of wheat came and entered the erstwhile rice regime of West Bengal. Gradually the food crisis in the region was over and agriculture of West Bengal faced a commercial movement. Cultivation of potato and mustard became increasingly profitable with rising prices and yields due to the arrival of high yielding seeds, development of irrigation and of technical implements. There started a shift of land from other (relatively less profitable) crop like wheat, rabi-pulses to potato and mustard. Simultaneously, most of the new plots brought under the umbrella of assured irrigation responded accordingly. Hence area under both of potato and mustard have been increasing at the cost of wheat and rabi-pulses.

Farmers in each place faced the task of allocating their increased area under cultivation between potato and mustard meticulously, on the basis of increasing profitability of one with respect to other and their managerial ability, which has however been increased with the development of technology. Moreover, the cultivation of potato is relatively more costly and risky[71] than the other, even though later, it is found to be more profitable in an even condition. Thus, increased land has been devoted for the cultivation of both in such a way as to balance between management and profit and also to disperse the risk. At individual farm level however, a substitution may take place if land is too scarce and there is a slack in the input constraints and managing capability. But it can not be analysed here, as no data at farm level is available from secondary sources in this regard.

Moreover, it is noticed that the coefficient of the two essential factors necessary for the expansion of area under cultivation, irrigation and chemical fertiliser, vary when they are combined with other explanatory variables to express their impact on acreage change. This is because the influence of any one of them is imparted on area under a crop through the impact of variation in other explanatory factors, explicitly introduced in the multivariate regression analysis.

Relationship between those explanatory variables, included in the regression equations of acreage under potato, boro rice and mustard is presented here in the form of two-way correlation table. All the variables in the table are expressed in logarithmic term except dummy variable (D). From the correlation table-7.1 it is evident that consumption of chemical fertiliser has a very strong correlation with yield of mustard, potato and also dummy variable. So any of them can be dropped from the estimation and that will not lead to a drastic fall in percentage of explained variation as most of the effect of one variable works through another, which is closely related to it. Here, only the use of yield and dropping of others will provide the coefficient which would reflect a joint influence of chemical fertiliser and other yield raising factors, not included in the model. Moreover, association among price of wheat, mustard and that of potato is very strong which is due to the general inflation that leads to a sustained rise in price of all crops over time more or less in the same manner. Hence total proceeds per unit of land in the post-Green Revolution period has increased in absolute sense for all crops but at different rate. This differential growth of proceeds can be attributed partly to inter-crop variation in yield growth as well as price revision. Correlation Table-7.2 also reveals that price of boro rice; chemical fertiliser and dummy variable are closely related in a two-way form. So dropping of any one of them will not lead to a significant loss of goodness of fit of the analysis of area responsiveness to each factor.

From the above analysis it is possible to throw some light on the impact of input (essential) factors on the growth of the acreage of crops under study. From the regression analysis, it is revealed that direct price and yield effect on acreage is always positive. This hypothesis is strictly followed when only price and yield of the crop under consideration are introduced in the regression equation. But when they are combined with many other variables, the statistical results are found to change. In fact, rainfall in the pre-sowing season is always welcome though from the foregoing discussion it has not emerged to be so important in any case. Actually, in the absence of rainfall, irrigation can act as an alternative inspiring force on the part of the farmers for the sowing of any crop, especially dry season crops. Higher yield and price of any crop are always likely to entice the farmers to allocate land for the cultivation of that crop. From the two variable regression equation of acreage on total proceeds per hectare of each crop under discussion, it is observed that farmers are significantly motivated by higher value of it. But it is not possible to draw any particular conclusion regarding the effect of proceeds per hectare of competitive crops on absolute acreage from the multivariate regression analysis when they are included in regression equation explicitly. Contradictory results are obtained from different equations. A separate analysis may be considered in this regard by fitting regression for ratio of area under any two crops on the ratio of prices or proceed per hectare keeping the others out of consideration. Here, proceed will be calculated by multiplying yield with price of previous year. In order to analyse a cobweb type of model the relative area of any two crops (say, potato and mustard) may be expressed as a function of relative price or per hectare proceeds. Symbolically,

$$Ln\ (A_p/A_m) = a_1 + b_1\ Ln\ (P_{p-1}/P_{m-1}) \qquad (6)$$

and

$$Ln\ (A_p/A_m) = a_2 + b_2\ Ln\ (P_{p-1}.Y_p/P_{m-1}.Y_m) = a_2 + b_2\ Ln\ (T_p/T_m) \qquad (7)$$

where A_p, A_m and P_p, P_m are area under potato, mustard and prices of those two respectively. T_p and T_m are total remuneration per hectare of the two crops respectively. Similar type of equations may be formed with respect to potato and wheat as well as aus and jute that earlier seemed to be competitive. The notations A_w, A_a and A_j will represent area under wheat, aus and jute. Similarly T_w, T_a and T_j will be the total proceeds per hectare of wheat, aus and jute respectively. The results obtained by regression are given below.

(i) $Ln\ (A_p/A_m) = 1.55 + \underset{(0.58)}{0.577}\ Ln\ (P_{p-1}/P_{m-1}),\ \underline{R^2} = \underline{0.0432}$

(ii) $Ln\ (A_p/A_w) = 0.5425 + \underset{(0.766)}{0.38}\ Ln\ (P_{p-1}/P_{w-1}),\ \underline{R^2} = \underline{0.0113}$

(iii) $Ln\ (A_a/A_j) = 0.78 + \underset{(0.263)}{0.284}\ Ln\ (P_{a-1}/P_{j-1}),\ \underline{R^2} = \underline{0.0502}$

(iv) $Ln\ (A_p/A_m) = -1.62 + \underset{(0.34)}{1.126}\ Ln\ (T_p/T_m)^*,\ \underline{R^2} = \underline{0.332}$

(v) $Ln\ (A_p/A_w) = -1.931 + \underset{(0.56)}{1.58}\ Ln\ (T_p/T_w)^*,\ \underline{R^2} = \underline{0.263}$

(vi)[72] $Ln\ (A_a/A_j) = 0.796 + \underset{(0.229)}{0.456}\ Ln\ (T_a/T_j)^{**},\ \underline{R^2} = \underline{0.152}$

It is ensued from the equation that the farmers are more concerned with relative changes in gross remuneration from a unit of land rather than that of prices only. This is clear from the slope coefficient, which is significantly positive in equation (iv), (v) and (vi) in spite of the fact that R^2s are not very high. In the first three equations, price ratio lagged one year explains very little of relative acreage change of any two crops.

Equation (iv) does not reflect a very strong competitiveness between aus and jute. The reason may be that, the farmers in the early years were to forgo either jute or aus cultivation in favour of the other. But now a days aus can even be cultivated on the same piece of land after the harvest of jute, though it is slightly delayed but its yield will generally not be affected due to this. The farmer can collect jute at a premature time and surrender a part of its possible production. Now, it is also possible to sow jute at some earlier time because of available irrigation facility, leaving sufficient time for the timely cultivation of aus after the harvest of jute. So they are now not so directly competitive as they were two decades ago. In Burdwan and also in West Bengal, during the decade of seventies area under aus observed a decelerating trend while that of jute noticed an increasing trend. During the next decades their movement subverted[73]. However, throughout the whole period aus observed a marginally net declining trend while that of jute an insignificant positive trend. As they do not appear to be highly competitive after the development of irrigation and high yielding short period crops, they do not show a variation, that can be compromised with the rational economic behaviour of a cultivator.

The variation in area ratio in relation to price ratio and relative proceeds evaluated at previous year's prices has been displayed graphically. A close look at the graphs from 7.1 to 7.6 reveals that price variation is much lower than the relative variation in proceeds per acre. Relative price fluctuation over a long period of time is negligible (from diagram 7.1 and 7.3) as prices of all the major crops vary over time in the more or less same way. Thus the major part of variation in relative proceeds per acre is attributable to relative fluctuation in yield. So variation in ratio of area between any two crops is found to be more associated with the variation in ratio of proceeds rather than the ratio of prices; though earlier it has been observed that the area under a crop varies significantly with a variation in absolute price of itself lagged one year, if all other conditions remain same.

7.5. An Alternative Approach

From the foregoing discussion the conclusion we may reach is that, irrigation is the leading supporting factor to bring about a sustained change in cropping pattern in line with the agricultural development. Availability and extensive use of chemical fertiliser is also another important condition for the extended cultivation of the crops concerned. All those factors are also related to a change in the cost of cultivation.

On the other side, yield and price factor play important attractive role in determining cropping choice of the farmers. From the regression analysis it is difficult to comment on the effect of variation in price and yield of competitive crops on the acreáge variation of a particular crop which is applicable in all conditions. Though expansion of irrigation, increasing availability of chemical fertiliser have brought about a positive change in area under boro rice, potato and mustard; their coefficients or elasticities change with the introduction of other variables in the model and some ambiguous results have been obtained. For example, in case of potato, equation 50 shows negative direct price effect and equation 45 shows a positive effect of yield of mustard on area under potato, which one cannot believe to be. From equation 53 and 55 also some observations are found which seem to be contradictory. It is thus very difficult to build up any irrefutable hypothesis regarding the cross effects from those equations. Moreover, in the above cases cost of production of a crop was not taken into account which when changes and not supported by revenue in spite of a rising price and yield may cause for an end of the production of any crop. So for the removal of ambiguity in the above behavioural analysis it requires a more subtle and rigorous explanation.

One explanation can be drawn from the accepted pattern of relationship between different crops that can be grown on a particular piece of land in a crop year (one complete crop cycle). The relationship among the crops in production are exposed through the overlapping sowing and harvesting seasons, which is manifested in the yield and output of crops[74].

Each and every crop has an ideal time of sowing and harvesting, which a rational farmer always tries to maintain under usual conditions. In a multiple cropping system some bottlenecks arise due to the overlapping timing of harvesting of a crop and that of sowing of its subsequent crop/crops, where crops within a cycle are cultivated in succession. The cycle repeats itself year after year and the combination of crops grown may change over the years depending upon the nature of effect that the cultivation of one crop has on its successors. Harvesting of any crop must be completed within a certain time to leave adequate time for the preparation of land to cultivate the next crop. The preparation time has been reduced to a great extent with the help of tractors, power tillers etc. and the completion of harvesting is also now possible in a much shorter time by mechanical devices. In addition to that, crops with

Chart-7.1

Diagram of changes in ratio of area (1970-71 to 1993-94) and prices (1969-70 to 1993-94) between potato and mustard over time in Burdwan

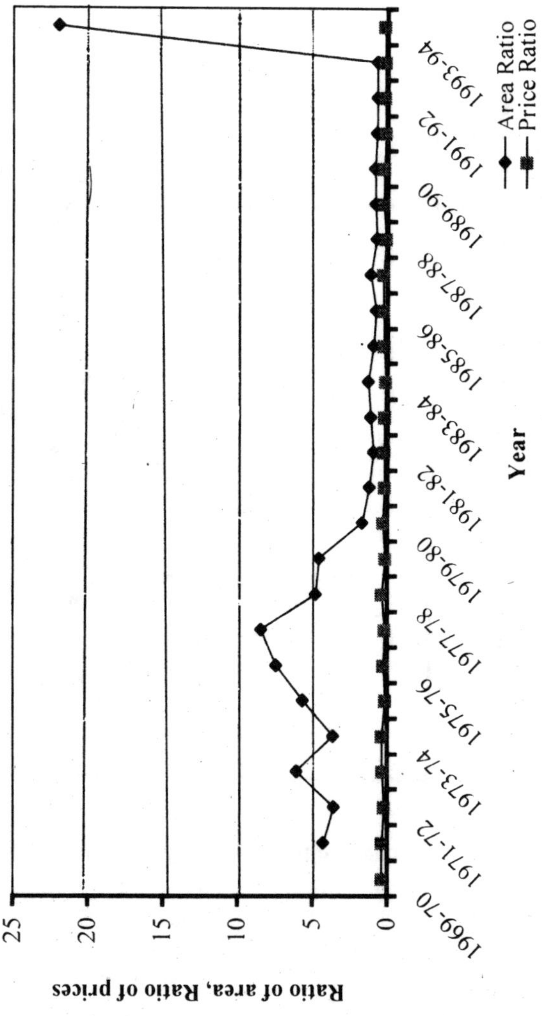

Chart-7.2

Diagram of changes in ratio of area and proceeds per hectare (evaluated at prices lagged one year) between potato and mustard during 1970-71 to 1993-94 in Burdwan

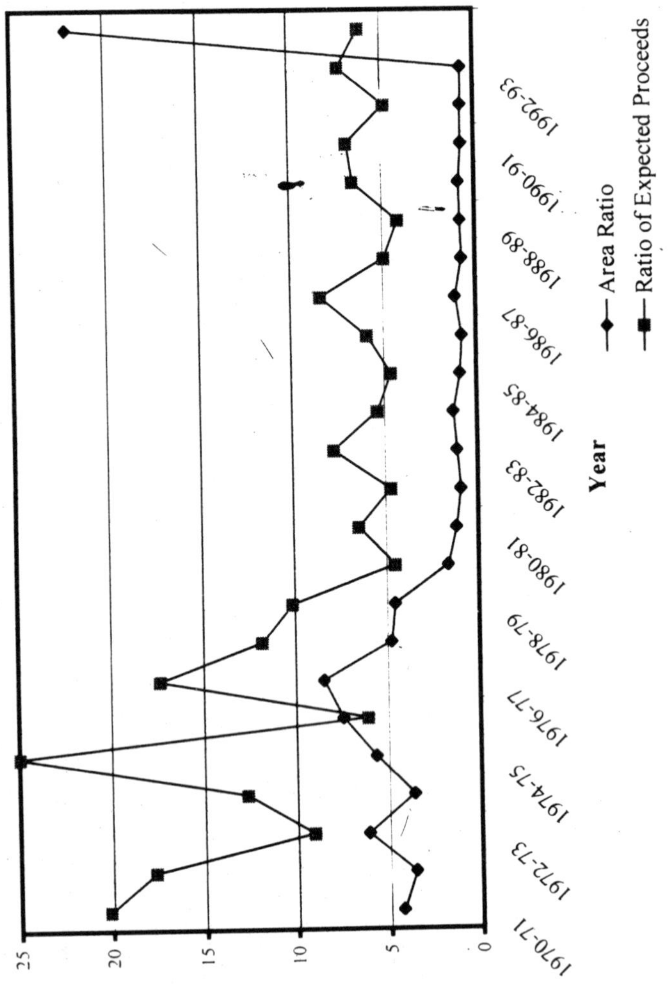

Chart-7.3

Diagram of changes in ratio of area (1970-71 to 1993-94) and prices (1969-70 to 1993-94) between potato and wheat over time in Burdwan

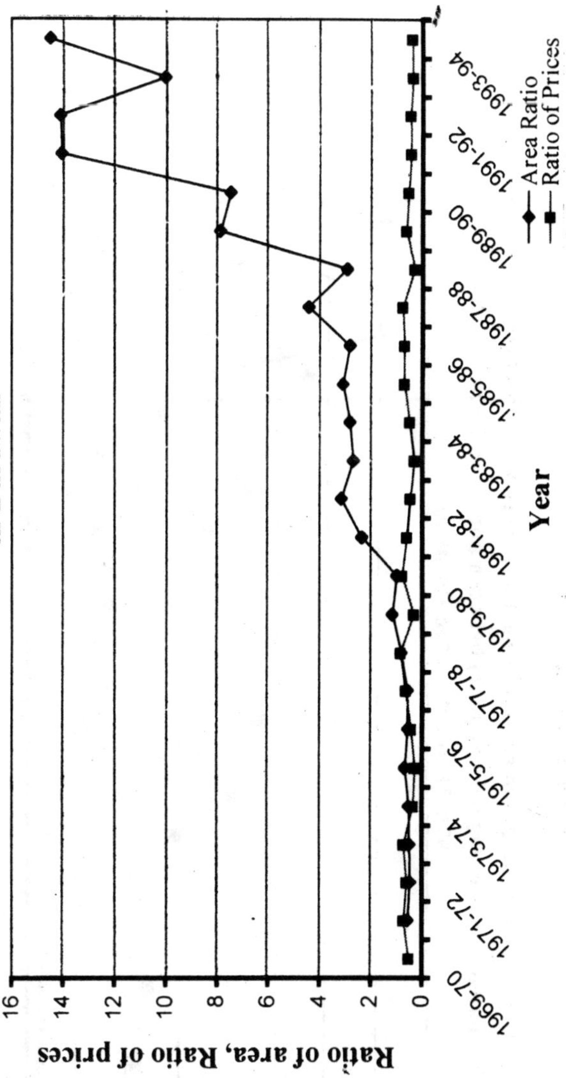

Chart-7.4

Diagram of Changes in ratio of area and proceeds per hectare (Evaluated at prices lagged one year) between potato and wheat during 1970-71 to 1993-94 in Burdwan

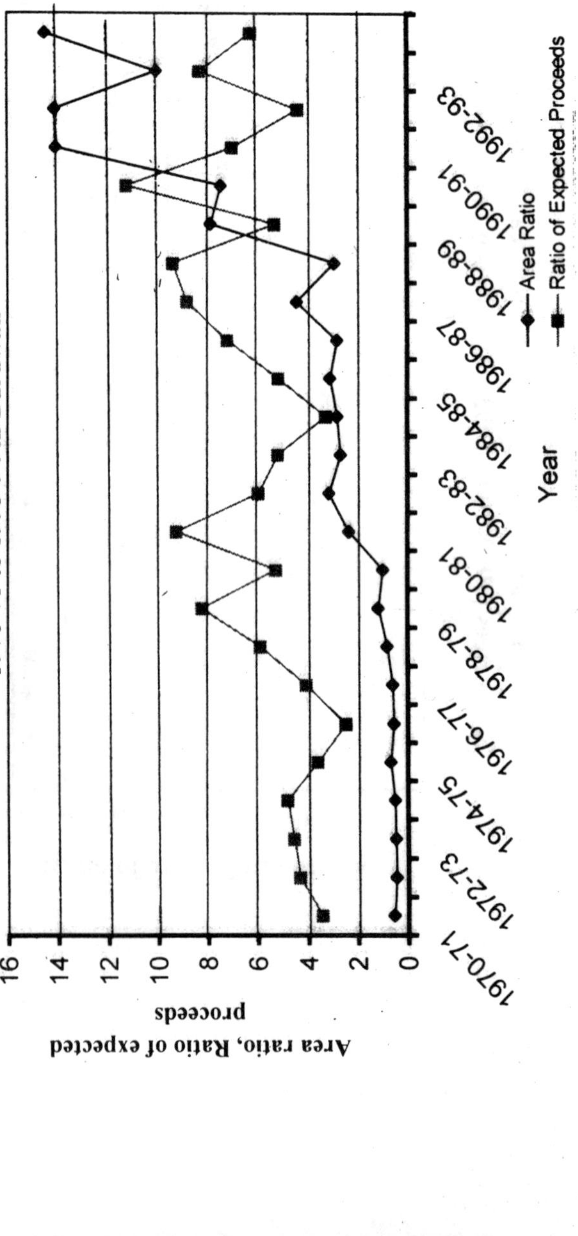

Chart-7.5

Diagram of changes in ratio of area (1970-71 to 1993-94) and prices (1969-70 to 1993-94) between aus and jute in Burdwan

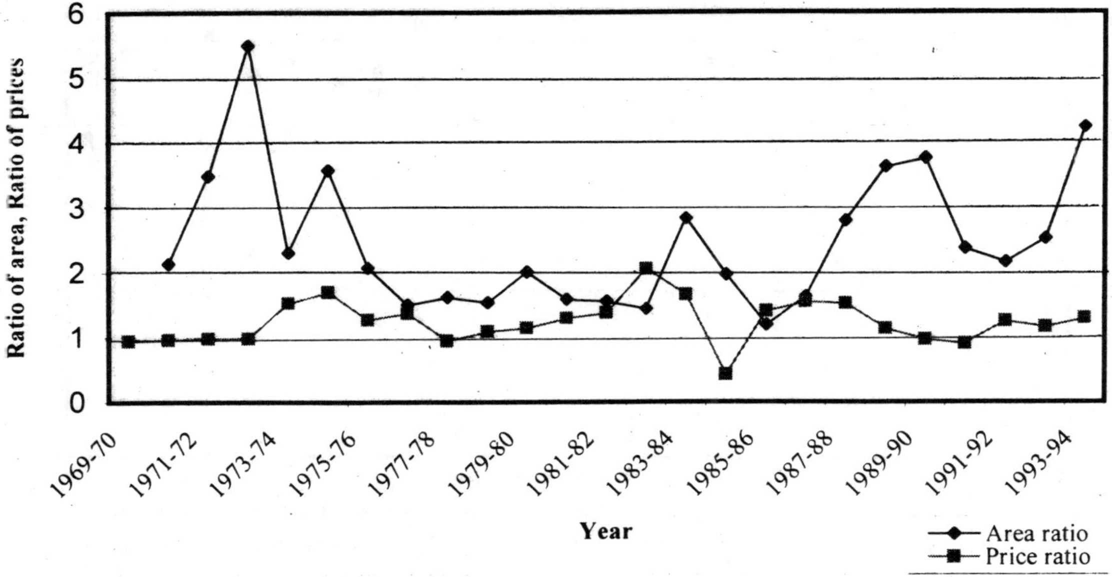

Chart-7.6

Diagram of changes in ratio of area and proceeds per hectare (Evaluated at prices lagged one year) between aus and jute during 1970-71 to 1993-94 in Burdwan

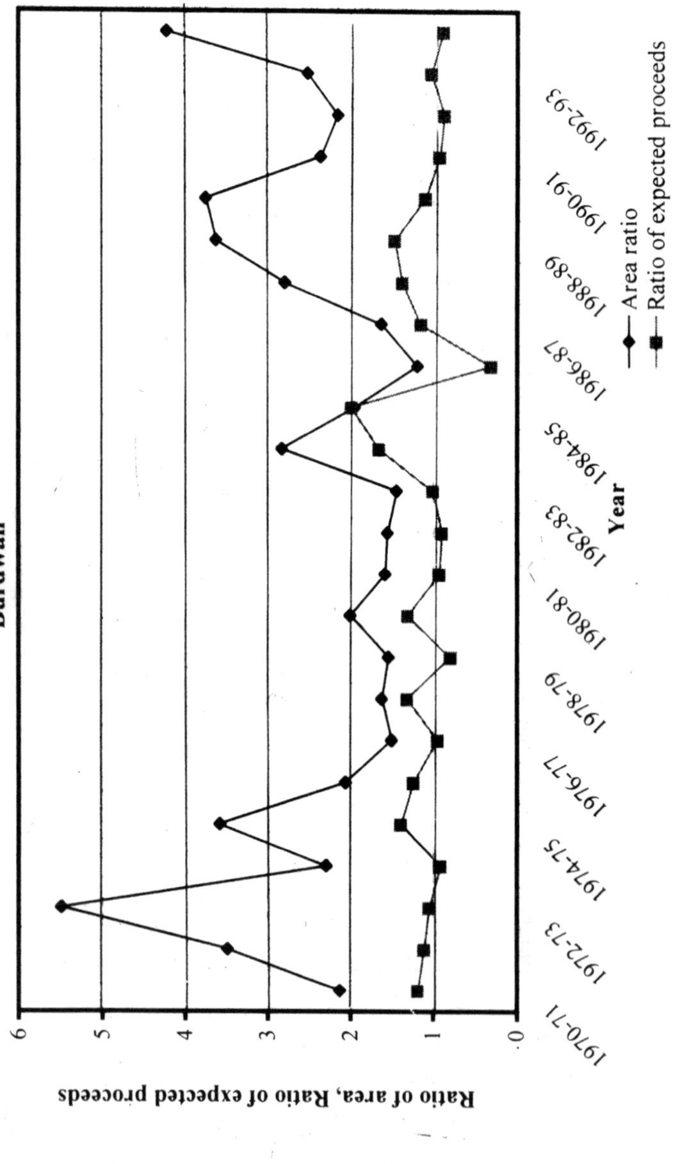

short period maturity and high yielding varieties are increasingly grown. But still there is a relationship because in many cases, ideal/natural timing of sowing and maturity has not changed significantly until a new variety emerges[75]. By ideal time of sowing we mean the duration of timing within which, the crop should be cultivated to get the best possible result with the usual application of other inputs; otherwise the yield will be affected or cost will be affected adversely. If any crop is cultivated at its usual time and inputs are used in an optimum proportion, then it will be matured at an ideal time (if no natural disturbances occur) and give optimum gross and net profit. The natural harvesting time of any crop may coincide with the natural sowing time of its immediate successors. So, if the latter is cultivated after the harvest of former on the same piece of land then performance of the latter will be delayed and productivity or profitability will be adversely affected. The same effect may be transmitted to the following crops due to the identical relationship. Sometimes premature crops are harvested to leave room for the next one. It is done if there is a possibility to compensate the loss incurred due to early or premature harvest by the next crop.

The case will not be similar where on the same plot of land cultivation of potato is preceded by aus and followed by boro rice to that one in which aus or high yielding varieties (H.Y.V.) aman, mustard or wheat and boro rice come in succession. In the two cases yield of boro rice and also cost of boro cultivation would be different. This is due to the differences in combination of crops in which it is grown. Empirically it is found that the cultivation of boro rice preceded by the harvest of wheat in February-March from the same plot of land is a late running performance and its productivity would be much lower even with usual application of other factors, than that if it had been sown earlier. However, if wheat is followed by jute or potato is followed by jute then the yield of jute is not affected due to this problem of matching of time. In the earlier case if the yield and profitability of wheat is not so high that it can overcompensate the expected loss of profit of boro rice due to its late sowing and harvesting, the farmers are supposed not to choose this combination. On the other hand if boro rice follows potato it also become too late and the yield of boro rice is likely to be adversely affected. Cost of potato cultivation is much higher than that of other crop but at the time of harvest, it leaves (the residual) much of fertiliser used and thus virtually very little amount of chemical fertiliser is needed for the following crop like boro rice, til etc. The pesticides' cost however increases because the invasions of pests are comparatively higher in case of late running crops[76]. Still the farmers may choose this combination if the productivity and net profit of potato is so high that it can overcompensate the expected loss of profit of latter. The farmers are supposed to choose a combination in such a way (to grow on the same field in a particular year) that they can disperse the risk and maximise expected profit.

Cultivation of some crops like potato, jute etc. leads to an increase in land productivity through preserving surplus fertiliser in case of potato and raising nitrogen content of land, in case of jute. This rising land productivity is utilised in the production of next alternative crop. The imputed value of rising land productivity due to the above reasons however can not be calculated directly by an economist but the task can be left to a biochemist or soil-scientist. What an economist can do is to compare the average yield of any crop (like boro rice) of different plots within same environment (having similar land character, water resources etc.) but grown after/in combination with different crops (such as, potato or mustard or local aman etc.). However, due to differences in former crop not only benefit, but also cost of the following crop differs; which is not very difficult to calculate.

Like yield and price or revenue, cost of cultivation is also an important instrument that can explain relative merit and demerit of different crops through an analytical framework of cost-benefit analysis, which is generally used to analyse the relative advantage and disadvantage of different enterprises. Though the farmers are more encouraged by higher gross revenue (as is evident from the earlier results) expected from each plot, cost of cultivation can also be regarded as instrumental in the determination of cropping pattern. The alternative possible combination of crops that can be harvested on a single plot in a crop year (which may be assumed to start with the cultivation of aus or aman and ends up with the harvest of boro rice, til or jute) can in this regard be evaluated to find out the net possible earning from each alternative combination. It can be used as one more reasonable explanation than that used earlier.

Rationale of this more subtle explanation arises out of the impact that the harvesting season of one crop has on the yield of the immediate next possible alternative crop, through the distortion of natural sowing and harvesting time on a fixed plot of land. Here the explanation is made on the basis of the assumption that land is a scarce factor and each plot is under optimum useable multiple cropping system (i.e., cropping intensity is almost 300 per cent). Even if irrigation is not available throughout the whole year and thus cropping intensity is less than optimum then also a similar explanation can be made under the unchanged existing condition. When the existing condition changes the pattern changes.

The frequently observed combinations in West Bengal,[77] particularly in Burdwan are identified first. These are: (i) high yielding aus, potato and boro rice, (ii) high yielding aus, potato and jute, (iii) high yielding aus, mustard and boro rice, (iv) high yielding aus, mustard and til, (v) high yielding aus, potato and til, (vi) high yielding aman, boro rice, (vii) high yielding aman, potato and boro rice, (viii) high yielding aman, mustard and til, (ix) local aman and boro rice,(x) high yielding aman, wheat and til, (xi) high yielding aman, wheat and jute, (xii) high yielding aman, potato and til, (xiii) high yielding aman, mustard and boro rice.[78]

Data on separate plot on which either of these combinations have been tried are not available from secondary sources. The farm management study conducted by the Evaluation Wing of the Directorate of Agriculture, Government of West Bengal presents data on cost, revenue and net benefit for different crops in different districts of West Bengal. The study is based on the sample survey technique of average farm family in which any of the combinations is tried on each plot belonging to a farm. The study made by the Evaluation Wing (latest, 36th volume, published in 1993-94 is available) would throw some light on the average yearly farm income emerging from different combination of crops and thus an understanding of the prospect of the crops/ combinations grown in the district/state may be possible. Here a cross section study of a particular year is being adopted. Most of the combinations noticed in the present days were absent in the early part of the seventies. So it is not possible to compare the relative profit of the present dominant combinations with the relative profit of the same in the early years of seventies after deflating by index of prices. At any time, any combination can be compared with the existing competitive combinations in term of their profitability and the combinations do change over time with the development of situation. The present study explains the rationality of farmers in a district or state (in aggregate) for preferring one particular combination in a given situation. Cost and benefits per acre for each individual crop in West Bengal during 1993-94 and cost-benefit of different combinations are presented in Table 7.3 and 7.4 respectively.

Table 7.4 shows that combination (vii) yields highest gross remuneration and also net remuneration over paid-out as well as total cost[79]. Next to it combination (i) and (ii) represent second and third highest gross turnover over other combinations as well as third and second highest net remuneration over paid-out cost compared to that of others. This explains the rationale behind the increasing choice of these combinations by the farmers. During monsoon season farmers have no other alternative but to choose highest profitable among different varieties of aus and aman. High yielding aman appeared to be the most profitable among them without having any adverse effect on the sowing time of next crops. Combination of it with potato and boro rice in succession yields most over paid-out cost as well as total cost; which appears to be an important reason behind this combination increasingly chosen in preference to others. So, the cultivation of potato and boro rice has been accelerated over the years. This does not indicate that, this combination gives highest profit in all the years. In any year due to any natural disturbance or any other reason it may give lower profit than any other combination. However it has the likelihood of yielding more than any other combination during most of the years under discussion. In future any other varieties of crop/crops may be generated and thus a new crop combination may be developed that will yield higher possible profit than that of any other combination. Then the farmers will tend to switch over to that combination if other conditions necessary for the cultivation of those crops are available.

In spite of high profitability of potato, during rabi season cultivators (especially the small cultivators) do not always remain in a position to cultivate potato to the extent they desire. This is because of the highest cost per unit of land and risk involved with the cultivation of potato. Demand-supply mechanism and storage facility also matters much in this case. This would provide another reason behind the expansion of mustard (mainly with the development of irrigation facility) in spite of much lower profit than potato over paid-out cost. The profitability consideration also provides the reason why growth of cultivation of mustard during nineties decelerated irrespective of a high growth in eighties as is observed earlier. However, the results of recent past suggest that choice of crops to be grown though a matter of cost-benefit in a commercial system, it is bound to come to a limit unless further technological breakthrough occur from time to time. A further technological breakthrough would bring a new cost-benefit relatives and thus a new cropping pattern may emerge accordingly.

7.6. Limitation

The main limitation of the above calculation is that the data on cost of individual crops for different combinations are not collected from the field on which the combinations have been exercised. Here evaluation of each combination is made after the calculation of cost and benefit of each crop from a sample of farms that cultivate the particular crops included in any of the combinations. The cost and benefit of each crop for different combinations would be different. Those types of data were not available from the secondary sources. Though it provides an analysis of average farm condition, examination of data based on farms exercising different combinations on different plots would provide a more logical analysis of the consistent choice of cropping pattern. Collection of data for aus (local) only from four farms in a particular district (that has been done in the study) to approximate the state average is also not a rational one. The best process would be to consider the data on separate combinations i.e., of individual crops in combination with several others in other season, separately from sample survey and to calculate distinct expenditure and revenue of different combinations.

NOTES

1 Geographical structure includes the location of the place, elevation and slopes of agricultural land and other agro-climatic conditions.

2 Competing crops are defined as crops among which area shifts can occur. In other words those are the potential rivals who compete for any plot in a particular place. Different places may face different crops to compete for attracting land areas.

3 If price of any crop, especially the expected price increases relative to that of others, it is generally supposed to tempt the farmers to increasingly allocate land, if possible to the production of that crop and vice versa. A systematic explanation of acreage response to price variation was given by Nerlove (1958), in his pioneering study, *Dynamics of Supply, Estimation of Farmer's Response to Price.* A useful analysis has also been found in Dharm Narain's pathbreaking work, *Impact of Price Movements on Areas under Selected Crops in India, published in 1965.*

4 Proceeds per acre means the price times yield per acre of the crop.

5 Narayanamoorthy A. (1997), "Crop Diversification and Yield Response to Fertilisers", *Productivity*, Vol. 38, No.1, April-June, pp. 118-125.

6 Production will not be the same, if these factors do not support favourably, even though the farmers opt for cultivating any crop (being tempted by high price or yield observed in the same or any other region) that requires essential services of these factors.

7 If the society is a self-sufficient village economy then need-based choice of cropping pattern is given much priority; the price or profit can not exercise much power to impress the farmer. While in a modern capitalist society the decision of the farmers is guided by profit motive. Production is organised mainly for market and thus price or profitability will be the major source of

inspiration for shifting area from one crop to another. While the factors like soil structure, rainfall, irrigation etc. are of much importance in all these situations. Untimely appearance of rainfall or lack of irrigation may throw some crop out of cultivation even though production is organised for making money. Prices of crops, which the farmers will not be able to cultivate due to any of the constraints, would not be considered in decision making.

8 Raj K.N., Sen A.K., Rao C.H.H. (ed.), (1988), *Dharm Narain, Studies on Indian Agriculture,* Oxford University Press, ch.1.

9 Any crop can not always remain relatively more or less profitable than the others can. It depends on the dynamic character of not only prices, but also of yields and cost of production which would change over time consequent to a changes in variation in techniques of production and vagaries of nature.

10 In earlier days most of the farmers could not cultivate potato on a large scale (or mainly on commercial basis) because it would require huge manual labour and cattle to plough. So it was not possible to complete the cultivation of many plots within the desired time period.

11 Soil structure and climate of South Bengal region are in general not suitable for the cultivation of tea. Different places of Southern West Bengal are favourable for the production of specific crops in different season owing to their specific soil structure and weather condition.

12 Even if full scale multiple cropping is not possible and cropping is done only once in a year, the inter-crop acreage shift is possible.

13 The implicit assumption here is that, though yield of different crops may change, the relative yield is most likely to remain unchanged.

14 The set of specific crops is determined by the profit motive and thus would change as profitability of crops expected by the farmer change.

15 Cropping intensity for the state as a whole (including the hilly region of northern part and semi-arid zone of Purulia and Bankura) was 125 in 1970-71 (Source: Government of West Bengal, Board of Revenue and Directorate of Agriculture, 1975, pp.71-72). The figure increased to 167 during 1990-91, as is observed from Agricultural Census of West Bengal, 1991. Now it has reached more than 200 according to the official statement of Directorate of Agriculture, Government of West Bengal. It is to be noted that full scale multiple cropping is not possible in all the places due to maximum limit of irrigation even with highly sophisticated technology. But many places where sufficient irrigation is available a nearly full-fledged multiple cropping is possible though some plots may remain fallow due to some other constraints.

16 It has already been discussed in chapter-3.

17 Nerlove M. (1958), *The Dynamics of Supply: Estimation of Farmers' Response to Price*, The John Hopkins Press, Baltimore.

18 Black J. D. (1924), " Elasticity of Supply of Farm Products", *Journal of Farm Economics*, Vol.6, No.2, April, pp.145-55.

19 Smith B. B. (1925), "Forecasting the Acreage of Cotton", *Journal of American Statistical Association*, New series, Vol.20, March, pp.31-47.

20 Bean L. H. (1929), "The Farmers' Response to Price", *Journal of Farm*

Economics, Vol.11, pp.368-85.

21 Cassels J. M. (1933), "The Nature of Statistical Supply Curves", *Journal of Farm Economics*, Vol.15, pp. 378-87.

22 Walsh R. M. (1944), " Response to Price in Production of Cotton and Cottonseed", *Journal of Farm Economics*, Vol.26, pp.359-72.

23 All of the above studies have explained acreage changes in relation to price variation, where the planned acreage is used as an approximation of planned output or supply.

24 Walsh R. M., (1944), op. cit.

25 Each year, some plots are usually abandoned in the midway of the season due to flood or drought. Sometimes it becomes very costly to tide over all those adverse situations and thus the cultivators may revise their target production of crops. Vagaries of nature may also be considered by them to form expectations regarding future yields, which is very difficult to include in a model.

26 Hicks J. R. (1946), *Value and Capital*, Oxford, pp.319-23.

27 Nerlove M., op. cit., Chapter 2 and 3.

28 Nerlove M., op. cit., pp .62-65.

29 Dharm Narain (1965), *Impact of Price Movements on Areas under Selected Crops in India: 1900-1939*, Cambridge University Press, ch.1.

30 Raj K. N., Sen A.K. and Rao C.H.H. (ed.), (1988), op. cit. Ch.1, pp.32-33.

31 Price is deflated to isolate the real change in price of crop whose acreage variation is to be analysed and to eliminate the variation in other economic factors. This is done to arrive at the conclusion regarding the effect of real change in price of crops under discussion on its acreage assuming other things as constant.

32 Raj K. N., Sen A.K. and Rao C.H.H. (ed.), (1988), op. cit. P.12; Walsh R. M., op. cit.

33 Raj K. N., Sen A.K. and Rao C.H.H. (ed.), (1988), op. cit. Ch.1, pp.12-13.

34 Since the area under any crop at any time displays the maximum amount that it can surrender to other crops, the competitive crops having a very small area under them would be kept out of the present analysis. A crop with a small area under it can not make a large difference to the area under crops being discussed about. So relative areas under crops could be used as the basis for weighing prices of crops under discussion. But the area under a crop though sets limit on the maximum area that it can lose; it sets no limit how little it may surrender. There is no compulsion for a crop occupying a large area under it, to lose in a big way. Besides, although a crop can not lose more than it has the area under the crop does not set a limit to its capacity to snatch area from other crops.

35 There are several other difficulties in setting a weight for deflating the price of a crop, whose acreage variation is to be explained. Some other arguments are also available in Raj et al (ed.), (1988), pp.11-18.

36 Sarkar G. K., (1988), *Jute in India, An Economic Analysis*, Oxford University

Press, Chapter-3.

(Earlier it was observed that either jute or aus could be grown on the same plot as a substantial part of their growing times were overlapping. So, one of them had to be sacrificed for the cultivation of the other. But now it is possible to cultivate both and though cultivation of aus become slightly delayed if it follows jute; it does not hamper the growth of following crops during the rest of the year. Sometimes, jute is cultivated earlier with the help of artificial irrigation or harvested earlier to make room for aus and a part of profit from jute is forgone).

37 Gulati A. and Sharma A. (1994), "Agriculture Under GATT: What it Holds for India", *Economic and Political Weekly*, July 16.

38 Vyas V. S. (1996), " Diversification in Agriculture: Concept, Rationale and Approaches", *Indian Journal of Agricultural Economics*, Vol.51, No.4, Oct.-Dec., pp. 636-643.

39 Nayyyar D. and Sen A. (1994), "International Trade and Agricultural Sector in India", in G. S. Bhalla (ed.), (1994), Economic Liberalisation in Indian Agriculture, Institute for studies in Industrial Development, New Delhi.

40 Narayanamoorthy A. (1997), op. cit.

41 Singhal M. and Gauraha A. K. (1997), "Crop Diversification in Madhya Pradesh: An Economic Analysis", Paper presented at the Annual Conference of Indian Society of Agricultural Economics.

42 Singh I. J., Rai K. N. and Karwasra J. C. (1997), "Regional Variations in Agricultural Performance in India", Paper presented at the Annual Conference of Indian Society of Agricultural Economics.

43 Sawant S. D. (1997), "Performance of Indian Agriculture with Special Reference to Regional Variations", *Indian Journal of Agricultural Economics*, Vol.52, No.3, July-September, pp. 353-73.

44 Chand R. (1996), "Diversification through High Value Crops in Western Himalayan Region: Evidence from Himachal Pradesh", Seminar Paper, Indian Society of Agricultural Economics, Oct.-Dec., pp. 652-63.

45 Bhalla G. S. and Singh G. (1996), "Recent Development in Indian Agriculture: A State Level Analysis", *Economic and Political Weekly*, Vol.32, No.19, March 29-April 4.

46 Dhindsa and Sharma, op. cit.

47 At that time India had to import much food to meet her domestic consumption need. A large part of food imports during the fifties came in the form of United States PL480 aid, with generous repayment conditions. For reference: (i) Government of India (1959), Report of the Foodgrains Enquiry Committee, (ii) Nilkantha Rath and V. S. Patvardhan, Impact of Assistance Under PL480 on Indian Economy, Gokhale Institute of Politics and Economics, Poona, 1967.

48 Even if there was no possibility of expansion of area under cultivation, by any means, price and yield forces could have worked within their substitutable limit.

49 This is reflected from the significant growth of gross cropped area and cropping intensity though net cropped area growth is not so significant.

50 Boyce (1987), op. cit., pp. 197-98.

51 In the regression analysis, variables like high yielding varieties of seeds, agricultural machineries (tractor, power tiller, pump-set etc.) are not explicitly introduced since continuous series of data on them are not available for any particular region. However, they can be utilised in case of analysing the inter-district variation.

52 Nerlove (1958), op. cit.

53 The same sort of explanation is appeared in Raj et. al. (ed.), op. cit., Ch.-1, pp. 25-26.

54 Though it is assumed that the positive bias of expectation of some farmers will offset the negative bias of that of some other, there is very likely the presence of a net upward bias. This follows from the optimism of farmers who expect to get back the performance in an ideal, undisturbed natural condition, which is the maximum possible limit and most often at least a few natural disturbances hamper yield levels differently.

55 The equation represents a modified Cobb-Douglas form of equation.

56 There is the likelihood of the presence of a time lag after which the effect (it has) would be realised.

57 Here figures in the parentheses represent standard error of the corresponding coefficient. *, ** and *** represent respectively that the coefficient is significant at 5%, 10% and 20% level of significance by two tailed test.

58 Yield of boro rice has not increased significantly over the period under discussion. In Burdwan the exponential rate of growth of yield of boro rice during the 1970-71 to 1993-94 period was only .102 per cent per annum. In the first half of the period the trend rate growth was negative due to uncertain irrigation and during the second half the rate was significantly positive.

59 The question has been raised in several studies regarding the developmental impact of rigorous land reform measures (mainly collection and distribution of vested land and operation barga) undertaken by the Government of West Bengal. Some former evaluators have argued that in the self evaluation made by the Government, results have been manipulated in order to inflate the success of the programs [Mallick R (1992), p.740, "Agrarian Reform in West Bengal, The End of an Illusion", *World Development*, Vol. 20, No.5, pp. 735-50]. Harriss (1993), Lieten (1990), C.H. Hanumantha Rao (1992) and Vaidyanathan (1988) have acknowledged the turnaround of agricultural performance in West Bengal was due to significant growth of irrigation, especially, ground-water irrigation.

60 Harriss J. (1993), loc. cit., Lieten (1990), loc. cit., Vaidyanathan (1988) loc. cit., Raychaudhuri and Sen (1996), ibid. Mallick (1992), loc. cit, Bardhan and Rudra (1977), ibid.

61 Cultivation of potato, boro rice are much costly affairs and so only distribution of small plots to the landless people does not ensure the cultivation of crops on commercial basis unless they are provided with financial and technical supports.

62 Raychaudhuri and Sen (1996), "Agricultural Reform and Productivity: Some

Important Lessons to be Learnt from West Bengal's Operation Barga", in Raychaudhuri and Sarker (Ed.) *Economy of West Bengal: Problems and Prospects*, pp. 24-25, Allied Publishers.

63 ardhan and Rudra (1977) report the same on the basis of inter-village comparisons in West Bengal, Bihar and Uttar Pradesh. The tenancy legislation also sparked large-scale evictions and concealment of tenancy.

64 Raychaudhuri and Sen (1996), in Raychaudhuri and Sarker (ed.), op. cit.

65 Harriss J. (1993), "What is Happening in Rural West Bengal, Agrarian Reform; Growth and Distribution", *Economic and Political Weekly*, June12, pp. 1237-1247.

66 Keynes J. M. (1957), *General Theory of Employment, Interest and Money*, London, p.51.

67 Cassels J. M. (1933), "The Nature of Statistical Supply Curves", *Journal of Farm Economics*, April, p.386. In this analysis of supply response to a change in price he has used acreage to approximate the output.

68 Raj, Sen and Rao (Ed), op. cit., p.11.

69 De U. K. (1998), " Regional Disparity in Agricultural Productivity in the state of West Bengal", *Productivity*, Oct.-Dec. pp. 508-515.

70 Here it is presumed that during rabi season, there is a maximum manageable area supprted by irrigation at any time on which any kind of rabi crop can be grown (though different rabi crops require different quantity of irrigation). So in any year with unchanged irrigation, if cultivation of any crop is to expand, area under any other must have to contract.

71 This is because, potato is more perishable than mustard and good storage facility is essential for its preservation if not sold immediately after the harvest. Thus the market of potato is relatively more unstable than mustard.

72 * means t value is significant at 5 per cent level and ** means t value is significant at 10 per cent level of significance by two tailed test.

73 Gradually jute faced stiff competition from other side i.e., from the emergence of synthetic substitutes. Thus gradual increase in uncertain price fluctuation has led to slight set back of jute. Still jute cultivation has been going in those places where it is more lucrative in the changing circumstances. Another problem faced by the cultivators is in connection with the collection of fibre from raw jute. This is because the work is done at a time when sowing of aus or aman is also being done.

74 This phenomenon has already been explained in detail in chapter-3.

75 Sometimes a little early maturity may however be observed for certain crops due to disproportionate application of inputs but not, without affecting yield rates.

76 The late running crops are usually more vulnerable to pests and different bacterias.

77 Though the regression analysis has been done for the district of Burdwan, Cost-benefit analysis here is made on the data of West Bengal average collected from Evaluation Branch, Directorate of Agriculture, Government of West Bengal. Since data for the district of Burdwan (in their study) have not been collected for all major crops cultivated in the district, an analysis of primary

survey in Burdwan will be presented later in support of the said argument in Chapter-9.

78 High yielding aman is the newly generated varieties of paddy that are now increasingly cultivated in place of traditional aman. The new one is generally planted in the month of July and harvested in October-November after which it is thus possible to grow mustard or potato. On the other hand the old varieties are planted normally in July-August and harvested in the month of December-January, after which cultivation of potato or mustard will become too late and the performance will not be good enough. However wheat can easily be cultivated as usual. Aman (HYV), potato and jute can also form another combination like aus (HYV), potato and jute; but the same is not popular because of uncertainty in the jute market.

79 Here gross and net remuneration means total revenue in value terms and net profit per acre of land in a whole year out of different combinations.

REFERENCES

1. Bandyopadhyay N. (1991), "Patterns of Change in Agrarian Structure with Special Reference to the Leftist Government in West Bengal", in N. Ansari (ed.), *Agrarian Structure, Land Reforms and Agricultural Growth in India*, Tata McGraw-Hill, New Delhi.
2. Bhalla G. S. and Singh G., (1996), op. cit.
3. Bose B. (1979), "Agrarian Programme of Left Front Government in West Bengal", *Economic and Political Weekly,* December 17, pp.2053-2060.
4. Boyce (1987), op. cit., pp. 197-98.
5. Chakraborty A. and Rudra A., (1973), "Economic Effects of Tenancy- Some Negative Results", *Economic and Political Weekly,* July 14.
6. Chand R. (1996), "Diversification through High Value Crops in Western Himalayan Region: Evidence from Himachal Pradesh", Seminar Paper, Indian Society of Agricultural Economics, Oct.-Dec., pp. 652-63.
7. Dasgupta B. (1980), *The New Agrarian Technology and India*, Macmillan, India.
8. Dhindsa and Sharma, op. cit.
9. Fertiliser Association of India (FAI) (1974); *Statistics on Fertiliser and Agriculture in Eastern India*, No.1, Calcutta: FAI Eastern Region, June.
10. Fertiliser Association of India, (1981), Fertiliser Statistics, 1980-81, New Delhi.
11. Fertiliser Association of India, (1994), Fertiliser Statistics, 1993-94, New Delhi.
12. Government of India (1959), Report of the Foodgrains Enquiry Committee.
13. Government of West Bengal, Bureau of Applied Economics and Statistics (BAES), *Economic Review*, Various Issues.
14. Government of West Bengal, *Statistical Abstract*, Various Issues.
15. Government of India: Area and Production of Principal crops in India (Various

Issues), Ministry of Agiculture, New Delhi.

16. Gulati A. and Sharma A. (1994), "Agriculture Under GATT: What it Holds for India", *Economic and Political Weekly,* July 16.

17. Harriss J. (1993), "What is Happening in Rural West Bengal, Agrarian Reform; Growth and Distribution", *Economic and Political Weekly*, June12, pp. 1237-1247.

18. Hicks J. R. (1946), *Value and Capital*, Oxford, pp.319-23.

19. Keynes J. M. (1957), *General Theory of Employment, Interest and Money*, London, p.51.

20. Narain Dharm (1965), *Impact of Price Movements on Areas under Selected Crops in India: 1900-1939*, Cambridge University Press, ch.1.

21. Narayanamoorthy A. (1997), "Crop Diversification and Yield Response to Fertilisers", *Productivity*, Vol. 38, No.1, April-June, pp. 118-125.

22. Nayyyar D. and Sen A. (1994), "International Trade and Agricultural Sector in India", in G. S. Bhalla (ed.), (1994), Economic Liberalisation in Indian Agriculture, Institute for studies in Industrial Development, New Delhi.

23. Nerlove M. (1958), *The Dynamics of Supply: Estimation of Farmers' Response to Price*, The John Hopkins Press, Baltimore.

24. Raj K.N., Sen A.K., Rao C.H.H. (ed.), (1988), *Dharm Narain, Studies on Indian Agriculture,* Oxford University Press, ch.1.

25. Rath Nilkantha and Patvardhan V. S., Impact of Assistance Under PL480 on Indian Economy, Gokhale Institute of Politics and Economics, Poona, 1967.

26. Sarkar G. K., (1988), *Jute in India, An Economic Analysis*, Oxford University Press, Chapter-3.

27. Sawant S. D. (1997), "Performance of Indian Agriculture with Special Reference to Regional Variations", *Indian Journal of Agricultural Economics,* Vol.52, No.3, July-September, pp. 353-73.

28. Singh I. J., Rai K. N. and Karwaşra J. C. (1997), "Regional Variations in Agricultural Performance in India", Paper presented at the Annual Conference of Indian Society of Agricultural Economics.

29. Singhal M. and Gauraha A. K. (1997), "Crop Diversification in Madhya Pradesh: An Economic Analysis", Paper presented at the Annual Conference of Indian Society of Agricultural Economics.

30. Vyas V. S. (1996), " Diversification in Agriculture: Concept, Rationale and Approaches", *Indian Journal of Agricultural Economics*, Vol.51, No.4, Oct.-Dec., pp. 636-643.

Table 7.1: Two-way Correlation Table-1

Variable	LnR	LnI	LnC	LnP_p	LnY_p	LnP_m	LnY_m	LnP_w	LnY_w	D
LnR	1	.198	.3246	.348	.1696	.2538	.3489	.2178	.1121	.384
LnI		1	.2671	.3477	.013	.2411	.1098	.259	-.127	.124
LnC			1	.744	.8095	.91	.8124	.823	-.420	0.88
LnP_p				1	.4218	.784	.5855	.7403	-.357	0.63
LnY_p					1	.735	.6615	.736	-.246	.716
LnP_m						1	.685	.877	-.367	.745
LnY_m							1	.538	-.374	.910
LnP_w								1	-.289	.612
'LnY_w									1	-.415

Note: Value in the ij[th] cell represents correlation between i[th] and j[th] variable.

Table 7.2 Two-way Correlation Table-2

Variable	LnR	LnI	LnC	LnP_b	LnY_b	D
LnR	1	0.198	0.324	0.133	0.198	0.368
LnI		1	0.267	0.296	-0.219	-0.043
LnC			1	0.91	-0.072	0.869
LnP_b				1	-0.087	0.770
LnY_b					1	0.320

Note: Same as Table 7.1.

Table 7.3 Cost Benefit Analysis of Different Crops in West Bengal on an Average Farm for the year 1993-94 (per acre)

Crop	Value of Output (Rs)	Cost of Cultivation (Rs)		Net profit (Rs) over	
		Paid-out Cost	Total Cost	Paid-out Cost	Total Cost
Aus (local)	2376.08	2072.17	3766.36	303.91	-1390.28
Aus (HYV)	3430.06	1727.81	2934.12	1702.25	495.94
Aman (HYV)	4544.92	1851.22	3982.0	2693.70	562.22
Boro (HYV)	5899.83	2791.86	5054.16	3107.97	845.67
Wheat	3662.85	2472.22	4225.58	1190.63	-562.73
Jute	6541.68	2565.61	5207.13	3976.07	1334.55
Mustard	3034.86	1915.67	3223.62	1119.19	-188.76
Potato	14389.04	8821.41	14255.35	5567.63	133.69
Til	2746.59	1407.10	2575.45	1339.49	171.14

Table 7.4 Gross and Net Benefit per acre for Alternative Possible Combinations in a Crop-Year (1993-94)

Combination	Gross Turnover (Rs)	Net Benefit (Rs) Over	
		Paid-out Cost	Total Cost
(i) Aus (HYV), Potato, Boro	25828.48 (2)	10860.46 (3)	1392.56 (6)
(ii) Aus (HYV), Potato, Jute	24360.78 (3)	11245.95 (2)	1468.24 (4)
(iii) Aus (HYV), Mustard, Boro	14474.3 (8)	6412.02 (9)	1070.11 (9)
(iv) Aus (HYV), Mustard, Til	9211.51 (12)	4160.93 (13)	478.32 (12)
(v) Aus (HYV), Potato, Til	20565.69 (5)	8609.37 (5)	800.77 (11)
(vi) Aman (HYV), Boro	13909.21(9)	6698.55 (8)	1608.6 (3)
(vii) Aman (HYV), Potato, Boro	28298.25 (1)	12266.18 (1)	1742.29 (1)
(viii) Aman (HYV), Mustard, Til	11681.28 11)	5566.65 (12)	828.05 (10)
(ix) Aman (Local), Boro	12554.3 (10)	6284.28 (10)	1325.15 (7)
(x) Aman (HYV), Wheat, Til	8646.42 (13)	5638.09 (11)	454.08 (13)
(xi) Aman (HYV), Wheat, Jute	16104.36 (7)	8274.67 (6)	1617.49 (2)
(xii) Aman (HYV), Potato, Til	23035.46 (4)	10015.09 (4)	1150.5 (8)
(xiii) Aman (HYV), Mustard, Boro	16944.07 (6)	7817.74 (7)	1419.84 (5)

Note: Figures in the parentheses represent ranks.

CHAPTER 8

INTER-DISTRICT DISPARITY IN THE APPLICATION OF MODERN AGRICULTURAL IMPLEMENTS AND CHANGES IN CROPPING PATTERN

8.1. Introduction

The earlier chapter has been devoted to a meticulous investigation of the major underlying causes behind the diversification of crop in West Bengal during 1970-71 to 1994-95. The major factors found to be responsible for the differential growth of acreage under crops or variation in cropping pattern are irrigation, synthetic fertiliser, price and yield. However, different sub-regions faced different crop-mix in different proportion consequent to differences in agro-climatological conditions coupled with disproportionate growth of technology in different fields and the aforesaid factors. All those above factors are interwoven in a well-knit agricultural production structure of the region. Because of their close inter-relationship, it is very difficult to draw a specific irrefutable hypothesis with regard to the process of diversification. There is no specific and concrete way of specifying a model involving both quantitative and qualitative variables where the variables are interrelated in different ways[1]. So it is very improper to make any definite conclusion regarding the above process.

The purpose behind the use of the two variable or multivariate regression analysis have been to find out a notion of relative importance of different production conditions and in contrast the role of price and non-price factors. The regression analysis of different types gives results, which are vulnerable to different sorts of criticisms. Absolute price and yield factors are found to be some important stimulating factors, whose direct effects are always positive and significant when the regression is run only on the two or either one of them separately. But if several other variables are included explicitly in the same model we get such results (especially the cross effects) as are not consistent with each other[2]. When area relative of any two competitive crops are expressed as a function of only price ratio of those two crops we do not obtain any significant result. But when the same is expressed as a function of ratio of proceeds per unit of area evaluated at previous year's prices, it provides a consistent result. This is the reflection of eagerness of cultivators, especially the commercial minded ones for earning higher and higher revenue from their limited holdings. If they act only on the basis of movements in price-relative, that would lead to an altogether different cases. The ratio of prices between any two competing crops remain more or less constant over the years as is evident from diagram 7.1, 7.3 and 7.5. This is because the nominal prices of all competing crops observe a more or less constant trend over a long period of time. Comparative yield growth is therefore of vital importance for the expansion of cultivation of potato, boro rice and mustard. The basic factors which lie beneath the differential rate of yield growth of different crops are the continuous changes in the capacity of irrigation, intensive use of synthetic fertiliser, development of high yielding varieties of seeds, increasing use of plant protective chemicals etc. Besides these, the other major factors to which disproportionate growth in acreage of crops in different districts can be attributed are identified as differential rate of diffusion of technology and adoption of agri-implements, differences in distribution of electricity in agricultural activities especially in irrigation which makes ground-water more accessible and cheap. As the data on minor irrigation, agri-implements etc. was not included in the previous chapter[3], here the emphasis will be put on the analysis of the variation in the inter-regional pattern of growth of these basic factors in contrast to the differential growth of area under cultivation of the said crops.

8.2. Irrigation

First of all, the case of irrigation is considered. In West Bengal canal, tube-wells, tanks, filter points and dug wells are the major sources of irrigation. Canal irrigation is mainly maintained by the government. There are three different types of government schemes for the development of canal irrigation system of the state. These are major (having cultural command area more than 10000 hectares), medium (having cultural command area between 2000 and 10000 hectares) and minor (having cultural command area up to 2000 hectares) schemes. The others are controlled by both private people and government. Government canals cannot provide water throughout the whole year in most places, despite a large commendable area of the state. Table-8.1 presents comprehensive data on *gross cropped area* under the canal irrigation. The triennia average of data collected from the *Department of Irrigation and Waterways*, Government of West Bengal and various issues of *Statistical Abstracts*, provide us important piece of information regarding the progress of government schemes in exploiting river water flow and utilising it in the production of crops.

The table reveals that since 1970-73 Burdwan has been always at the top position followed by Birbhum, Bankura and Hooghly. But it is also evident that proportion of *gross cropped area* covered by canal irrigation in Burdwan, Hooghly, Darjeeling has been decreasing over time. The implication is that area under canal irrigation has not increased at the same pace as that of *gross cropped area*. In other words, acreage of cultivation in the rabi and summer season has increased more due to the expansion of minor irrigation. A remarkable achievement has been noticed after 1970, in the field of ground water irrigation, made possible by shallow tube-well (STW), deep tube-well (DTW), submersible pumps etc. Accelerating spread of area under minor irrigation schemes, sponsored by the government and under private ownership has brought a momentous change in agrarian scenario in those districts. Table 8.2 shows that, a notable growth of ground-water irrigation structure has taken place at differential rate in different districts of West Bengal.

It is observed that around 59 per cent of *gross cropped area* and 40.8 per cent of *net cropped area* were under potential source of irrigation in West Bengal during 1988. The corresponding figures during 1973 were roughly 25.5 and 22 per cent respectively. It was a remarkable achievement. Ground-water structures have further progressed vigorously after 1988 mainly under the initiative of the private people depending upon their resource position and potential water reserves in their respective areas.

An inter-district comparison reveals that Burdwan and Hooghly are the two leading districts in terms of proportion of *net* and *gross cropped area* under the irrigation potential of government canals and ground-water sources. These are the main causes of rapid progress and diversification of agriculture in these two districts. In this estimation it is assumed that all the deep tube-wells (DTW), submersible pumps, shallow tube-wells (STW) are able to irrigate with full potential in all the three seasons of the year. Whereas, open dug well, filter points and government canals can supply water only in one-season and river pumps twice of the three crop seasons in each year. It is true that all the shallows and deep tube-wells are not of equal capacity and not operated in full-swing at all times due to several constraints (low voltage problem in electricity supply, problem of water table that goes far down during dry summer and machinery failures etc.). The results exhibit the potential capacity of the state and districts, which can be put under irrigation if all the sources function in the ways presented above. It is also observed from Table 8.2-A that percentage of *net cropped area* covered by all sources is highest in Burdwan throughout the entire period under consideration. The proportion was 65.38 per cent during 1973 and increased to roughly 90 per cent during 1988, of which around 8 and 26 per cent were the share of ground-water sources during 1973 and 1988 respectively. In other words, the share of ground-water has increased by more than three times during the said period which has further increased after 1988 but data on all of these are not available. Data on only growth of potential irrigation structure under different government irrigation schemes are available up to 1994-95, which have been taken into consideration later in table-8.3. Burdwan, Hooghly and Birbhum have been the three major districts receiving irrigation on more than fifty per cent of their *net sown area*; whereas, Purulia and Cooch Behar have been the worst sufferers in this respect in 1979.

In 1988 around 90, 77 and 73 per cent of *net sown area* were under all these sources in Burdwan, Hooghly and Birbhum respectively. The corresponding proportions in Purulia and Cooch Behar were 11.74 and 13.4 per cent. In 1988, Jalpaiguri and Darjeeling were at the lowest rung of area coverage by irrigation sources. Substantial achievement has taken place in the district of Nadia, Which has improved ranking from seven to four. Only 16.73 per cent of *net sown area* were under irrigation in 1973 and increased to 60.55 per cent in 1988. 24-Paraganas also experienced significant improvement in the net sown area under irrigation from only around 5 per cent to 27 per cent, though there was no significant change in its relative ranking.

There has hardly been any significant development of the area under government canals in West Bengal which had increased from around 11 per cent to only 13.6 per cent of *gross cropped area* through 1970-73 to 1991-94 as is evident from table-8.1. In terms of percentage of *net sown area* covered by government canals, the figure increased nearly by 3 per cent from 15.86 to 18.82 during 1973 to 1988 i.e., in 15 years.

The change that occurred in this field was mainly due to the progress in the districts of Burdwan, Bankura, Birbhum, Midnapore, Purulia and Howrah after the completion of several river valley-projects under major and minor irrigation schemes of the government.

Despite hardly any facility of canal irrigation the districts, like Nadia, 24-Paraganas, West Dinajpur and Malda have been successful in bringing a major part of *gross cropped area* under assured irrigation. Nadia became the third district in terms of extent of *gross cropped area* under irrigation. Still now Burdwan, Hooghly and Nadia are the three front runners, whereas the districts of Purulia, Bankura have started progressing significantly after 1981 in the race of catching up. Much of the private irrigation schemes have been developed by the initiative of private people on their own interest which has not been fully covered in this analysis due to non-availability of data. A comparison of data in table-8.3 and those of 8.4 reveals that major part of shallow tube-well (and also the low capacity deep tube-wells (LDTW) and submersible pump-sets) are under private ownership and management.

Number of shallow tube-wells is quite different between the two tables. Whereas 3342 shallow tube-wells (STW) were under Government or public irrigation scheme in 1987-88 (in table-8.4) the corresponding number from census of West Bengal was 366542 in 1988 (from table-8.3). The figures were 60573 and 155621 during 1973-74 and 1981 under the total of public and private management and ownership. On the other hand, under public irrigation system the figure was only 3369 in 1979-80. Though the years were not identical in the two corresponding tables, the figures of 1979-80 and 1981 as well as 1987-88 and 1988 of the two tables are weakly comparable. The increase in huge differences implies the heavy rate of growth of shallow tube-wells under private ownership. Number of STW under public management has decreased to 3231 in 1994-95 since many of STW has been converted to low capacity, middle capacity and high capacity deep tube-well. Among them, there was a mushroom growth of submersible pumps or low capacity DTW. This conversion had taken place to cope with the problem of gradual lowering of the water table and increasing demand year after year. Over the years, water table has gone downwards faster in districts having a rapid expansion of ground-water set-up. The densely situated shallows, submersibles etc are now facing problem of low water table and fellow owners are enmeshed in competition of raising the power and capacity of their establishments to exploit water as much as possible. Ground-water exploitation through filter point and open dug well has been the other important ways in the district of Purulia, Midnapore, Bankura, Jalpaiguri and Cooch Behar, where the establishment of DTW and STW are very difficult and costly and hence uneconomic to the very small private cultivators. In 1994-95 there were only 148 DTWs of different capacity under public minor irrigation schemes in the district of Bankura and there was nothing in Purulia and Darjeeling. Hooghly, Burdwan and Nadia are the three leading districts where these establishments have made a favourable impact in the expansion of cultivation of crops in all the seasons. Many of the low capacity deep-tubewells have been established by the private people for their own use and to conduct irrigation business, for their additional income. This has been encouraged by the extension of loan advanced by different financial agencies and government. Number of STW under government schemes has decreased since many of them have been converted to low capacity deep-tubewell (LDTW) or middle capacity deep-tubewell (MDTW) and with only few new establishments. The same is true also for private people as difficulty of lifting water by STW has increased with rising demand. Still, very poor farmers are now setting STW as well as LDTW. But the census data were not available. So it is not possible to give a contemporary picture of the private sector. However, it can be safely asserted that the role of private irrigation system occupies an important place in the ground-water irrigation of West Bengal, especially in the districts where, these sources are cheap and easily accessible.

8.3. Chemical Fertiliser

Let us now consider the consumption of chemical fertiliser, which has observed an enormous growth in the post-Green Revolution period in West Bengal and facilitated rapid expansion of cultivation. Adoption of more chemical fertiliser is another example of employment of modern technological inputs in the cultivation of crop. Three types of chemical fertilisers are generally used in most cases. These are nitrogenous (N), phosphatic (P) and potassic (K). Though, a mild difference is present in the use of these categories in the production of different crops, their use has increased over time with the growing commercialisation and diversification of crops. It has been observed that cultivation of boro rice, potato and mustard has increased at the cost of other low value crops. As more and more land are withdrawn from cultivation of other crops like jowar, bazra, ragi, small millet, wheat, pulses etc and shifted to increase the area sown of the aforesaid crops along with the general increase in *gross cropped area*, requirement of chemical fertilisers also increases. This is because; those high value crops are relatively more fertiliser intensive[4]. It is also true that increased use of chemical fertiliser is complementary to an improved irrigation system[5]. Data on the use of chemical fertiliser of N, P and K categories and their aggregates are collected at the district level from different issues of Statistical Abstract, Economic Review of West Bengal. Three-year moving average of use of chemical fertiliser per thousand hectares is then calculated and displayed in table-8.5.

It is observed that the use of nitrogenous, phosphatic and potassic fertiliser has increased in aggregate by nearly seven times through 1972-75 to 1991-94 in West Bengal. On the average during 1972-75 the figure was 14.87 tonnes per thousand hectares and increased to 96.62 tonnes per thousand hectares during 1991-94. The district level figures reveal that Howrah, Hooghly, Burdwan and Birbhum were at the foremost positions all the times with a mild change in order. Howrah and Hooghly were always at top two positions alternately, whereas Burdwan was at number three or four in the relative ranking of the districts. The district, which has improved its position significantly, is Darjeeling. The ranking improved from 9 in 1972-75 to 3 in 1991-94. The use of chemical fertiliser however has increased in absolute amount in all the districts. The districts, where the use is higher than the state average are Howrah, Hooghly, Darjeeling, Burdwan, Birbhum and Malda. In Nadia and 24-Paraganas, the application of chemical fertiliser per thousand hectares has increased by over 5 and 6 times respectively without any significant change in their relative rankings. In Howrah the consumption of chemical fertiliser in 1991-94 was around 8 times of that of 1972-75, which was the highest ever increase compared to the other districts. The table also reveals that, use of chemical fertiliser and/or its growth rate was very high in districts where the growth of acreage under boro rice, potato and mustard had taken place at a relatively rapid rate. Though the use of chemical fertiliser in Midnapore and Nadia is still below the state average, growth in these districts has taken place at a noticeable rate as they were initially very low user but gradually adjusting themselves. In addition to these above, use of other chemicals, supplementary foods of the plants are now increasingly used in the cultivation of commercial crops to enhance yield.

8.4. Modern Agricultural Implements

Diversification and development of crop cultivation in any region is also related to the use of modern agricultural implements. Like irrigation and chemical fertiliser, application of modern, improved technical implements like, increase of diesel engine/ pump-set, electric pump-set for irrigation (along with DTW, MDTW etc.), power tiller, tractor and sprayer/duster are all important aspects of agricultural growth in West Bengal. Use of these instruments help, rapid adjustment of crop cultivation over different seasons with the changing motive/outlook of the cultivators. For example the growth of tractors, power tillers and developed irrigation machineries facilitated accelerated acreage of boro rice and potato since 1970. For quick completion of cultivation of potato on an extensive area, within a small, stipulated time, use of tractor and power tiller instead of simple plough is essential. Similarly, modern pump-sets if electrified help raising capacity of farmers to sow boro rice on more and more areas.

However the use of these instruments has not spread uniformly over different districts of West Bengal and thus can be viewed as a symptom of presence of inter-district disparity of cropping pattern movement and growth of agriculture. Available data on these aspects are very limited. Table-8.6 shows the application of main implements in agricultural activities during 1972, 1982 and 1989 in different districts of West Bengal.

From the table it is evident that the number of all the implements has increased manifold during 1972-1989 in the agricultural use of West Bengal. The number of diesel engines together with electric pump-sets, the chief instruments of ground-water irrigation has increased from merely one per thousand hectares in 1972 to over 52 per thousand hectares in 1989. Beyond 1989 also there has been an enormous growth of all type instruments, data of which are not presented here. Number of tractors was only 0.102 in 1972 and in 1989 it went up to 0.737 per thousand hectares, in spite of the fact that tractors are also used in some other business (such as transportation) activities. Number of power tillers and sprayers operated by power were respectively 0.393 and 0.459 per thousand hectares in 1982. They have increased to 0.946 and 5.567 per thousand hectares during 1989. It is also clear from the inter-district comparison that Burdwan, Hooghly, Nadia, Howrah, 24-Paraganas are relatively more advanced in these respects compared to the other districts of the state. It is no wonder that these districts observed faster rate of growth of cultivation of boro rice, potato and mustard as considered earlier.

8.5. Observation

The above discussion reveals that the districts which observed larger growth of area under boro rice, mustard and potato (the newly emerging cash crops), also displayed relatively faster growth in the use of agricultural implements, which are used to plough field, lift water from river as well as underground sources and agricultural transportation. These, districts have improved their positions significantly in the use of chemical fertiliser, irrigation and other modern agri-inputs in raising productivity of land. Despite the presence of disparity in adoption of modern technology all the districts of the state have noticed a trend of modernization over time in respect of use of all these major inputs and agricultural machineries[6]. The differential rate of diffusion of technology is instrumental in causing widespread imbalances in diversification of crop and growth of agricultural production and productivity. This difference in adoption pattern can be attributed to differences in general level of awareness of farmers of various regions, which is influenced by their level of education, media contact, urban influence, demonstration and initiative by different agencies and government itself, as well as their financial position and availability of technical instruments that facilitate the easy expansion of agriculture and diversification of cultivation. The growth of market also has a feed back effect on the use of these instruments or methods of cultivation, through the changing opportunities that, necessitate the urgent growth of specific categories of crops which in turn requires utilisation of new methods and instruments. Therefore there is much scope for further research on whether and how variation in scientific knowledge based technological change, embodied in new biological, chemical and mechanical inputs or disembodied technical change, farmer's educational level affect the diversification process. Also one can consider the variation in government infrastructure, number of bank branches (from where farmers can take loan), variation in temperature (e.g., number of cool months (temperature less than 18°C)), soil moisture capacity index etc. to explain the regional variation in diversification.

NOTES

1 Gujrati D. (1984), *Basic Econometrics*, Mc-Graw Hill, Singapore, ch. 9 and 13.

2 This is due to the interaction of several inter-dependent factors used as explanatory variables in the model.

3 For the lack of availability of data all of them could not be included in the regression analysis.

4 It is noticed from the data on cost of cultivation as presented in the study on Farm Management and Cost of Production of crops in West Bengal, 1993-94 (conducted by the Evaluation Wing, Directorate of Agriculture, Government of West Bengal) that the fertiliser cost of potato, boro rice is relatively more than that of other crops.

5 Dasgupta B. op cit.

6 Use of high yielding seeds is not considered here due to the lack of data at district level.

Table 8.1 Percentage of Gross Cropped Area Irrigated by Government Canals in West Bengal (District-wise)

District	1970-73	1977-80	1984-87	1991-94
Burdwan	46.99 (1)	49.36 (1)	45.51 (1)	43.81 (1)
Birbhum	37.001 (2)	40.36 (2)	42.43 (2)	40.90 (2)
Bankura	19.60 (4)	35.14 (3)	41.10 (3)	39.55 (3)
Midnapore	10.59 (5)	14.60 (5)	15.78 (5)	15.17 (5)
Howrah	3.57 (7)	3.04 (9)	4.20 (8)	3.18 (8)
Hooghy	27.4 (3)	27.33 (4)	27.26 (4)	22.19 (4)
24-Paraganas	---	---	---	2.82 (9)
Nadia	---	---	---	---
Murshidabad	7.92 (6)	8.67 (6)	8.26 (6)	7.59 (6)
West Dinajpur	---	----	---	---
Malda	---	---	---	---
Jalpaiguri	2.95 (8)	2.29 (10)	1.74 (10)	1.39 (10)
Darjeeling	2.77 (9)	3.55 (8)	2.48 (9)	0.584 (11)
Cooch-Behar	0.056 (11)	---	0.095 (11)	0.125 (12)
Purulia	0.786 (10)	4.39 (7)	7.22 (7)	6.69 (7)
West Bengal	11.335	13.39	13.83	13.57

Sources: (i) Department of Irrigation and Waterways, Government of West Bengal.
(ii) Government of West Bengal, Bureau of Applied Economics and Statistics, *Statistical Abstract (various issues).*
(iii) Government of West Bengal, Bureau of Applied Economics and Statistics, *Economic Review (various issues).*

Note: (i) Figures in the parentheses represent rankings.
(ii) The Sign--means the value is nil or negligible.

Table 8.2 (A) Potential Percentage of Net Cropped Area under Irrigation in West Bengal (Districtwise)

District	Ground Water			Canal Irrigation			Total		
	1973	1981	1988	1973	1981	1988	1973	1981	1988
Burdwan	7.97	13.41	25.93	57.41	52.48	63.61	65.38 (1)	65.89 (1)	89.54 (1)
Birbhum	3.45	5.13	13.4	50.83	49.97	59.57	54.27 (3)	55.1 (3)	72.97 (3)
Bankura	2.59	5.28	12.5	31.69	42.29	43.02	34.29 (4)	47.57 (4)	55.51 (3)
Midnapore	3.46	6.11	17.08	14.03	18.79	21.86	17.50 (6)	24.9 (7)	38.94 (7)
Howrah	9.53	11.79	14.33	3.74	4.13	5.31	13.27 (8)	15.92 (9)	19.63 (10)
Hooghy	15.82	30.00	39.5	46.16	35.25	37.7	61.98 (2)	65.25 (2)	77.2 (2)
24-Paraganas	4.92	13.03	26.79	---	---	---	4.92 (11)	13.03 (10)	26.79 (9)
Nadia	16.73	36.22	60.55	---	---	---	16.73 (7)	36.22 (5)	60.55 (4)
Murshidabad	10.64	22.44	39.57	12.91	11.71	12.05	23.55 (5)	34.15 (6)	51.62 (6)
West Dinajpur	6.06	9.30	16.28	0.38	---	---	6.4 (10)	9.3 (11)	16.28 (11)
Malda	11.35	17.44	27.62	---	---	---	11.35 (9)	17.44 (8)	27.62 (8)
Jalpaiguri	0.91	1.72	6.79	3.28	2.07	1.93	4.19 (13)	3.79 (15)	8.72 (14)
Darjeeling	0.19	1.98	2.32	4.47	5.92	5.70	4.66 (12)	7.85 (12)	8.02 (5)
Cooch-Behar	2.35	6.27	13.16	0.04	0.11	0.23	2.39 (14)	6.38 (14)	13.39 (12)
Purulia	0.16	1.60	2.68	1.09	4.83	9.06	1.24 (15)	6.43 (13)	11.74 (13)
West Bengal	6.12	11.97	21.97	15.86	16.45	18.82	21.98	28.42	40.79

Sources: (i) Government of West Bengal, Directorate of Irrigation and Waterways.

(ii) Government of West Bengal, State Water Investigation Directorate, A Report on Ground Water Structures in the State of West Bengal, Calcutta, Nov. 1982

(iii) Report of census of Minor Irrigation Schemes in West Bengal, 1988.

Note: (i) Data of 1973 do not include area under dug well and filter point.

(ii) Data include both private and public irrigation system.

(iii) In the calculation of potential capacity, deep-tubewells, shallows and submersible pumps are considered to provide irrigation maximum in all the three seasons while, river pumps in two full-seasons and filter-point, open dug-well, canals to give only in one season of the year.

(iv) Area under canal water includes area covered by Government canals (under major and minor schemes) only.

(v) Capacity of river life irrigation in 1981-82 is calculated from the data of 1979-80 as those data for 1981-82 is calculated from the data of 1979-80 as those data for 1981-82 were not available.

(vi) Figures in the parentheses represent rankings.

(vii) ---means the value is ineligible.

Table 8.2 (B) Potential Percentage of Gross Gropped Area under Irrigation in West Bengal (Districtwise)

District	Ground Water			Canal Irrigation			Total		
	1973	1981	1988	1973	1981	1988	1973	1981	1988
Burdwan	17.49	30.72	52.46	44.90	42.41	44.32	62.39 (1)	73.13 (2)	96.78 (1)
Birbhum	7.41	11.34	27.15	39.24	40.35	42.13	46.65 (3)	51.69 (4)	69.28 (5)
Bankura	6.06	11.93	28.16	27.22	36.97	37.27	33.28 (4)	48.9 (5)	65.43 (6)
Midnapore	8.10	14.25	37.56	12.01	16.26	17.84	20.11 (8)	30.51 (10)	55.4 (8)
Howrah	22.55	27.23	26.50	3.16	3.41	3.62	25.71 (7)	30.64 (9)	30.12 (11)
Hooghy	29.84	58.80	69.41	31.70	24.31	23.20	61.57 (2)	83.11 (1)	92.61 (3)
24-Paraganas	12.87	32.88	60.82	---	---	---	12.87 (10)	32.88 (7)	60.82 (7)
Nadia	30.85	66.05	95.00	---	---	---	3.85 (5)	66.05 (3)	95.00 (2)
Murshidabad	18.56	39.31	69.14	8.14	7.52	7.23	26.70 (6)	46.83 (6)	76.37 (4)
West Dinajpur	11.41	15.79	32.01	0.28	---	---	11.69 (11)	15.79 (11)	32.01 (10)
Malda	18.84	30.66	47.75	---	---	---	18.84 (9)	3.66 (8)	47.75 (9)
Jalpaiguri	2.59	4.24	12.62	3.21	1.87	1.39	5.8 (12)	6.11 (14)	14.01 (15)
Darjeeling	0.29	2.29	8.31	2063	2.84	7.72	2.92 (14)	5.13 (15)	16.03 (13)
Cooch-Behar	4.88	10.69	21.94	0.03	0.08	0.13	4.91 (13)	10.77 (12)	22.07 (12)
Purulia	0.31	2.52	4.23	1.06	5.18	9.88	1.37 (15)	7.7 (13)	14.11 (14)
West Bengal	13.17	25.83	45.28	12.37	12.94	13.67	25.54	38.77	58.95

Sources: Same as Table -8.2 (A),
Notes: Same as Table 8.2 (A)

Table 8.3 Ground-Water and River-life Irrigation strength of West Bengal (Number)

District/Year	1973*			1981**					1988			
	DTW	RLI	STW	DTW	RLI	STW	FP	DW	DTW	RLI	STW	DW
Burdwan	301	191	7114	362	237	15808	762	184	390	266	37047	391
Birbhum	40	65	3107	49	91	4480	385	646	50	103	14661	713
Bankura	59	65	1632	82	130	3554	671	7045	55	175	13002	8053
Midnapore	152	212	6234	302	267	10322	499	22129	304	365	43789	26328
Howrah	79	46	1411	122	56	1154	37	--	132	95	1177	--
Hooghy	240	219	5720	350	262	17571	301	75	376	316	23512	59
24-Paraganas	213	115	8080	253	140	27323	5973	164	256	211	60262	--
Nadia	510	239	7620	603	272	28494	6750	1	588	319	61137	--
Murshidabad	368	264	6880	434	302	22973	7070	--	402	340	52699	--
West Dinajpur	116	270	4837	142	270	8816	4123	2748	133	345	22640	1381
Malda	128	347	5586	178	353	10127	1179	5	177	381	20101	6
Jalpaiguri	33	7	409	37	27	1005	181	604	40	71	4370	1370
Darjeeling	1	1	--	1	11	157	7	44	4	23	814	231
Cooch-Behar	15	15	1943	49	23	3836	3128	8158	51	88	11331	3763
Purulia	--	12	--	--	55	1	--	25506	--	100	--	18290
West Bengal	2255	2068	60573	2964	2496	155621	31066	67309	2958	3198	366542	60585

Sources: (i) *Government of West Bengal, Directorate of agriculture,
(ii) **A Report on Ground water structure in the state of West Bengal, State Water investigation Directorate, Government of West Bengal, Calcutta, Nov. 1982.
(iii) Government of West Bengal, Directorate of Irrigation and Waterways.

Notes: (i) --indicate the values in nil
(ii) DTW→Deep tubewell, STW → Shallow tubewell,, RLI → River lift irrigation, FP → Filter point, DW → Dug Well.

Table 8.4 Progress of Minor Irrigation Projects (Ground and River-life Irrigation) in West Bengal under Government Minor Irrigation Schemes in West Bengal (Number)

District/Year	1979-80			1987-88			1993-94						1994-95					
	DTW	RLI	STW	DTW	RLI	STW	HDTW	MDTW	LDTW	Total DTW	RLI	STW	HDTW	MDTW	LDTW	Total DTW	RLI	STW
Burdwan	301	237	408	332	266	408	443	19	114	576	265	510	447	24	176	647	259	101
Birbhum	45	91	--	46	103	--	47	19	--	66	103	--	42	20	12	74	98	--
Bankura	64	130	--	66	175	--	67	18	--	85	181	--	45	20	83	148	180	24
Midnapore	172	267	187	223	365	187	297	16	130	443	399	187	190	20	217	427	387	71
Howrah	89	56	30	93	95	30	94	12	--	106	95	30	79	20	--	99	91	--
Hooghy	240	262	361	261	316	361	317	11	180	508	316	361	312	17	276	605	304	80
24-Paraganas	228	140	318	252	211	318	266	20	12	298	211	396	246	39	59	334	208	356
Nadia	517	272	600	532	319	600	612	28	216	856	319	943	591	32	228	851	299	758
Murshidabad	383	302	936	402	340	909	479	18	162	659	354	1161	469	32	150	651	343	748
West Dinajpur	116	270	200	134	345	200	209	8	--	217	345	404	308	11	--	319	333	407
Malda	128	353	239	164	381	239	242	9	24	275	381	395	257	11	24	292	347	232
Jalpaiguri	33	27	--	33	71	--	46	--	--	46	77	174	46	--	--	46	77	202
Darjeeling	1	11	--	1	23	--	1	--	--	1	23	--	--	--	--	--	23	--
Cooch-Behar	15	23	90	15	88	90	24	--	--	24	95	276	30	--	--	30	95	252
Purulia	--	55	--	--	100	--	--	--	--	--	133	--	--	--	--	--	128	--
West Bengal	2332	2496	3369	2554	3198	3342	3144	178	838	4160	3297	4837	3062	236	1225	4523	3172	3231

Sources: (i) *Government of West Bengal, Directorate of agriculture,
(ii) Government of West Bengal, Directorate of Irrigation and Waterways.

Notes: (i) Figures related to Minor irrigation Schemes of the Government of West Bengal
(ii) --indicate the values in nil
(iii) DTW → Deep tubewell, STW → Shallow tubewell,, RLI → River lift irrigation, FP → Filter point, DW → Dug Well.

Table 8.5 Consumption of Chemical fertiliser per thousand hectate of Gross Cropped Area in West Bengal (District-wise)

(Tonne/thousand hectare)

District	1972-75	1977-80	1984-87	1991-94
Burdwan	22.55 (4)	49.80 (3)	87.63(3)	125.42 (4)
Birbhum	24.59 (3)	37.40 (5)	64.84 (6)	124.62 (5)
Bankura	20.62 (5)	32.58 (6)	48.05 (10)	71.62 (14)
Midnapore	10.87 (10)	23.34 (9)	44.84 (11)	72.94 (12)
Howrah	34.01 (2)	78.93 (1)	172.91 (1)	276.62 (1)
Hooghy	41.68 (1)	78.22 (2)	165.28 (2)	183.60 (2)
24-Paraganas	16.099 (7)	28.20 (7)	60.85 (7)	97.94 (7)
Nadia	17.96 (6)	42.03 (4)	59.13 (8)	87.17 (8)
Murshidabad	14.40 (8)	20.92 (11)	54.89 (9)	80.49 (10)
West Dinajpur	3.53 (14)	15.306 (12)	38.88 (12)	57.72 (15)
Malda	10.34 (11)	24.13 (8)	69.59 (5)	106.18 (6)
Jalpaiguri	4.126 (13)	7.67 (15)	21.75 (15)	72.17 (13)
Darjeeling	12.05 (9)	22.29 (10)	80.09 (4)	164.435 (3)
Cooch-Behar	3.395 (15)	9.803 (14)	36.55 (14)	76.46 (11)
Purulia	6.317 (12)	13.97 (13)	37.30 (13)	84.42 (9)
West Bengal	14.87	30.06	60.67	96.62

Sources: (i) Fertiliser Association of India, *Fertiliser Statistics, (various issues)*

(ii) Government of West Bengal, Bureau of Applied Economics and Statistics, Statistical Abstract (various issues).

Notes: Figures in the parentheses represent rankings.

Table 8.6 Number of Principal Agricultural Implements per Thousand Hectares of Gross Cropped Area (District-wise) in West Bengal

District/year	Diesel Engine 1972	Diesel Engine 1982	Diesel Engine 1989	Electric Pumpset 1972	Electric Pumpset 1982	Electric Pumpset 1989
1	2	3	4	5	6	7
Burdwan	0.872 (5)	50.656 (2)	65.44 (5)	0.684 (8)	2.446 (3)	5.268 (6)
Birbhum	0.178 (12)	19.574 (9)	40.41 (8)	0.103 (9)	1.091 (7)	6.621 (4)
Bankura	0.265 (10)	22.747 (7)	35.15 (9)	0.14 (8)	0.323 (10)	1.33 (10)
Midnapore	0.894 (4)	32.842 (6)	71.463 (3)	0.10 (11)	1.999 (5)	3.95 (8)
Howrah	8.56 (1)	34.38 (5)	49.144 (7)	0.69 (2)	1.855 (6)	11.375 (2)
Hooghy	1.777 (2)	110.73 (1)	87.503 (1)	0.007 (14)	4.219 (2)	8.047 (3)
24-Paraganas	0.74 (6)	43.206 (4)	70.017 (4)	0.259 (6)	2.121 (4)	5.797 (5)
Nadia	0.70 (7)	48.808 (3)	73.221 (2)	1.109 (1)	10.755 (1)	14.861 (1)
Murshidabad	0.531 (8)	22.414 (8)	54.658 (6)	0.60 (4)	0.604 (8)	5.131 (7)
West Dinajpur	0.248 (11)	5.82 (11)	24.80 (10)	0.179 (7)	0.222 (12)	1.096 (11)
Malda	0.178 (13)	12.313 (10)	17.217 (11)	0.325 (5)	0.311 (11)	2.773 (9)
Jalpaiguri	0.44 (9)	--	3.445 (12)	0.103 (10)	--	0.516 (12)
Darjeeling	0.171 (14)	--	3.232 (13)	0.012 (13)	--	--
Cooch-Behar	1.362 (3)	3.89 (13)	2.911 (14)	0.042 (12)	0.581 (9)	0.20 (13)
Purulia	.111 (5)	4.183 (12)	2.606 (5)	--	0.110 (13)	0.172 (14)
West Bengal	0.763	29.78	47.656	0.299	1.975	4.630

Contd.. . . .

Table 8.6 concld.

District/Year	Power Tiller 1982	1989	Tractor 1972	1982	1989	Power Opearated Sprayer/Duster 1982	1989
1	8	9	10	11	12	13	14
Burdwan	.358 (3)	1.173 (4)	.233 (2)	1.661 (1)	3.882 (1)	0.185 (8)	1.747 (1)
Birbhum	.116 (7)	.259 (8)	.160 (1)	.155 (6)	.696 (5)	0.142 (9)	.753 (7)
Bankura	.063 (9)	.102 (10)	.028 (15)	.052 (9)	.547 (6)	.118 (10)	.463 (10)
Midnapore	.143 (5)	1.613 (3)	0.43 (13)	.093 (7)	.329 (10)	.417 (2)	.595 (9)
Howrah	2.656 (2)	3.537 (2)	.34 (1)	.438 (3)	.856 (3)	.363 (3)	1.047 (5)
Hooghy	4.696 (1)	7.277 (1)	.065 (10)	1.041 (2)	1.545 (2)	.595 (1)	1.212 (4)
24-Paraganas	.332 (4)	.959 (5)	.154 (5)	.274 (4)	.477 (8)	.295 (5)	1.222 (3)
Nadia	.074 (8)	.264 (7)	.139 (6)	.189 (5)	.840 (4)	.348 (4)	.360 (11)
Murshidabad	.019 (12)	0.51 (12)	.065 (11)	.042 (11)	.250 (11)	.268 (6)	.128 (13)
West Dinajpur	.012 (13)	0.19 (13)	0.32 (14)	0.41 (12)	.547 (7)	.050 (12)	.638 (8)
Malda	.119 (6)	.328 (6)	0.84 (8)	0.54 (8)	.005 (14)	.006 (13)	.888 (6)
Jalpaiguri	--	.142 (9)	.165 (3)	--	.360 (9)	--	1.708 (2)
Darjeeling	--	--	0.73 (9)	--	--	--	--
Cooch-Behar	.062 (10)	.073 (11)	0.48 (12)	0.21 (13)	.122 (13)	.204 (7)	0.22 (12)
Purulia	.038 (11)	--	.102 (7)	.047 (10)	.163 (12)	0.72 (11)	0.12 (14)
West Bengal	.393	.946	.102	.281	.737	.459	5.567

Sources: (i) Live Stock Census Report of West Bengal, 1982
(ii) Govermnet of West Bengal , Bureau of Applied Economics and Statistics, *Statistical Abstract, (various issues).*

Note: (i) Figures in the parentheses represent rankings.
(ii) -- indicated the value is not available.

CHAPTER 9

AN EMPIRICAL ANALYSIS WITH RESPECT TO THE DISTRICT OF BURDWAN

9.1 Background

The district of Burdwan is an important agricultural district of West Bengal. The south central district, Burdwan is bounded on three sides north, east and south by the districts of Birbhum, Murshidabad, Nadia, Hooghly, Bankura and Purulia and on the West by the state of Bihar. Total area of the district is 7024 square kilometres. The district is situated between latitudes 23^0 53^1 – 22^0 56^1 North and longitudes 88^0 25^1 - 86^0 48^1 East.[1]

Most of the agricultural and non-agricultural activities are found in the district. Thus the district occupies an important position in both the agricultural and industrial activities of the state. The industrial activities are mostly concentrated in the north-western part while the vast southern part is mainly confined to agricultural and agro-based industrial activities. Despite a good industrial base, the economy of the district is predominantly agricultural. The sector provides livelihood to most of the population of the district and there is no sign of significant decrease in agricultural dependence during the last two decades. Around 52.5 per cent of main workers are engaged in agricultural activities according to 1991 Census Report[2]. The figure was 54.8 per cent in 1970-71[3]. For its particular agro-climatic condition the district is capable of growing a good number of crops. Soil is partly alluvium and partly lateritic, which show very good response to the application of fertilisers and manures. Rainfall is also moderate.

The district occupies 8.05 per cent of total area of the state and ranks third, after 24Paraganas and Midnapore in terms of area. It constitutes respectively 8.65 and 8.67 per cent of total cultivable area and net sown area of the state in 1994-95. Comparatively much higher percentage of total foodgrains produced in the state is contributed by the district. In 1994-95 it was 12.82 per cent, the second highest among all the districts of the state. Yield of foodgrain was the highest (27.87 thousand Kg. Per hectare) in Burdwan in 1994-95, which implies that the production per unit of total cultivable area and net sown area were also highest among all the districts[4]. All these figures are depicted in table-9.1. It is also observed that, production of foodgrain in 1994-95 was 3.41 and 3.59 tonnes per hectare of total cultivable area and net sown area respectively. Because of its remarkable contribution to the state's total foodgrain production the district is recognised as the granary of West Bengal.

Explanations of the earlier chapters reveal a continuous change in cropping pattern in the district (like the state) since 1970-71. The change in inter-crop variation in acreage has taken place largely in favour of boro rice, potato and oilseed, the principal component of which is mustard. However rice continues to remain the principal component of agricultural production of the district. The alluvium soil, normal and moderate rainy season is highly conducive to the cultivation of paddy. Despite the geographical and agro-climatic factor noted above, socio-economic, technological and institutional factors act as guiding force behind the changing cropping pattern of the district. A change of all these has been reflected in the movement of cropping pattern. It has been found that acreage of oilseeds, boro rice and potato has increased at relatively rapid rate than that of others and at the cost of pulses, wheat and inferior crops like jowar, bajra etc. Farmers were attracted by the fabulous remuneration of those advancing crops and their plans were supported by the development of necessary factors such as; irrigation, machineries needed for the fast growth of cultivation of those crops. As the district is over-saturated with the production of food articles, commercialisation has been expedited with the advancement of technology, market or exchange facilities and infrastructural systems. The evolution of sophisticated implements, high yielding seeds, and fertilisers has made those crops relatively more attractive (in terms of profit) than the others grown in their respective seasons. It has also been observed that the expansion of those crops happened to be in accordance with the farmers' objective of generating maximum possible surplus from their limited holdings (in a crop year) at a least possible risk.

In the final section of chapter-7, the hypothesis of choice by comparison of revenue or profit of alternative crops in a progressive situation has been further strengthened by considering the profit expected from the cultivation of different possible combination of crops, grown in successive seasons of the year on the same plot. When alternative combinations are open to choice, it has been noticed that the most profitable combination is in line with the lucrative crops. But the explanation lacks one thing that the profitability of a combination had been calculated simply by aggregating the profitability of each crop within that particular combination; where the data on output and cost of a crop represent the average of output and cost of all sample plots, on which the crop has been grown. On some of the sample plots the crop grown (in a particular season) say, potato (in winter) may be followed by boro rice (in summer) and in the same way on some other plots mustard may be followed by boro rice. In these two different cases cost and output of boro rice and so its profitability would be different due to just, differences in preceding crop. On a particular plot the preceding crop may affect the cost and output of the current seasons crop. In the same way the choice of present season's crop may affect the cost and output of the successor to be grown during the next season. Therefore the use of same data on cost and benefit of each crop forming different combinations is not so appropriate. As the cost and output differs for different combinations it will be more appropriate; if it is possible to collect data on cost and benefit of each crop for separate cases i.e., from different sample plots on which different combinations are followed. In this chapter the same sort of analysis has been done for the district of Burdwan.

9.2 Methodology Adopted

The analysis has been made on the basis of primary data collected from 60 sample farms chosen 20 from each of three villages in Madhabdihi block of southern Burdwan. The block in southern Burdwan is well developed in agricultural sphere and the three contiguous villages are chosen purposively as those villages were known for several years where agricultural development has taken place at rapid strides. Most of the land of those villages are now within the purview of multiple cropping and thus it is possible to have cross section data on cost and output or simply profit of major crops grown in that area with different preceding crops and succeeding crops on separate plots of land. Moreover, there are very good marketing facilities and co-operative and other banking facilities, which help rapid expansion of commercialisation of agriculture. There are good irrigation facilities mostly under private irrigation system and a few under government canals, river lift irrigation as well as government provided deep tube-well. The canals provide irrigation mainly in monsoon season whereas the shallow tubewells, deep tube-wells and submersible pumps can function throughout the whole year. Now many of the shallow tube-wells and submersibles are electrified and a few are running with diesel engines. The development of marketing facilities, banking system and diffusion as well as innovation of technology has led to the diversification of crop in those villages. This is despite the fact that the diversification may also take place in a traditional system as inter-crop comparison was always possible through imputed benefit-cost criterion in every socio-economic condition. It is also true that the profitability criterion is applicable for the selection of crops to be grown in any system within their capacity. All these have earlier been explained in chapter-7. The farmers cultivate crops for their own use as well as for marketing. Production is operated with the help of own as well as hired labour. Even the small peasants hire labour for their cultivation work and sometimes they hire out their own labour when they are free.

From each village 20 farms have been selected by simple random sampling without replacement. The chosen farms are found to be mostly small (more than one hectare but less than two hectares), marginal (below one hectare) and medium (above two hectares and up to four hectares) category. From each scientifically selected farm various data relating to the availability of irrigation facilities, topology of plots, price about the inventory and live stock with its value and the repair, if any etc. are collected. The sets of information like utilisation of family labour and hired labour, quantity and value of seeds, fertilisers used, manures, quantity and share of landowner (if leased in), cost of machinery (pump-set, power tiller etc.) incurred for each crop (hired or own) are collected. Data on quantity of land allocated to each crop in a particular season corresponding to the portion of its area, used for different crops in the preceding and subsequent season have been collected. All the relevant information relating to expenditure and revenue have been collected for each crop separately corresponding to different preceding crops. The profitability of each crop corresponding to different preceding crops has been calculated. Thereafter a flow chart has been prepared that shows the flow of land in aggregate of all the sixty farms together. Profitability of major combinations have been calculated and compared to observe whether there is any relationship between the profitability of different combinations and flow of land allocation towards the production of crops involved in different combinations.

9.3. Observation

Flow of land in aggregate of all the sample farms during 1993-94 are presented in diagram-9.1. From the flow chart it is evident that out of total area (242 acre) cultivated in the kharif season by all the farms during 1993-94, 166.5 acre was used for high yielding aman, 52.5 acre for local/traditional aman and 23 acre for high yielding aus. At that time, local aus varieties were not in the fields of those farmers. In the rabi/ winter season land used for the cultivation of potato, mustard, wheat was 58.2, 54.5 and 4.6 acre respectively, while the others were grown in 18.8 acre of land. Here others include onion, lentil and other rabi pulses[5]. Some other winter crops, vegetables are although grown in good amount, have not been considered in the present survey as they do not constitute very large portion of total land and also not the main crop of the region. During the next season 11.5, 26.6 and 115.5 acre of land are used respectively for jute, til and boro rice. Here it is noticed that in the kharif season high yielding aman, in the winter season potato and in the summer season boro rice occupies the largest proportion of land cultivated during the respective season. Not only that the flow of land over the seasons is highest for the combination of high yielding aman; potato and boro rice (No. 7 in table-9.2). It is followed by the combination local aman, boro rice (i.e., combination 13) and combination of high yielding aman, mustard, boro rice (i.e., combination 12).

Here it is not actually followed from the flow-chart-9.1. The chart reveals only the flow of area from each crop in one season to other crops in the following season. However flow of land towards a particular combination means the quantity of land on which all those crops included in that particular combination were cultivated successively in that particular crop year. Here *it is calculated separately by asking how much of area on which say, potato was cultivated in earlier season is used for cultivation of aus/aman (H.Y.V./local varieties in the preceding season and also how much that was used for boro rice and how much for til or jute in the following season. Similarly how much of land on which say H.Y.V. aman was grown during summer was used for mustard cultivation and how much for others in the following season.* This is plotted more clearly in flow-chart-9.2. *Yield and input used of such separate fields are also collected and that was very difficult but manageable only for these limited sample farms.*

Cost and benefits per acre for different combinations in 1993-94 of the selected sample are presented in table-9.2. Here total cost includes, cost of seed, expenditure on labour (bullock, human and machine like tractor or power tiller) if hired and for owned bullock, tractors etc. and family labour, which is calculated at the going market rate as they could earn if hired out those, irrigation charges (even if the farm own irrigation set up then its running cost, depreciation of machinery, electric bill if electrified are considered), organic or synthetic fertiliser, pesticides as well as the rent of leased in land (in case of owner cultivator how much he/she could get if leased out), transportation and marketing cost.[6] Revenue includes value of main and by-product only. It is however very difficult to find out the cost and revenue of different plots with different combinations and thus to calculate the corresponding revenue and cost because expenditure mainly on fertiliser, pesticides for growing a particular crop and its yield changes for differences in crop grown in preceding season on the same plot, as explained earlier. Here all these informations are collected for each crop corresponding to different preceding crop form each farm family separately. Then the corresponding cost and revenue are calculated taking the data of all combinations of all the sample firms together. Thereafter profit per acre of each combination is calculated by subtracting total cost from total revenue of the corresponding combination.

From the Table-9.2 it is revealed that the profitability per acre of high yielding aman (calculated at Rs 3691.19) is greater than that of high yielding aus (Rs 2747.5) and local aman (Rs 1622.5). Thus in the monsoon season, high yielding aman, became the most popular variety to the farmers. Generally potato is not cultivated after local aman on the same plot because normal sowing time of potato is greatly distorted by the cultivation of local aman. Local aman is harvested during the month of December. If potato is cultivated after that then, its productivity will be much lower than that of earlier sown one and so would be the profitability. Normal level of yield of potato remains unaffected if it is grown after aus or high yielding, short period aman, since the ideal sowing time of potato is not affected due to the cultivation of those varieties of crops. If there is no distortion of ideal time of sowing, during winter season potato is observed to be the most profitable crop among all the rabi crops. If boro rice is cultivated after potato the profitability (Rs 821.31) is found to be more than the profit of jute (Rs 649.5) and also of average profit of til (Rs 797.12). That is however far less than the profit earned when boro rice is cultivated after local aman or mustard which is calculated at Rs 3263.33. Average profit of boro rice remains more or less same when it is grown after local aman or mustard. Still combination 7, (high yielding aman, potato, boro rice) remains the most profitable combination yielding a net profit of Rs 7071.9 during 1993-94.

A comparative analysis of flow-chart-9.2 and table-9.2 reveals that the flow of acreage towards the combination including local aman and boro rice is also very high despite much lower net profit. One reason may be that, now-a-days local aman is generally grown on the fields, far away from the residential places of the farmers where despite adequate irrigation facility rabi crops are not cultivated on a large scale because of the problems of transportation, management and protection. For early harvesting and resulting transportation problem short period crops are generally not grown on far interior fields and so are the rabi crops like mustard, potato. Only boro rice is cultivated after local aman; in the span of January-April, that is found to be the more profitable crop than any other crop grown in that season. Moreover, in those areas many farmers grow boro rice on their own land and thus enjoy in addition to the net profit over total cost (as shown in table-9.2) the amount of rent that is usually paid by a sharecropper to the land owner. Though mustard yield net negative profit over total cost including rent; it is mainly preferred by those, who cultivate with the help of family labour and those who grow on their own land. Those two types of farmers generally do not emphasise on their own labour and rent of self owned land. This is also clear from the fact that they do not give much weightage on the value of self-labour and rent of self owned land in their profit approximation.

9.4. Conclusion

The conclusion we may reach out of the above discussion on the basis of the results obtained from the sample survey is that, farmers in decision making always consider the profit of different crops. Along with that they consider the number of crops that can be grown in successive seasons of the year. So the farmer prefers that combination of crops from which he can derive maximum possible net revenue at least possible risk. In acreage allocation availability of inputs, location of plots and technology of cultivation of crops also play some important roles. Stability of long run flow of income that can be obtained from their limited land is also considered by the rational farmers. Above all it follows that relative profitability expected by the farmers from different combinations of crops, that can be grown in any existing situation (for given resources and technology) plays the ultimate role in planning of acreage.

NOTES

1 Source: *Economic Review* of West Bengal 1994-95, Bureau of Applied Economics and Statistics, Government of West Bengal.

2 *Census of India, 1991*, Series-1, Paper-2 of 1992.

3 *Census of India, 1971*, Series-1, Primary population total.

4 The proportions of net sown area and foodgrains' production to the state's total have been rising during 1970-71 to 1994-95. It was noticed from the Agricultural Census Report, 1970-71 that the corresponding figures were 8.22 and 11.13 per cent respectively. Proportion of area under foodgrains in the district to state's total figure also increased from 8.55 per cent in 1970-71 to 9.56 per cent in 1994-95.

5 Two types of onion are generally grown. One in the purely rabi season and the other is normally cultivated in January-February and harvested in March-April.

6 One may also consider the interest on capital invested (loan or owned) for the cultivation of each crop but it will raise complicacy of calculation. The quantity of available capital also affects the cultivation of crops and that too differ for different size of farms. Here some farm takes loan from bank in a season but use on different purposes, inputs like fertilizer, pesticides are purchased on terms of payment after harvest at some higher prices. Not only that farmer spent throughout the whole cropping season (from sowing to harvest and marketing) and it is not included to avoiding complicacies in computation.

Table 9.1 Percentage Share of Each District to State's Total Area, Total Cultivable Area, Net Sown Area, Production of Foodgrains and Production of Foodgrains per Total Cultivable Area, Net Sown Area and Yield at District Level in 1994-95

District	Total Area	Total Cultivate Area	Net Sown Area	Production of Foodgrains	Production of Foodgrains per (tonnes per hectare)		Yield of Foodgrains (Kgs/Hec.)
					Total Cultivate Area	Net Sown Area	
Burdwan	8.05 (3)	8.65 (3)	8.67 (3)	12.82 (2)	3.41 (1)	3.59 (1)	2787 (1)
Birbhum	5.21 (9)	5.62 (9)	5.67 (9)	6.35 (8)	2.60 (6)	2.72 (6)	2231 (5)
Bankura	7.93 (4)	7.21 (6)	6.94 (6)	7.49 (5)	2.39 (8)	2.62 (8)	2314 (4)
Midnapore	15.25 (2)	15.06 (1)	15.33 (1)	17.48 (1)	2.67 (4)	2.77 (5)	2124 (8)
Howrah	1.57 (15)	1.55 (15)	1.44 (15)	1.65 (14)	2.44 (7)	2.79 (4)	1820 (11)
Hooghly	3.60 (14)	4.04 (13)	4.19 (13)	5.66 (9)	3.23 (2)	3.28 (2)	2602 (2)
24 Paraganas	15.48 (1)	11.72 (2)	12.25 (2)	11.29 (3)	2.21 (9)	2.24 (10)	2010 (9)
Nadia	4.51 (10)	5.31 (10)	5.50 (10)	6.37 (7)	2.76 (3)	2.82 (3)	2189 (7)
Murshidabad	6.132 (7)	7.19 (7)	7.46 (5)	8.25 (4)	2.64 (5)	2.69 (7)	2220 (6)
West Dinajpur	6.131 (8)	8.19 (4)	8.22 (4)	7.04 (6)	1.98 (11)	2.08 (11)	1767 (12)
Malda	4.27 (11)	5.23 (11)	5.24 (11)	4.91 (10)	2.16 (10)	2.28 (9)	1933 (10)
Jalpaiguri	7.12 (5)	5.66 (8)	5.88 (8)	2.29 (13)	0.93 (15)	0.95 (15)	1135 (15)
Darjeeling	3.75 (13)	2.75 (14)	2.62 (14)	1.55 (15)	1.29 (13)	1.43 (14)	2501 (3)
Cooch Behar	3.93 (12)	4.42 (12)	4.56 (12)	2.89 (12)	1.50 (12)	1.54 (13)	1253 (14)
Purulia	7.07 (6)	7.36 (5)	6.02 (7)	3.95 (11)	1.24 (14)	1.59 (12)	1620 (13)
West Bengal	100	100	100	100	2.30	2.43	2077

Source: (i) Government of West Bengal, Bureau of Applied Economics and Statistics, *Statistical Abstracts* (1994-95).
(ii) Government of West Bengal, Bureau of Applied Economics and Statistics, *Economic Review*, (1994-95).

Note: Figures in the parentheses represent rankings.

Table - 9.2: Allocation of land Towards Different Combinations and Net Benefit per Acre over Total Cost in the Selected Area (1993-94)

Combination of Crops	Area Total(Acre)	Profit over Total Cost per acre in a Crop Year (Rs)
(1) Aus (H. Y. V.), Potato, Boro	4	2747.5 + 2559.41 + 821.31 = 6128.22 (6)
(2) Aus (H.Y.V.), Potato, Jute	1	2747.5 + 2559.41+ 649.5 = 5956.41 (9)
(3) Aus (H. Y. V.), Mustard, Boro	6	2747.5 + (-5.86) + 3263.33 = 6004.97 (8)
(4) Aus (H. Y. V.), Mustard, Til	1	2747.5 + (-5.86) + 619.00 = 3360.64 (14)
(5) Aus (H. Y. V.), Potato, Til	1.8	2747.5 + 2559.41 + 797.12 = 6104.03 (7)
(6) Aman (H.Y.V.), Boro	8	3691.19 + 3263.33 = 6954.52 (3)
(7) Aman (H.Y.V.), Potato, Boro	34.4	3691.19 + 2559.41 + 821.31 = 7071.91 (1)
(8) Aman (H.Y.V.), Mustard, Til	3.5	3691.19 + (-5.86) + 619 = 4304.33 (11)
(9) Aman (H.Y.V.), Wheat, Til	1.4	3691.19 + (-846.29) + 619 = 3463.9 (13)
(10) Aman (H.Y.V.), Wheat, Jute	0.5	3691.19 + (-846.29) + 649.5 = 3494.4 (12)
(11) Aman (H.Y.V.), Potato, Til	10.7	3691.19 + 2559.41 + 797.12 = 7047.72 (2)
(12) Aman (H.Y.V.), Mustard, Boro	24.5	3691.19 + (-5.86) + 3263.33 = 6948.66 (4)
(13) Aman (Local), Boro	31.4	1622.5 + 3263.33 = 4885.83 (10)
(14) Aman (H.Y.V.), Potato, Jute	5.0	3691.19+2559.41+649.5 = 6900.1 (5)

Note: Figures in the parentheses represent ranks.

Flow Chart 9.1

Flow of Acreage in Aggrage over the seaons in the selected Area during 1993-94 (in acre)

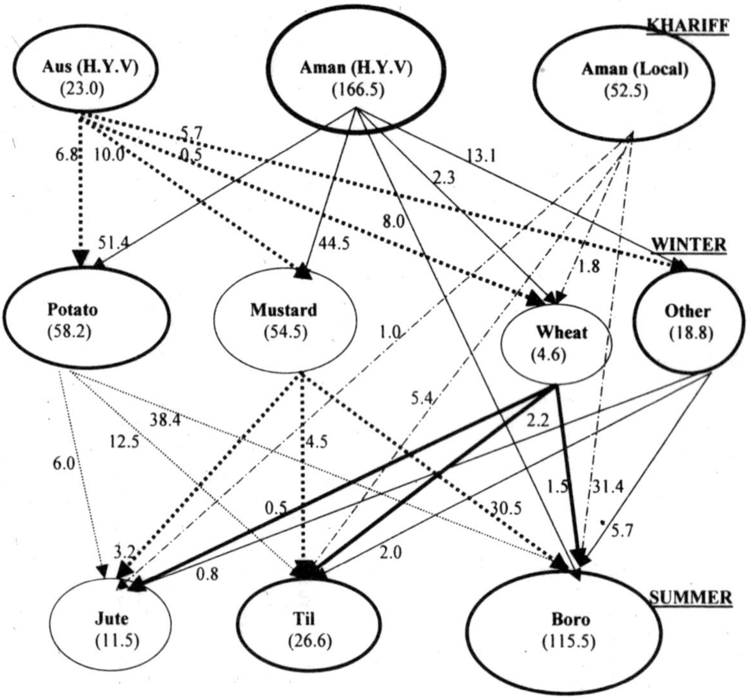

Flow Chart 9.2

Complete Flow of Acreage over the seaons in the selected Area during 1993-94 (in acre)

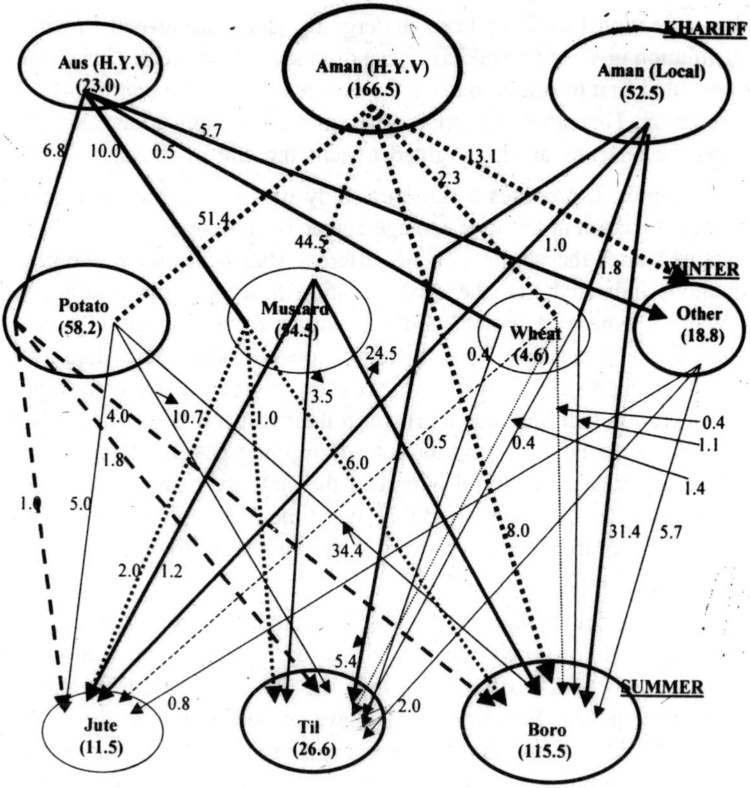

Chapter 10

Epilogue

10.1 Summary of Findings

The nature, consequence and the basic causes for the crop diversification that have been undergoing since the arrival of Green Revolution in West Bengal have been discussed elaborately. This chapter is devoted first to briefly outline the observations of the entire forgoing discussion. Thereafter the conclusions and policy implications emanated from the analysis are highlighted toward the end of the discussion.

Chapter 3, provides a rigorous study of the nature of changes in cropping pattern in terms of acreage allocation among the crops. Results obtained after the application of different statistical and econometric methods indicated that the diversification has taken place largely in favour of boro rice, potato and oilseeds as a whole, whose primary component is mustard. The diversification has taken place largely in favour of high value crops or towards the crops with relatively higher remuneration than the others grown in their respective seasons. This is clear from the positive contribution of cropping pattern change on the increasing total agricultural output of the state over time as discussed in chaper-6. It is also observed that over time high yielding varieties of each crop occupied major portion of the land used for the cultivation of each of them.

Area under foodgrains in absolute unit, however, observed an increasing rate of growth because of increasing rate of growth of area under cereals which offset more than the deereaing rate of decline in area under pulses. Superior cereals have gained in area at the cost of area under inferior cereals (like jowar, bajra, ragi, small millet etc.,) wheat and pulses. Among cereals, paddy especially boro rice has experienced significantly increasing rate of growth in area under cultivation.

Among the major rabi crops sharp decline in area under wheat has been observed while that of potato and mustard has increased at the cost of other relatively low remunerative crops.

Inter-district variations in cropping pattern change have been varied and divergent. Significantly larger rate of increase in area and proportion of area under boro rice was noticed in all the South Bengal districts except Purulia and Malda, West Dinajpur, Coach-Behar in the north. In the early years the rate of growth was much higher in Burdwan, Hooghly and Nadia, the three relatively advanced districts while the case was reversed for other districts. Deceleration in the rate of growth was noticed in those three front runner districts whereas acceleration was observed in other districts. Wheat, one of the major rabi crops in earlier years, experienced sharp decline in area under cultivation in central region (Burdwan, Birbhum, Bankura, Howrah and Hooghly) while all the northen districts recorded a positive trend of the same in terms of absolute and proportion of area. Sizeable growth in absolute and proportion of area under potato have been observed in the southern districts like Hooghly, Burdwan, Midnapore and Howrah in descending order and only in Jalpaiguri in the north. Area under oilseeds as a whole especially mustard, has increased but a decelerating rate in most of the major oilseed producing districts. Absolute area of jute remained more or less same in most of the districts while the other cash crop sugarcane recorded a sharp decline in absolute area in all the districts.

Variability and instability of acreage growth also differs among the crops and across the districts and also between sub-periods. Variability of area under boro rice was much significant in the earlier period than the latter sub-period in the districts where the growth was also rapid but irrigation was uncertain in early years of development. In the districts of drought prone zone like Purulia and Bankura both variability and instability were insignificant since there was vert little scope for boro rice cultivation in the earlier periods due to the lack of assured irrigation. The development of irrigation though started later (as is clear from chapter 8) the growth was rather slow but smooth. The districts with high growth in area under non-food crops observed greater instability in all those crops. Growth of wheat in a the northern region of the state was associated with greater instability. Instability of growth of area under cereal crops as a whole was significant in the southern districts where the growth was significant but variability of growth of leading cereal, aman rice has been reduced over time in the major growing district(s) like Burdwan, Midnapore, Nadia, Murshidabad in the south and West Dinajpur, Malda and Jalpaiguri in the north.

Output of different crops also changed broadly in the same way as the area under crops. Production of boro rice, potato and oilseed as a whole particularly mustard increased vigorously while that of pulses, wheat and other cereals like jowar, bajra, ragi etc. has decreased significantly. Though production of wheat had increased during the earlier years, it has been declining since 1979-80. Inter-district disparity in the production of boro rice and oilseed decreased along with the increase in production while inter-district variability in case of potato followed an increasing trend with the increase in its production. Reduction in inter-district disparity in case of boro rice and oilseed implies than the laggard districts have advanced faster in these fields than the erstwhile-developed districts. Despite slower rate of growth in area and production, rice remains the first crop in terms of area and output. Production of foodgrains was highly concentrated in the developed districts of southern part. Though absolute production of foodgrains has increased in all the districts, proportional contribution to state's total production of the formerly backward district has risen while that of others has fallen. Production of wheat experienced an increasing trend in all the northern districts while it recorded a negative trend in most of the southern districts. In absolute districts. In absolute among production of jute also increased disproportionately in all the districts despite an insignificant change in its acreage.

Like area and production, inter-crop and inter-district variation in yield growth was also varying and divergent. Throughout the entire period 1970-71 to 1994-95 yield of foodgrains has experienced significantly positive rate of growth despite short-term variation in growth rate. Yield of cereals as a whole increased at a rate higher than that of pulses. Among cereals, yield of rice experienced a significantly higher rate of growth than that of wheat. However among different varieties of rice, yield of boro-rice recorded very slow rate of growth. Among non-food crops yields of oilseed experienced highest exponential rate of growth, which was followed by potato and jute.

Inter-district variation in composite productivity indices was observed to increase over the years. Disparity in yield has however decreased in case of boro rice, wheat, pulses, potato and sugarcane whereas it has increased in case of other crops. Burdwan and Hooghly have always been at the top two positions in terms of composite agricultural productivity while Darjeeling, West Dinajpur and Cooch-Behar were always among the bottom five districts in the relative rankings. Nadia has been observed to advance at a relatively faster rate than the other districts in terms of composite productivity.

Component analysis of Chapter 6 revealed that intensive cultivation of crops through rising yield has significantly contributed to the total increase in agricultural production of the state. Irrespective of the contribution is by no means negligible. The explanation revealed that the choice of combination of crops to be grown in a cyclic order in a crop-year or cropping pattern at any given situation has an important bearing on the total revenue from the agricultural crop activities. From the analysis it is also clear that though in the earlier sub-period area growth was much significant and that was possible through rising net sown area and bringing more and more land under multiple cropping system, later it became increasingly difficult to increase total area under cultivation. The stress therefore shifted on to yield and cropping pattern component. Impact of yield growth and cropping pattern component became more and more significant with the passage of time. Significantly large contribution of yield-cropping pattern interaction component also indicated the increasing allocation of land towards the high yielding of high value crops.

Changes in cropping pattern have been due to several reasons. The regression analysis has given some basic information about the important causes for the rapid growth of area under boro rice, potato and oilseed (particularly mustard) during 1970-71 to 1993-94. Though the impetus for raising acreage of aforesaid crops/ crop groups has come from different sources, the basic and ultimate criterion for increasingly allocating land towards those crops is net of gross revenue. In the early stages of Green Revolution it was believed that the small farmers would be less commercial minded and allocate maximum portion of land for the cultivation of food crops whereas the large farmers would be more commercial minded and allocate a large portion of land for the cultivation of cash crops.[1] But in the modern age of commercial movement that concept has gradually faded away. Even the small farmers can easily collect their required commodities from the market in exchange of money earned by selling the commodities produced by them. Over time profit motive is becoming more and more dominant criterion. At any given technical knowledge and available other resources, farmers will choose to grow those crops successively in different and also the cultivation of those specific crops are guided by the changing technology and available supporting inputs that facilitates easy cultivation of those specific crops. Institutional changes are also found to play some role in alternative situations.

The main supporting factor that has prompted boro rice to emerge as one important cash crop in the development of irrigation. Chemical fertilizer also has substantial impact on the acreage growth of boro rice. Irrigation is the leading input of boro rice as it is grown during summer time and regular supply of water is essential for paddy cultivation. Chemical fertilizer and yield growth has led to the acceleration of area under potato and oilseed especially mustard. Irrigation development has also boosted up the growth of area under potato and mustard though it is not clear from the regression equation. Actually expansion of groundwater irrigation in West Bengal has important bearing on the growth of cultivation of potato, mustard and boro rice along with canal irrigation. But it is not incorporated into the regression analysis due to the lack of systematic date. However, it isclear from the inter-district disparity in acreage growth of those crops in relation to variation in groundwater irrigation as explained in Chapter 8. Moreover there is a correlation between the growth of irrigation, consumption of chemical fertilizer and yield of boro rice and dummy variable shows a significantly positive impact of land reforms on acreage growth of oilseed and also on that of boro rice. Simultaneous expansion of area under potato and mustard during winter was possible due to expansion of area under cultivation during that season. Though a substitution of acreage between them was possible both were practised in order to reduce the problem of management and finance as well as to disperse risk involved in the cultivation of crops.

The extended version of regression analysis also reveals that direct price effect lagged one year is much strong in case of acreage allocation decision of the farmers. Moreover it is observed that even if any one of the price and yield has no significant impact on acreage growth, direct effect of expected total proceed per unit of area evaluated at prices lagged one year is much significant. Therefore the revenue from the cultivation of each crop is one of the important criteria which when increase relative to other crops induce the farmers to increasingly allocate their land resources from the cultivation of that crop. The diversification or inter-crop acreage shift has been reinforced due to the advancement of technology in different fields that makes up the conditions necessary for the cultivation of desired crops along with the maintenance of economic feasibility.

The extend versions, however, exhibit some kind of contradictory results emanated from the cross price and yield effects. The contradictions arise mainly due to the specific nature of inter-correlation among the explanatory variables. Though cross effect of changes in price and yield of wheat on area under potato is negative, the effect of variation in price and yield of mustard, on area under potato is completely opposite (though not significant). The main reason is that in the early years of development much of land used to remain uncropped during winter and summer seasons (owing mainly to lack of irrigation). With the expansion of capacity of irrigation a large portion of uncultivable land became available for cultivation during that time. Though initially food crop production was given special emphasis, later when the country became self-sufficient in foodgrain production, rapid commercialization set in. With the arrival HYV seeds, development of irrigation and other complex agricultural implements as well as revision of prices both mustard and potato became profitable. In spite of differences in their profitability; on consideration of the problem of management, financial positions, relative cost components and risk involved in the production of various crops farmers were goaded to allocate the increasing area under cultivation between potato and mustard in an optimum proportion. This is the main reasons for the growth (at different rates) of area under both potato and mustard.

Relative revenue per unit of area evaluated at prices lagged one year is found to play more important role in the acreage allocation between any two competing crops than the relative prices lagged one year. Coefficient of dummy variable that reflects the impact of land reform measures undertaken by the left-front government of West Bengal after 1978-79 is found to be significantly positive only in case of oilseed as a whole and boro-rice but insignificant in other cases. There is much doubt about the contribution of land reform measures in mobilising land towards the newly emerging commercial crops from other uses. Just by looking at the performances of the beneficiaries of the programme (as has been done in several cases) it is not possible to comment on the impact of the land reforms on changes in cropping pattern unless their role in the process of diversification is compared with that of same category of non-beneficiaries, Moreover, the surplus lands are generally distributed among the landless or marginal farmers. According to Bharm Narain those farmers are less commercial minded that the big farmers.[2] Again if these beneficiaries do not receive adequate financial and technical support it is not possible for them to go for producing those highly commercial crops.

It is also important to note that growth of area under any crop is not only dependent on the profitability of that crop and that of crops which can be grown during the same season but also on the profitability of other crops grown during other seasons. This is because of the close dependence of profitability of different crops that are grown in successive seasons on the same plot. This type of dependence occurred due to overlapping harvesting and sowing seasons of crops that can be cultivated in successive seasons on the same plot of land. From the last section of chapter 7 it is clear that though irrigation, chemical fertilizer availability and its application, development of technology in other fields were the key factors for the expansion of cultivation of boro rice, potato and oilseed in the post-Green Revolution period; it was the gross and net profit from each unit of area throughout the whole crop-year (a year within which maximum three major crops can be grown successively on the same plot) that provided the ultimate ground and guided the farmers of the region to increasingly allocate land for the production of those crops. The combination of crops that cam possibly be grown in successive seasons on the same plot over each year yielding highest expected profit, is given the top priority, provided technology and other inputs are available sufficiently to support the cultivation of those crops. As technology and thus cost of cultivation, constellation of price change, relative profitability of different combination changes, choice of crop-combination or crop rotation changes accordingly. In the same way future prospects of crops always invite new technology and innovation takes place to accelerate the growth of desired crops. It is observed from chapter 8 that the districts having experienced rapid expansion and diffusion of modern technical inputs and implements also recorded rapid growth of area under relatively faster growing crops during 1970-71 to 1993-94.

The same result has also been observed from the analysis of data collected from some farm families of the district of Burdwan. It has been found from chapter 9 that the relative profitability of crop-combinations is of vital consideration for the allocation of land resources towards the cultivation of different crops in different seasons of the years.

10.2 Conclusion and Policy Implication

Crop diversification is an essential dynamic feature of agricultural development. It is closely associated with the process of agricultural growth. With the changing agricultural scenario, technological advancement and changes in institutional conditions, pattern of crops grown changes. Besides that, cropping pattern and its movement diverge across the region on account of differences in the agro-climatic, social, technical and economic factors. Sometimes a new cropping pattern is introduced by the farmers in each region that is best suited to changing technology and available input resources and from which they can earn more. There is always coherence between the changing cropping pattern and variation in technology, availability of resources and market structure. Changes in cropping pattern in important from the point of view of employment of labour force, steady flow of income of the farmers from their limited land holdings as well as environmental sustainability. Proper choice of cropping pattern can solve many problems faced by the people, where there is no scope for raising net area under cultivation.

It is clear from the overall discussion that irrigation was the primary input that facilitated the growth of acreage of boro rice, potato and mustard that have experienced a rapid growth at the cost of area under other lower value crops. These three crops have emerged as newly commercial crops of the region dominating the importance of former commercial crops like jute, sugarcane etc. Though boro rice is a food crop, it is now-a-days grown mainly for earning profit. Moreover, the districts having easy access to irrigation sources experienced more rapid expansion of cultivation of the aforesaid crops than the districts where irrigation development started later. Again fluctuation of acreage growth was very high in the early years of Green Revolution which got reduced with the passage of time and more rapidly in the districts, which recorded swift expansion or irrigation. The districts having easy access to irrigation sources experienced deceleration of growth after the exhaustion of all easily available irrigation sources with existing technology. However, where the process of irrigation started later the expansion still continued with accelerated pace and reduced variability as well as instability of growth.

It is therefore important to emphasise more on technological development to bring about a new breakthrough, so that the maximum possible and difficult sources of irrigation can be exploited and the development process can be continued. Not only that, special programmes that have already been launched for the development of arid zone should be reframe for assured irrigation throughout all seasons of the year. Then it would be possible to reduce the inter-district disparity in acreage growth of those crops and also agricultural development.

Sometimes cropping pattern changes may not be a sequel to mere agricultural development. A new cropping pattern may be introduced to fulfil the desired targets. For instance, production of foodgrains (specially, wheat) was given tremendous emphasis at the time of acute food shortage in the country to reduce deficiency in the supply of food. For this HYV seeds were imported and irrigation development projects were started to support the programmes. In order to introduce a new cropping pattern technological changes best suited to the cultivation of desired crops in best possible way were invited. If all the resources are fully utilised and there is no short-term scope for changing technology, choice of crops best suited to the agro-climatic and existing technological conditions gives highest possible remuneration. Sometimes government policies (e.g. government price policy) are framed to encourage the production of some crops and discourage some others.[3]

In spite of the programmes undertaken by the government for drought prone areas, it was found that many districts are lagging behind in raising area under the desired crops or introducing a new cropping pattern. River water-flows should be utilised more properly and channelised to reduce the quantity of unused land in winter and summer along with the perfect cropping choice. Generation of more and more crop varieties with drought, flood resistant capacities should be encouraged in the governments research and development programmes which can also solve the problems to some extent. Even in the relatively advanced area, where deceleration of growth of area under boro rice, potato etc. (despite much of land remain unused in the off-monsoon season) has set in due to exhaustion of already available irrigation sources, new sources are to be searched or difficult sources will have to be utilised to use optimally the unused land during the off-monsoon season. Hundred percent relief from monsoon dependence is never possible but proper management of available water (river flows and ground water) can in many cases solve the problems.

Besides this, disproportionate growths of agricultural implements are found to be partly responsible for the disproportionate expansion of area under boro rice, potato and mustard. Use of tractor and power tiller has raised the capacity of management and converted the lands hitherto left fallow (or used otherwise), suitable for potato cultivation. In this context the use of agro-implements in the state is still below Punjab. The government should take steps to expand the use of those implements especially in the districts where the use is at very low level. Finance in this case is also a great problem. Though the small farmers can utilise these technologies from machine market, they can not take full advantage of them due to peculiar nature of market and other problems. It thus requires the development of cooperatives for supplying and maintaining the machines that can be of great help to the small and marginal farmers. Government schemes can be developed to advancé loans and the existing schemes should be handled effectively.

Regarding land reforms, it can be said that it is not by itself conducive to proper cropping pattern growth. The marginal farmers cannot by themselves use the allocated land properly as they in most cases suffer from resource crunch and lack of information. Even if there is available resources like irrigation, agro-machinery, which can be hired they cannot take the full benefit of modern technology. It is also not possible for them to maintain separate establishments for those things. They thus require to be provided with adequate government assistance and technical support to enable them to use lands efficiently, otherwise the objectives of land reform measures will be left partially successful. The *panchayats* in the rural areas can play an important role in this regard. Panchayats can identify the eligible farmers who require proper training and different facilities and also arrange the programmes in appropriate ways. In case of resource management the panchayat can make different arrangements (for better utilisation of groundwater and ponds, timely allocation of government subsidized modern seeds, development of local communication etc.) and make more and more people aware of different programmes and facilities extended by the government and other institutions.

Sometimes farmers are unable to take risk of cultivating some crops, due to greater fluctuation of market price of low storage capacity of nondurable crops etc. In those cases government can take steps to provide proper information sufficiently in advance and to take measures for market stabilisation. Development and maintenance of good infrastructure is also another essential criterion for the channelisation of inputs and outputs throughout the whole region which can help farmers making better choice for the use of their land and other resources in best possible ways.

10.3 Further Scope for Research

There is much room for further improvement of the analysis by incorporating the role of institutional changes on crop diversification. Though in this book (chapter-7) the impact of land reforms has been examined, the role of economic reforms, institutions like commercial banks, government policies, cooperatives, NGO, etc., have not been considered.

It may be enriched by analysing the changes in institutional setting with other quantitative information in an inter-linked fashion. Biological innovations that have been taking place largely in public sector, depending on investment in research and development of human capital, are also not less important in regard to the productivity of agriculture. Education improves that farmer's ability to collect and use information and to adjust with the changes in prices, markets and technology. Hence thee factors may be incorporated as explanatory variables in analysing the process of diversification. Also the average temperature variation in different regions (like the number of cool months), moisture content of the soil, market infrastructure etc. may be incorporated in the analysis of regional variation of diversification.

Above all the analysis is done taking the case of average farmer, as majority of farmers in West Bengal is middle category. However the same analysis may be extended to different category of farmers.

REFERENCES

1. Raj, Sen, Rao; op cit.
2. Dharm Narain (1965), op. Cit.
3. Gulati (1994), op. Cit.

Definitions

Area - Gross Cropped Area Elasticity: Ratio of rate of change in area under a particular crop to the rate of change in gorss cropped area.

Bullock Days: The number of days spent by a pair of bullocks on field crop operations. The cost of bullock days is calculated at the going market rate, paid by the farmers and the same rate is also used to evaluate the days spend by the owned pair/pairs of bullocks.

Competing Crops: Crop those are potential rivals, complete for area in a particular place or in other words, it indicates the crops among which area shifts can occur. Different regions may face different crops to complete for attrating land areas.

Crop Combination/Crop-mix: It means the combination of crop that can poosibly be grown in different seasons in a crop year/crops cycle viz. aus rice, potato, boro rice; aman (H.Y.V.), potato, jute; or aus rice, musted and ill.

Crop Year/ Crop Cycle: It is a period which starts with a particular sowing season (like the sowimg of aus rice) after which cultivation of the preceding crop (aus rice in our example) is again possile. In this book a period ranges from July-August to next July-August is considered to be a crop year within which maximum number of crops can be cultivated almost uniformly year after year.

Gross Turnover: Total amoung of gross revenue obtained per unit of land (acre) from each combination of crops i.e., sum of price times yield of crops in each combination.

Human Labour Days: Labour days actually spend on crop cultivation through harvesting either by family members or hired (permanent/ casual) labour. In this study different kinds of labour days (e.g., male, female and child) are evaluated at the actual wage rate paid by the farmers for each category. The evaluation of the family labour used for cultivation is also done at the going market rate.

Leased in Land: It represents the area leased in by a cultivator under any form of contract. It may be recorded or unrecorded.

Owned Land: It consists of all lands (cultivable and uncultivable) under the heritable possession of the household. In other words, it is the land over which the farmer has occupancy right. A farmer may possess a piece of land with or wihtout selling right. Thus the land allocated to landless people, marginal farmers etc. through the scheme of redistribution of vested land are included in this category.

Paid-out Cost: It includes cost incurred on human labour (hired/owned), bullock labour days, machine labour days (tractor, power tiller - hired/owned), seed, manure, fartilisers, plant protective chemicals, depreciation, irrigation charge (hired/owned), land revenue, marketing cost etc. Here seeds, manure may be home produced or purchased. The cost of each of the item is evaluated at the purchase price, and added together to obtain total paid-out cost. Cost of hiring (if not owned) of threshers, sprayers, bullock cart for transportation are also included.

Pull Factors: Factors those attract farmers to come forward to cultivate some crops at the existing state of technology and other conditions of farming viz. relative price, yield or profitability of competing crops.

Push Factors: Factors those enable the farmers or create conditions congenial to grow/cultivate crops e.g. irrigation during summer season without which it is impossible to cultivate boro rice.

Total Cost: Includes paid out cost plus rent paid for leased in land, interest on loan if any and rental value of own land.

Value of Output: Includes value of main product and also of by product, which is calculated for each crop seperately and also for each combination. Evaluation is done at the harvest prices.

Select Bibliography

Acharya, S. (1989), "Agricultural Wages in India: A Disaggregated Analysis", *Indian Journal of Agricultural Economics,* Vol. 44, No. 2, April-June, pp. 121-129.

Acharya, S. (1994), "Marketing Environment for Farm Products- Emerging Issues and Challenges", *Indian Journal of Agricultural Marketing,* Vol. 8, No. 2, July-December.

Acharya, S. (1994), *Aspects of Agricultural Transformation of Burdwan*, M. Phil Dissertation (unpublished), Department of Economics, University of Burdwan.

Ahluwalia, M. S., (1978), "Rural Society and Agricultural Performance in India", *Journal of Development Studies*, Vol. 14, No. 3, pp. 298-323.

Ahmed, S. (1966), "On the Theory of Induced Invention", *Economic Journal*, Vol. 76, No. 2, pp. 344-357.

Alagh, Y. K. and Sharma, P. S. (1980), "Growth of Crop Production: 1960-61 to 1978 - 79-is it Decelerating?", *Indian Journal of Agricultural Economics,* Vol. 35, pp. 104-18.

Bandyopadhyay, A. (1977), "Cereal Crop Growth Pattern in Punjab and Bengal-Study in Contrast", *The Economic Times*, April 7 & 8.

Bandyopadhyay, A. (1981), "Contract System of Cultivation in Summer Rice: A Case Study of Reverse Tenancy in North 24-Paraganas in West Bengal"; Centre for Regional, Ecological and Science Studies in Development Alternatives Transactions (Calcutta), Vol.1, No. 1, pp. 199-216.

Bandyopadhyay, A. (1996), "Growth and Instability in the Production of Main Cereal Crop of West Bengal and Punjab-Haryana, 1950-51 to 1984-85 - A Note", *Indian Journal of Agricultural Economics*, Vol. 44, No. 2, April-June, pp. 168-176.

Bandyopadhyay, D. (1980), *Land Reforms in West Bengal*, Calcutta: Information and Cultural Affairs Department, Government of West Bengal.

Bandyopadhyay, D. (1991), "Grass Roots Justice: Law, System and People", *Economic and Political Weekly*, September 28.

Bandyopadhyay, N. (1975), "Changing Farms of Agricultural Enterprise in West Bengal", *Economic and Political Weekly*, Vol. 10, No. 17, pp. 700-701.

Bandyopadhyay, N. (1991), "Patterns of Change in Agrarian Structure, with Special Reference to the Leftist Government in West Bengal", in N. Ansari (Ed.), *Agrarian Structure, Land Reforms and Agricultural Growth in India*, Tata Mc Graw-Hill, New Delhi.

Bardhan, P. K. (1973), "Size, Productivity and Returns to Scale: An Analysis of Farm Level Data in Indian Agriculture", *Journal of Political Economy*, Vol. 81, No. 6, pp. 1370-86.

Bardhan, P. K. (1976), "Variations in Extent and Farms of Agricultural Tenancy: Analysis of Indian Data across Regions and over Time", *Economic and Political Weekly*, Vol. 11, Nos. 37-38, pp. 1505-11 and 1541-46.

Bardhan, P. K. and Rudra, A. (1978), "Interlinkage of Land, Labour and Credit Relation, An Analysis of Village Survey Data in East India", *Economic and Political Weekly,* Annual Number, February.

Bardhan, P. K. and Rudra, A. (1980), "Labour, Employment and Wages in Agriculture: Results of a Survey of Villages in West Bengal", *Economic and Political Weekly,* November 8.

Barker, R. (1979), "Adoption and Production Impact of New Rice Technology – The Yield Constraints Problem", in International Rice Research Institute (IRRI), *Farm Level Constraints to High Rice Yields in Asia: 1974-77*, Los Banos: IRRI, pp. 1-26.

Barnum, H. N. and Squire L., (1978), "Technology and Relative Economic Efficiency", *Oxford Economic Paper*, Vol. 30, No. 1, pp. 181-98.

Basu, S. K. and Mukherjee, S. B. (1962), *Evaluation of Damodar Canals (1959-60): A Study of the Benefits of Irrigation in the Damodar Region*, London: Asia Publishing House.

Bean, L. H. (1929), "The Farmers' Response to Price", *Journal of Farm Economics*, Vol.11, pp.368-85.

Bhaduri, A. (1973), "Agricultural Backwardness under Semi-feudalism", *Economic Journal*, Vol. 83, No. 1, pp. 120 - 37.

Bhalla, S. (1978), "The Role and Sources of Income and Investment Opportunities in Rural Savings", *Journal of Development Studies*, Vol. 5, pp. 259-81.

Bhalla and Singh, (1997), " Recent Development in Indian Agriculture: A State Level Analysis", *Economic and Political Weekly*, March, 29, pp. A.8 - A.12.

Bhalla, G. S. and Alagh, Y. K. (1979): *Performances of Indian Agriculture: A Districtwise Study*, Sterling Publisher, New Delhi.

Bhalla, G. S. and Tyagi, D. S. (1989): Patterns in Indian Agricultural Development – A District Level Study, *ISID*, New Delhi.

Bharadwaj, K. (1974), *Production Conditions in Indian Agriculture: A Study Based on Farm Management Surveys*, Department of Applied Economics, Occasional Paper No. 33, Cambridge; Cambridge University Press.

Bhattacharjee, B. K. (1982), "A Note on Conservation and Development of Water Resources in West Bengal", Calcutta: State Water Investigation Directorate, typescript.

Bhaumik, S. K. (1993), *Tenancy Relations and Agrarian Development. A Study of West Bengal,* Sage, New Delhi.

Black, J. D. (1924), " Elasticity of Supply of Farm Products", *Journal of Farm Economics*, Vol.6, No.2, April, pp.145-55.

Bose, B. (1979), "Agrarian Programme of Left Front Government in West Bengal", *Economic and Political Weekly*, December 17, pp. 2053-2060.

Boyce, J. K. (1987), *Agrarian Impasse In Bengal, Institutional Constraints to Technological Change*, Oxford University Press.

Bray, F. (1986), *The Rice Economics: Technology and Development in Asian Societies*, Basil Blackwell, Oxford, U. K.

Burman, S. (1982), *Specio Temporal Aspects of Agriculture in Burdwan District*, Ph.D. Dissertation, Department of Geography, University of Burdwan.

Cassels, J. M. (1933), "The Nature of Statistical Supply Curves", *Journal of Farm Economics*, Vol.15, pp. 378-87.

Census of India, 1981, Series-1, Primary Population Total.

Census of India, 1991, Series-1, Paper-2 of 1992.

Chakraborty, A. and Rudra, A. (1973), "Economic Effects of Tenancy-Some Negative Results", *Economic and Political Weekly,* July 14.

Chand, R. (1996), "Diversification through High value Crops in Western Himalayan Region: Evidence from Himachal Pradesh", Seminar Paper, Indian Society of Agricultural Economics, Oct.-Dec., pp. 652-63.

Chattopadhyay, B. (1983), "Growth and Fluctuations in Foodgrains Output Since Independence", *Ecoscience*, Vol. 3, No. 1.

Chow, G. C. (1960), " Test of Equality between Subsets of Coefficients in Two Linear Regression," *Econometrica*, 28, pp 591-605.

Dandekar, V. M. (1994), *The Indian Economy 1947-92: Volume-I, Agriculture*, Sage, India.

Dantwala, M. L., (1996), "Self-Sufficiency and Allocative Efficiency: Case of Edible Oils", *Economic and Political Weekly*, Vol. 31, No. 27, July 6, pp. 1784-85.

Dantwala, M. L., (1996), "My Academic Dialogues: Agricultural Price Policy and the Green Revolution", *Indian Journal of Agricultural Economics*, Vol. 51, Nos. 1 & 2, January-June, pp. 51-59.

Das, K. K. (1967), *Some Socio-Cultural Factors Affecting Attitude of Farmers towards HYV of Paddy*, Master's Dissertation, Bidhan Chandra Krishi Viswavidyalaya.

Dasgupta, B. (1980), *The New Agrarian Technology and India*, Macmillan, India.

Dasgupta, B. (1984), "Sharecropping in West Bengal from Independence to Operation Barga", *Economic and Political Weekly*, Review of Agriculture, June, A 85- A 96.

Datta, P. K. (1981), "Statistics of Bargadars and Extent of Barga Cultivation in West Bengal: An Analytical Study", Calcutta: Directorate of Land Records and Surveys, Government of West Bengal, *mimeo.*

De, U. K. (1998), " Regional Disparity in Agricultural Productivity in the State of West Bengal", *Productivity*, Oct.-Dec., pp. 508-515.

De, U. K. (2000), "Diversification of Crop in West Bengal : A Spatio-Temporal Analysis", *Artha Vijnana*, Vol. XLII, No.2, June, pp. 170-182.

De, U. K. (2000-01), "Cropping Pattern and Agricultural Development in West Bengal during 1970-71 to 1994-95", *The Indian Economic Journal*, Vol.48, No.4, April-June, pp. 68-77.

Desai, G. M. and Singh, G. (1973), *Growth of Fertiliser Use in Districts in India: Performance and Policy Implication*, Ahmedabad: Indian Institute of Management.

Desai, G. M. (1982), *Sustaining Rapid Growth in India's Fertiliser*

Consumption: A Perspective Based on Consumption of Use, Washington: International Food Policy Research Institute Research Report, No. 31, August.

Dhawan, B. D. (1975), "Economics of Ground Water Utilisation", *Economic and Political Weekly*, Vol. 10, No. 25 and 26, pp. A 31- A 42.

Dhawan, B. D. (1979), "Trends in Tubewell Irrigation, 1951-78", *Economic and Political Weekly*, Vol. 14, No. 51 and 52, pp. A 143- A 154.

Dhawan, B. D. (1983), "Impact of Irrigation on Instability in Farm Output: A Case Study of Tamil Nadu State", *Economic and Political Weekly*, Vol. 18, No. 39, pp. A 109- A 116.

Dhawan, B. D. (1988): *Irrigation in Indian Agricultural Development: Productivity, Stability, Equity*, Sage, New Delhi.

Dhindsa, K. S. and Sharma, A. (1995), "Analysis of Cropping Pattern Changes in Punjab During 1965-66 to 1990-91", *Indian Economic Review*, Vol. XXX, No. 1, Jan.-June, pp. 69-87.

Dwivedi, H. and Rudra, A. (1973), "Economic Effects of Tenancy: Some Further Negative Results", *Economic and Political Weekly*, Vol. 8, July 21, p. 28.

Fertiliser Association of India (FAI), (1974), *Statistics on Fertiliser and Agriculture in Eastern India*, No. 1, Calcutta, FAI Eastern Region, June.

Fertiliser Association of India (1981), *Fertiliser Statistics*, 1980-81, New Delhi.

Fertiliser Association of India (1994), *Fertiliser Statistics*, 1993-84, New Delhi.

Ganguli, B. N. (1938), *Trends of Agriculture and Population in the Ganges Valley: A Study in Agricultural Economics*, London, Methuen.

Ghose, A. K. and Saith, A. (1976), "Indebtedness, Tenancy and the Adoption of New Technology in Semi-feudal Agriculture", *World Development*, Vol. 4, No. 4, pp. 305-319.

Ghose, A. K. (1979), "Farm Size and Land Productivity in Indian Agriculture: A Reappraisal; *Journal of Development Studies*, Vol. 16, No. 1, pp. 27-49.

Ghosh, A. (1991), "Eighth Plan: Challenges and Possibilities- Agriculture and Irrigation", *Economic and Political Weekly*, 6th April.

Gill, K. S. (1992), " Diversification of Agriculture in Punjab: Progress and

Possibilities", *Agricultural Situation in India*, Vol. 17, No. 5, August.

Government of India, (1995), Directorate of Economics and Statistics, Ministry of Agriculture, *Agricultural Statistics at a Glance,* New Delhi.

Government of India, (1994), Directorate of Economics and Statistics, Ministry of Agriculture, *Indian Agriculture in Brief*, New Delhi.

Government of India, Ministry of Agriculture, Area and Production of Principal crops in India (Various Issues), New Delhi.

Government of India, Directorate of Economics and Statistics, Ministry of Agriculture, *Agricultural Wages in India, (Various issues)*, New Delhi.

Government of India, Directorate of Economics and Statistics, Ministry of Agriculture and Irrigation, *Agricultural Prices in India, 1963-74, (Various issues)*, New Delhi.

Government of India, Directorate of Economics and Statistics, Ministry of Agriculture, *Agricultural Prices in India, 1993-94, (Various issues)*, New Delhi.

Government of India (1959), Report of the Foodgrains' Enquiry Committee.

Government of India, Ministry of Agriculture, *Agricultural Situation in India, 1993-94, (Various issues)*, New Delhi.

Government of West Bengal, Bureau of Applied Economics and Statistics (BAES), *Economic Review*, (Various Issues), Calcutta.

Government of West Bengal, Bureau of Applied Economics and Statistics (BAES), *Statistical Abstract*, (Various Issues), Calcutta.

Government of West Bengal, Evaluation Wing, Directorate of Agriculture, Study on Farm Management and Cost of Production of Crops in West Bengal, (Various Issues), Calcutta.

Government of West Bengal, Evaluation Wing, Directorate of Agriculture, *Agricultural Census of West Bengal*, (Various Issues), Calcutta.

Government of West Bengal, conduct by Land and Land Reforms Department and Evaluation Wing, Directorate of Agriculture, Agricultural Census of West Bengal, (Various Issues).

Griffin, K. B. (1974), *The Political Economy of Agrarian Change*, Macmillan, London.

Gulati A., (1989), "Structure of Effective Incentives in Indian Agriculture-

Some Policy Implications", *Economic and Political Weekly,* Vol. 24, No. 39, Sept. 30, pp. A 124- A 132.

Gulati, A. and Sharma, A. (1994), "Agriculture under GATT: What it holds for India", *Economic and Political Weekly*, July 16.

Haque, T. (1996), "Diversification of Small Farms in India: Problems and Prospects", in T. Haque (Ed.) (1996), *Small Farm Diversification: Problems and Prospects*, National Centre for Agricultural economics and Policy Research (ICAR), New Delhi.

Harriss, J. (1993), "What is Happening in Rural West Bengal, Agrarian Reform; Growth and Distribution", *Economic and Political Weekly*, June12, pp. 1237-1247.

Hati, A. K. and Rudra, A. (1973), "Calculation of Efficiency Indices of Farmers", *Economic and Political Weekly,* Vol. 8, No. 13, pp. A 17- A 20.

Hayami, Y. and Keijiro, O. (1995), "Beyond the Green Revolution: Agricultural Development Strategy into the New Century", in Jock R. Anderson (Ed.), (1995), *Agricultural Technology: Policy Issues for the International Community*, CAB International with World Bank, Wallingford, Oxon, U. K.

Hazell, Peter B. R. (1982), *Instability in Indian Foodgrains Production,* Research Report No. 30, International Food Policy Research Institute, Washington D.C., U. S. A.

Herdt, R. W. and Capule, C. (1983), *Adoption, Spread and Production Impact of Modern Rice Variety in Asia*, Las Banos: International Rice Research Institute.

Hicks J. R. (1946), *Value and Capital*, Oxford, pp. 319-23.

Hossain, M. M. (1981), "Cropping Systems and Estimation of Area and Production of Aus and Broadcast Aman Rice in Low-lying Areas of Bangladesh, 1980-81", Joydebpur: Bangladesh Rice Research Institute, Division of Agricultural Economics, November, mimeo.

Johanson, L. (1972), *Production Functions*, North-Holland, Amsterdam.

Johl, S.S. and Sandhu, H.S. (1970), Existing and Suggested Cropping Patterns by the Type of Farming Areas in Different Districts of Punjab and Haryana, 1969-70. Department of Economics and Sociology, Punjab Agricultural University, Ludhiana.

Joshi, P. K., Singh, O. P., Rao, K. V. G. K and Singh, K. N. (1987), "Sub-

Surface Drainage for Salinity Control: An Economic Analysis", *Indian Journal of Agricultural Economics*, Vol. 42, No. 2, April-June, pp. 198-206.

Joshi, P. K. and Tyagi, N. K. (1991), "Sustainability of Existing Farming System in Punjab and Haryana- Some Issues on Groundwater Use", *Indian Journal of Agricultural Economics*, Vol. 46, No. 3, July-Sept., pp. 412-421.

Kaur, P. and Sethi, K. (1994), "Inter-district Variation in Agricultural Productivity in Punjab", *Agricultural Situation in India*, June, p. 167.

Keynes J. M. (1957), General Theory of Employment, Interest and Money, London, p.51.

Kahlon, A. S. and Tyagi, D. S. (1983), *Agricultural Price Policy in India*, Allied Publishers, New Delhi.

Khan, A. R. (1968), *Scientific Farming in India- An Introduction*, Orient Longman, New Delhi.

Khusro, A. M. (1971), "Structural Change in Indian Agriculture", Conference on Agriculture and Economic Development, Tokyo, September.

Krishnaji, N. (1975), "State Intervention and Foodgrain Prices", *Social Scientist*, Vol. 3, Nos. 6 & 7, pp. 75-90.

Krishnaji, N. (1980), "Measuring Agricultural Growth", Indian Society of Agricultural Economics, pp. 31-41.

Krishnaji, N. (1990), "Agricultural Price Policy: A Survey with Reference to Indian Foodgrain Economy", *Economic and Political Weekly*, June 30, pp. A 54 - A 63.

Krishnan, T. N. (1965), "The Marketable Surplus of Foodgrains", *Economic Weekly*, Vol. 17, Annual Number, February.

Koutsoyiannis A, (1977), *Theory of Econometrics* (2nd ed.), Macmillan Press, London.

Kumar, P. (1996), "Structural Change in Consumption and Small Farm Diversification", in T. Haque (Ed.), (1996), *Small Farm Diversification: Problems and Prospects*, National Centre for Agricultural Economics and Policy Research (ICAR), New Delhi.

Lau, L. and Yotopoulas, P. (1971), "A Test for Relative Efficiency and Application to Indian Agriculture", *American Economic Review*, Vol. 61, No. 1, pp. 94-109.

Lee, J. H. (1981), "A Review of the Theory of Technological Change in Agriculture: Biases and Substitutability", *Journal of Rural Development*, (Korea), Vol. 4, No. 1, pp. 55-56.

Lieten, G. K. (1990), "Depeasantisation Discontinued: Land Reforms in West Bengal", *Economic and Political Weekly*, Vol. 25, No. 40, pp. 2265-71.

Lieten, G. K. (1992), *Continuity and Change in Rural West Bengal*, Sage Publication, Delhi.

Mallick, R (1992), p.740, "Agrarian Reform in West Bengal, The End of an Illusion", *World Development*, Vol. 20.

Mehra, Shakuntala, (1981), *Instability in Indian Agriculture in the Context of the New Technology*, Research Report No. 25, International Food Policy Research Institute, Washington D. C., U. S. A.

Mellor, J. W. and Desai, G. M. (Ed), (1986), *Agricultural Change and Rural Poverty*, Oxford, Delhi.

Minhas, B. S. and Vaidyanathan, A. (1965), "Growth of Crop output in India, 1951-54 to 1958-61: An Analysis by Component Elements", *Journal of the Indian Society of Agricultural Statistics*, Vol. XVII, No. 2, December, pp. 230-252.

Minhas, B. S. (1966), " Rapporteur's Report on Measurement of Agricultural Growth", *Indian Journal of Agricultural Economics*, Vol. XXI, No.4, Oct.-Dec.

Mishra, V. N. (1971), " Growth of Crop Output in Gujarat: A Component Analysis", *Anvesak*, Vol.1, No. 1, June, pp. 1-15.

Mitra, T. K. (1989), "Growth and Instability of Agricultural Prices in West Bengal: A Note", *Indian Journal of Agricultural Economics*, Vol. 44, No. 1, Jan.-March, pp. 67-71.

Mody, A. (1980), "Population Growth and Commercialisation of Agriculture: India, 1890-1940", Trivandrum; Centre for Development Studies, working paper No. 117.

Mruthyunjya and Kumar, P. (1989), "Crop Economics and Cropping Pattern Changes", *Economic and Political Weekly*, Dec. 23-30, pp. A 159 – A 166.

Mukherjea, S. N. (1956), *A Brief Agricultural Geography of West Bengal*, Calcutta; Government of West Bengal.

Mukherjee, B. and Mukhopadhyay, S. (1995), "Impact of Institutional Change on Productivity in a Small Farm Economy: Case of Rural West Bengal", *Economic and Political Weekly*, August 26.

Mukherjee, S. et. al. (1994), Differential Impact of Modern Rice Technology in West Bengal, ISPAR and ISI, Calcutta.

Nadkarni, M. V. (1984), "Irrigation and Rural Development: A Sceptical View", *Economic and Political Weekly*, Vol. 19, No. 26, pp. A. 67- A. 73.

Nadkarni, M. V. and Vedini, K. H. (1996), "Accelerating Commercialisation of Agriculture: Dynamic Agriculture and Stagnating Peasants", *Economic and Political Weekly*, Vol. 31, No. 26, June 29.

Nanavati, A. and Patel, B. C., (1994), "Inter-district Variation in Agricultural Productivity in Gujarat", *Productivity*, Vol. 35, No. 2, July-Sept.

Nair, N. K. (1976), "Contribution of Fertilisers to Foodgrain Production in India: Some Estimates", *Productivity*, Vol. XVII, No. 1, April – June.

Narain Dharm, (1965), *Impact of Price Movements on Areas Under Selected Crops in India: 1900-1939*, Cambridge University Press.

Narain Dharm, (1972), "The Changing Agricultural Structure", *Yojana*, Vol. XVII, Nos. 15 and 16, August 15.

Narain Dharm, (1977), "Growth of Productivity in Indian Agriculture", *Indian Journal of Agricultural Economics*, Vol. XXXII, No.1, Jan.-Mar., pp.1-44.

Narayanamorthy, A. (1997), "Crop Diversification and Yield Response to Fertiliser, *Productivity*, Vol. 38, No. 1, April – June, pp. 118 – 126.

Nayyar, D. and Sen, A. (1994), "International Trade and Agricultural Sector in India", in G. S. Bhalla (Ed.) (1994), *Economic Liberalisation and Indian Agriculture*, Institute for Studies in Industrial Development, New Delhi.

NCAER, (1966), *Cropping Pattern in Punjab*, New Delhi.

Nerlove, M. (1958), *The Dynamics of Supply: Estimation of Farmers' Response to Price*, The John Hopkins Press, Baltimore.

Pandey, V. K. and Sharma, K. C. (1996), "Crop Diversification and Self-Sufficiency

in Foodgrains", *Indian Journal of Agricultural Economics*, Vol. 51, No. 4, Oct. – Dec., pp. 644 – 651.

Parikh, A. (1966), "Statewise Growth Rate in Agricultural Output; An Econometric Analysis", *Artha Vijnana*, Vol. 8, No. 1, March, pp. 1-52.

Pathak, S. and Majumdar, A. K. (1978), "Multivariate Regression Analysis of Adoption Behaviour of Jute Farmers", *Indian Journal of Extension Education*, July – December.

Patnaik, U. (1972), "Mode of Production in Indian Agriculture", *Economic and Political Weekly*, Vol. VII, No. 40, Sept. 30.

Patnaik, U. (1972), "Development of Capitalism in Agriculture", *Social Scientist*, Vol. 1, Nos. 2 & 3, Sept. and Oct.

Patnaik, U. (1971), "Capitalist Development in Agriculture", *Economic and Political Weekly*, Vol. VI, No. 39, Sept. 25.

Raj, K. N. (1959), "Employment and Unemployment in the Indian Economy: Problems and Classification, Measurement and Policy", *Economic Development and Cultural Change*, Vol. 7, No. 3, Part – 1, p. 258.

Raj, K.N., Sen, A.K. and Rao, C.H.H. (Ed.), (1988), *Dharm Narain: Studies on Indian Agriculture,* Oxford University Press.

Ranade, C. G. (1980), " Impact of Cropping Pattern on Agricultural Production", *Indian Journal of Agricultural Economics*, Vol.35, No.2, April-June.

Rao, C. H. H., (1975), *Technological Change and Distribution of Gains in Indian Agriculture*, The Macmillan Company of India Ltd., Delhi.

Rao, V. M., Nadkarni, M. V. and Deshpande, R. S. (1980), "Measurement of Growth and Fluctuations in Crop Output: An Approach Based on the Concept of Non-systematic Component", in Indian Society of Agricultural Economics, 1980, pp. 21- 30.

Rao, C. H. H. (1992), "Agricultural Policy and Performance", in B. Jalan (Ed.), The *Indian Economy: Problems and Prospects*, Delhi, Viking.

Rath, Nilkantha (1977), "Performance of Agriculture in Maharashtra, 1960 – 1972", Gokhale Institute of Politics and Economics, Pune, (*mimeo*).

Rath, Nilkantha (1980), "A Note on Agricultural Production in India During 1955 – 78", *Indian Journal of Agricultural Economics*, Vol. 35, April – June, pp. 94 – 104.

Rath, Nilkantha and Patvardhan, V. S., (1967), *Impact of Assistance Under PL480 on Indian Economy*, Gokhale Institute of Politics and Economics, Poona.

Ray, S. K. (1983), "Growth and Instability in Indian Agriculture", Delhi: Institute of Economic Growth, June, (*mimeo*).

Ray, Pradipto et. al. (1988), *Agricultural Innovation Among Indian Farmers*, NICD, Hyderabad.

Roychoudhuri, A and Sarker, D. (Ed.), (1996), *Economy of West Bengal: Problems and Prospects*, Allied Publishers, Calcutta.

Rudra, A. (1983), "Non-Maximising Behaviour of Farmers: Crop Selection", *Economic and Political Weekly*, Vol. 18, No. 48, Nov. 26, pp. 2032 – 55.

Rudra, A. (1983), "Non-Maximising Behaviour of Farmers: Crop Selection", *Economic and Political Weekly*, Vol. 28, No. 40, Oct.-1, pp. 1717 – 22.

Rudra, A. (1971), "Capitalist Development in Agriculture – Reply", *Economic and Political Weekly*, Vol. VI, No. 45, Nov.-6.

Rudra, A. (1975), "Sharecropping Agreements in West Bengal", *Economic and Political Weekly*, Vol. 10, No. 39, pp. A 58 – A 63.

Sagar, Vidya. (1980), " Decomposition of Growth Trends and Certain Related Issues", *Indian Journal of Agricultural Economics*, Vol.35, No.2, April-June, pp. 42-59.

Saha, A. (1996), "Adoption of Modern Agricultural Technology in Rice Cultivation in West Bengal", in Roychoudhury and Sarkar (Ed.), *Economy of West Bengal, Problems and Prospects*, Allied Publishers, Calcutta.

Saha, A. and Swaminathan, O. M. (1994 a), "Agricultural Growth in West Bengal During the 1980s: A Disaggregation by Districts and Crops", *Economic and Political Weekly*, March 26.

Saha, A. and Swaminathan, O. M. (1994 b), "Agricultural Growth in West Bengal", *Economic and Political Weekly*, June 30.

Sarkar, G. K. (1988), *Jute in India, An Economic Analysis*, Oxford University Press, Ch. - 3.

Sarkar, G. K. (1995), *Agriculture and Rural Transformation in India*, Oxford, University Press, Calcutta.

Sarkar, A. (1997), "On the Relationship Between Price and Output Seasonality in

Backward Agriculture", *Indian Economic Review*, Vol. XXXII, No. 1, pp. 107 – 115.

Sastri, A. V. K. (1960), " Relative Contribution of Area and Yield to Increased Production of Wheat During the First Plan", *Agricultural Situation in India*, Vol. XV, No.5, August. pp. 481-486.

Sawant, S. D. (1997), "Performance of Indian Agriculture with Special Reference to Regional Variations", *Indian Journal of Agricultural Economics,* Vol.52, No.3, July-September, pp. 353-73.

Sawant, S. D. and Achutan, C. V. (1995), "Agricultural Growth across Crops and Regions: Emerging Trends and Patterns", *Economic and Political Weekly*, March 25, Review of Agriculture, A. 2 – A 13.

Sen, A. K. (1962), "An Aspects of Indian Agriculture", *Economic Weekly*, Vol. 14, No. 4 – 6, (Annual Number), pp. 243 – 246.

Sen, S. R. (1971), *Growth and Instability in Indian Agriculture*, Firma K. L , Mukhopadhyay, Calcutta.

Sen, A. and Sengupta, R. (1995), "The Recent Growth in Agricultural Output in Eastern India, with Special Reference to the Case of West Bengal", Unpublished Paper presented at a workshop on 'Agricultural Growth and Agrarian Structure in Contemporary West Bengal and Bangladesh, Calcutta, January 9-12, 1995.

Sengupta, S. (1996), "Agrarian Policies and Pattern of Rural Change in South

Bengal", in Roychoudhury and Sarkar (Ed.), *Economy of West Bengal, Problems and Prospects*, Allied Publishers, Calcutta.

Shastri, C. P. (1958), "Input – Output Relations in Indian Agriculture", *Indian Journal of Agricultural Economics,* Vol. 13, No.2, pp. 35 - 42.

Singhal, M. and Gauraha, A. K. (1997), "Crop Diversification in Madhya Pradesh: An

Economic Analysis", Paper presented at the Annual Conference of Indian Society of Agricultural Economics.

Singh, I. J., Rai, K. N. and Karwasra, J. C. (1997), "Regional Variations in Agricultural Performance in India", Paper presented at the Annual Conference of Indian Society of Agricultural Economics.

Smith, B. B. (1925), "Forecasting the Acreage of Cotton", *Journal of American Statistical Association*, New series, Vol.20, March, pp.31-47.

Smith, B. B. (1928), (Factors Affecting the Price of Cotton", U. S. *Department of Agricultural Technical Bulletin*, No. 50, January, pp. 19–24.

Sondhi R. and Singh K., (1975), " Component Analysis of Food Grain Economy of India", *Journal of Social and Economic Studies*, Vol. III, No.2, Sept.

Srinivasan, T. N., (1979), " Trends in Agriculture in India, 1949-50 to 1977-78", *Economic and Political Weekly*, 14 (30-2), Special Number, 1283-94.

Suryanarayana, M. H. (1995), "PDS Reform and Scope for Commodity-Based Targeting", *Economic and Political Weekly*, Vol. 30, No. 13, April 1, pp. 687 – 695.

Theil, H. (1967), *Economics and Information Theory*, North Holland Publishing Co., Amsterdam.

University of Burdwan, (1992), *Technology Adoption in Agriculture in West Bengal: Socio-Economic Perspectives*, Report of ICAR Research Project, Department of Geography, June.

Vaidyanathan, A. (1977), "Performance and Prospects of Crop Production in India" *Economic and Political Weekly*, Vol. 12, Nos. 33 & 34, Special Number, August.

Vaidyanathan, A.(1977), "Constraints on Growth and Policy Options: Reply", *Economic and Political Weekly*, Vol. 12, No. 51, December 17.

Vaidyanathan, A.(1987), "Irrigation and Agricultural Growth", *Indian Journal of Agricultural Economics*, Oct. – Dec.

Venkataramanan, L. S. and Prahaladachar, M. (1980), "Growth Rates and Cropping Pattern Changes in Agriculture in Six States: 1950-75", *Indian Journal of Agricultural Economics*, Vol. 35, No. 2, April – June.

Visaria, P. (1995), "Rural Non-Farm Employment in India: Trends and Issues for Research", *Indian Journal of Agricultural Economics*, Vol. 50, No. 3, July- September.

Vyas V. S. (1996), "Diversification in Agriculture: Concept, Rationale and Approaches", *Indian Journal of Agricultural Economics*, Vol. 51, No.4, Oct.- Dec., pp.636-643.

Walsh R. M. (1944), " Response to Price in Production of Cotton and Cottonseed",

Journal of Farm Economics, Vol.26, pp.359-72.

World Bank (1990), *Agricultural Diversification: Policies and Issues from East Asian Experience*, Agriculture and Rural Development Department, Washington, D.C., U.S.A.

Index